Divide & Conquer

D0771774

In the series STUDIES IN TRANSGRESSION,
edited by DAVID BROTHERTON

John C. Quicker and Akil S. Batani-Khalfani, *Before Crips: Fussin',
Cussin', and Discussin' among South Los Angeles Juvenile Gangs*

John M. Hagedorn, *Gangs on Trial: Challenging Stereotypes and
Demonization in the Courts*

Series previously published by Columbia University Press

ROBERT D. WEIDE

Divide & Conquer

RACE, GANGS, IDENTITY, AND CONFLICT

TEMPLE UNIVERSITY PRESS

Philadelphia | Rome | Tokyo

TEMPLE UNIVERSITY PRESS
Philadelphia, Pennsylvania 19122
tupress.temple.edu

Library of Congress Cataloging-in-Publication Data

Names: Weide, Robert D., 1978– author.
Title: Divide & conquer : race, gangs, identity, and conflict / Robert D.
   Weide.
Other titles: Studies in transgression.
Description: Philadelphia : Temple University Press, 2022. | Series:
   Studies in transgression | Includes bibliographical references and
   index. | Summary: "This book reveals the roots of interracial conflict
   between gangs in Los Angeles. The author argues that violence and
   mistrust between racialized gangs are the result of state and media
   efforts to popularize racial ideology to serve capitalistic and colonial
   interests and interrupt class solidarity"—Provided by publisher.
Identifiers: LCCN 2022000505 (print) | LCCN 2022000506 (ebook) |
   ISBN 9781439919460 (cloth) | ISBN 9781439919477 (paperback) |
   ISBN 9781439919484 (pdf)
Subjects: LCSH: Gangs—California—Los Angeles. | Ethnic
   conflict—California—Los Angeles. | African Americans—Relations with
   Mexican Americans. | Race awareness—United States. | Identity
   politics—United States. | Capitalism—Social aspects—United States. |
   LCGFT: Ethnographies.
Classification: LCC HV6439.U7 L7884 2022 (print) | LCC HV6439.U7 (ebook)
   | DDC 364.106/60979494—dc23/eng/20220408
LC record available at https://lccn.loc.gov/2022000505
LC ebook record available at https://lccn.loc.gov/2022000506

Printed in the United States of America

9 8 7 6 5 4 3 2 1

To my son Francisco Buenaventura . . .

May we leave a better legacy for our children

than we inherited ourselves.

CONTENTS

ACKNOWLEDGMENTS

I thank my parents who sacrificed and endured so much to see me become the scholar I am today. I thank my wonderful wife for all her support caring for both me and our young son while I was writing and revising this manuscript. I owe my eternal gratitude to my primary academic mentor, David Charles Brotherton, who provided me with both the intellectual and professional foundations on which I anchor my academic career. I also express my profound gratitude to my primary graduate program adviser at New York University (NYU) and dissertation co-chair, Craig Calhoun, without whose steadfast support I would have likely ended my academic career before it ever got started. I also thank Juan Corradi, who generously agreed to co-chair my dissertation, as well as Jeff Goodwin and James Diego Vigil, both of whom also served on my dissertation committee and not only offered their intellectual guidance but also opened up their hearts and their homes to me as well.

I also thank my early advisers in graduate school at NYU. I thank Troy Duster and Ann Morning, who laid the foundations of my thinking on issues of race and identity. I thank Ruth Horowitz and Lynne Haney, who introduced me to the field of ethnography, and David Greenberg, who introduced me to the field of criminology. I thank my undergraduate advisers Eric R. A. N. Smith, John Sutton, and Mary Vogel for encouraging me to apply to graduate school. I thank all of the faculty who generously guided and mentored me when I was in graduate school: Elijah Anderson, Dalton Conley, Jeff Ferrell, David Garland, Kathleen Gerson, Doug Guthrie, John Hagedorn, David Halle, Mark Hamm, Keith Hayward, Jack Katz, Jayne Mooney, Greg Snyder, Florencia Torche, and the late Betty "Jo" Dixon and Jock Young. I thank my editor, Ryan Mulligan, for his patient guidance and the production team at Temple University Press; the peer referees selected by the editor; and colleagues, students, and mentors who provided me with invaluable feedback on earlier versions of what became this book: Alex A. Alonso, Darryl Barthé, David Brotherton, Craig Calhoun, Randol Contreras, Juan Corradi, Jeff Goodwin, Jorge David Mancillas, Ann Morning, Manuel Pastor, Clint Terrell, and James Diego Vigil. Alex also generously contributed photographs and created the map that appears in the Introduction. I express my gratitude for the generosity of my old friends, Estevan Oriol and Mark "Mister Cartoon" Machado, for their support.

I thank my colleagues Luoman Bao and Sheera Joy Olasky for sharing their statistical expertise and their time to help me complete the quantitative aspects of both my dissertation and this book. I thank everyone at the numerous gang intervention and prisoner reentry programs I work with in Los Angeles for all their generosity and support, including Homeboy Industries, 2nd Call, and the Southern California Ceasefire Committee. I express my gratitude to all my dedicated research assistants over the years: Lami J. Glenn, Diana Grijalva, Gabriel Lopez, Tamia Morrow, Luis Orellana, Christopher Ortunio, Ryan Rising, Rayceana Rocha, Gustavo Subuyuj, and Galinda Villegas. Finally, I thank my colleagues at Cal State LA who have mentored me through my early career and helped me navigate academic politics on our campus: Scott Bowman, Wai Kit Choi, Gabriella Fried Amilivia, Roseann Giarrusso, Gretchen Peterson, and Jackie Teepen.

This book would not have been possible without each and every one of you. You are all so very much appreciated.

Divide & Conquer

INTRODUCTION

Divide et impera: divide and you will rule; divide and you will grow rich; divide and you will deceive the people, blind their reason, and mock justice.

—PIERRE-JOSEPH PROUDHON, *Qu'est-ce que la propriété?*[1]

On the morning of Monday, February 5, 1996, as the warm sun began to cut through the chilly morning fog layer the Westside of Los Angeles is known for, two high school students—fourteen-year-old Eduardo "Eddie" Gamez and sixteen-year-old Aldo Dominguez—were walking to Dorsey High School, as they did every morning. They were accompanied by another friend who was unenrolled at the time: fourteen-year-old Alberto Ruiz. The boys were painting graffiti along the street behind the school as they made their way to campus when a vehicle pulled up abruptly and a twenty-six-year-old African American man, Anthony Jerome "Flash" Smith, emerged with a gun and yelled, "Fuck Faketeen!" He fired multiple times, hitting Alberto in the arm, Aldo in the buttocks, and Eddie in the lower back. Aldo and Alberto were able to run away and save themselves. Eddie, however, was incapacitated on the ground from the initial round to the lower back. Flash approached him and fired multiple times into his chest and head. He then dropped a red rag (handkerchief) on Eddie's body, returned to the vehicle, and drove off. Eddie died in a local hospital later that week.[2] Flash remains in prison, serving a life sentence for murder, as of the time of this writing.

Eddie, Aldo, and Alberto were childhood friends of mine. None of them were members of the local 18 Street gang Flash apparently thought he was

---

1. Proudhon (1840) 1873, 96, translation by the author.
2. Krikorian 1996.

targeting. We were all "tagbangers," members of a local crew that claimed the Palms and Westside Village neighborhoods of West Los Angeles as our territory. We enjoyed painting graffiti all over the city, wherever we could, but violence was endemic to our existence. Our coterie of teenage delinquents drew its membership from local schools, including Culver City Middle School, Culver City High School, Palms Middle School, Hamilton High School, and Dorsey High School, and many of us had connections through family and friends to the hegemonic *Sureño*-affiliated gangs in our community, Culver City 13 and 18 Street.[3]

Flash was seeking revenge for the murder of one member and the severe wounding of another member of a local African American gang, the Black P Stones (Bloods), in a shooting on 10th Avenue outside the Mid City Swap Meet the week before. He had apparently mistaken the boys for 18 Street gang members. Not long before Eddie's murder, we had played a friendly game of football on the recreational yard at Palms Middle School with another local crew from Venice we were friends with. Afterward, we went to a local Shakey's Pizza restaurant on Sepulveda Boulevard in Culver City, adjacent to the Fox Hills Mall, to eat pizza, drink soda, and play video games, as children are wont to do. That is the last memory I have of Eddie before he was murdered on his way to school a few weeks later.

While Eddie's death was devastating for his family, our cohort of teenage delinquents took it in stride. Hyper-criminalization and the normalization of violence were unquestioned aspects of our existence at the time. We had grown up in Los Angeles during the peak years of the violent crime rate, in the late 1980s and the early 1990s, and had grown indifferent to the sectarian conflicts and regularly occurring murders of peers in our community. Shootings were so common when I was growing up that it was rare for anyone even to call the police when a shooting occurred, as long as no one was laid out on the ground dead or wounded. Funerals for young men and boys were such a regular occurrence in our world that they had assumed a sort of ritualistic quality, not only as a tribute to another life lost, but as another opportunity for childhood friends to pledge their allegiance to local gangs and plan their retaliation so that a funeral in one community would inevitably be followed by others in a neighboring community. Thus, we were unfazed by Eddie's death—or anyone else's, for that matter. We lived in a world where mothers buried their sons instead of sons burying their mothers. Death was a way of life for us, and we took for granted the seeming inescapability of deadly violence in our lives.

---

3. *Sureño*-affiliated gangs are those that identify and align with predominantly Chicano prisoners from Southern California in carceral contexts, often, though not always, denoted by the number 13 at the end of the name of the gang.

It wasn't until years later that I began to question the circumstances that had led to and followed Eddie's murder. The murder had occurred in the context of a racialized gang conflict that had erupted only a few years earlier between a local *Sureño*-affiliated gang, West Side 18 Street, and local African American Blood-affiliated gangs, the Black P Stones and the Rolling 20s Neighborhood Bloods. Interracial sectarian conflict between African American and Chicano gangs was so endemic to our existence at the time that we never thought to question the racial animosity that had been instilled in us by our families and peers, and by our role models in the community: the Original Gangsters (OGs) and *veteranos* we idolized. Nor were we cognizant of the influence institutions that serve the interests of American oligarchy such as academia, the media, and law enforcement had on our understandings of ourselves and one another and the conflicts among us. Moreover, while racialized gang conflict had only recently emerged as a proximate line of division between predominantly African American Crip- and Blood-affiliated gangs on one side and predominantly Chicano *Sureño*-affiliated gangs on the other in our community, we were oblivious to the historical foundations of that division and conflict, which had been laid long before our time.

While this is a book that appears on its face to be about gangs, it is also a book about the race concept and, particularly, its contemporary iteration in ethnonationalist ideology and identity politics. An ethnography of gangs in Los Angeles, *Divide & Conquer* provides a case study in how racialized identities and nationalist ideology function to divide subordinate labor populations, thereby turning them against one another—the classic *divide and conquer* stratagem of capitalist labor management. While there is nothing new about the race concept serving as a vehicle for labor division, what is significant about the modern era is where the boundaries of division lie and who enforces them. Since the invention of the race concept as a self-regulating vehicle for labor management and social control around the turn of the eighteenth century, race has served as the primary line of division among labor populations in the United States, undermining labor solidarity and preventing coordinated resistance to shared economic, social, and political subordination.[4] As sociologist Immanuel Wallerstein explains, "If one wants to maximize the accumulation of capital, it is necessary simultaneously to minimize the costs of production (hence the costs of labour-power) and minimize the costs of political disruption (hence minimize—not eliminate, because one cannot eliminate—the protests of the labour

---

4. Allen 1997; Isenberg 2016; Morgan 1975; Roediger and Esch 2012; Smedley 2007.

force). Racism is the magic formula that reconciles these objectives."[5] Racism exists, not as an evil unto itself, but as a vehicle to facilitate labor exploitation by dividing labor populations into opposing racialized factions.

The race concept is a self-regulating system of labor management and social control because it employs labor populations themselves as the agents of enforcement for the racial regime that undermines their own solidarity. From the inception of the modern race concept in North America, the white labor population had been the primary enforcement mechanism of the race regime. At first, white labor populations had to be sold on the merits of racism, but over time they realized the comparative status and material privilege—the "wages of whiteness"—created by the subjugation of nonwhite populations in an explicitly white supremacist society, and many of them embraced it.[6] While there is undeniably profound anxiety among white Americans over the diminishing dividends paid on the "possessive investment in whiteness," many still do.[7] The very explicit and legal subjugation of nonwhite populations in the United States continued essentially unabated from the inception of black chattel slavery around the turn of the eighteenth century until the Civil Rights Movement era in the 1960s, when such explicitly legal racial prejudice was ostensibly outlawed. While the toothless Civil Rights Acts of 1964 and 1968 by no means ended racial oppression in America, the Civil Rights Movement ushered in a new era that had been developing in the United States since the early twentieth century. Throughout the Jim Crow era, and black chattel slavery before it, the racism of white Americans had always been the primary enforcement mechanism of racial boundaries.

However, in the post–Civil Rights Movement era, people of color have become the new sheriff in town, themselves zealously policing the boundaries that maintain the salience of racial taxonomies. As sociologist Rogers Brubaker of the University of California, Los Angeles, has astutely observed, in the wake of the collapse of the Civil Rights Movement, "claims to blackness began to be more closely policed than claims to whiteness."[8] In the contemporary era, people of color themselves have become the enforcers of the racial boundaries that have been used for centuries to divide, exploit, and subjugate them, embracing the very ethnoracial categories that make their continued division, exploitation, and oppression possible in the first place. Increasingly, people of color have deputized themselves as the *identity police*, the agents of exclusion, enforcing the ostensibly rigid boundaries

---

5. Balibar and Wallerstein 1991, 33.
6. On the wages of whiteness, see Roediger (1991) 2007.
7. Lipsitz 2006.
8. Brubaker 2016, 60.

and incontestable sanctity of racialized identities not only between themselves and white America, but also between themselves and other similarly situated communities of color. Racialized identities, whose salience are owed entirely to their role as vehicles for material oppression, labor management, and social control, have been reconceived as a badge of honor, a point of pride, a form of private property to be jealously defended at all costs: *a cult of identity.*

In the post–Civil Rights Movement era, identitarian discourse has proved hegemonic in both academia and the mainstream media. In the process, class-consciousness and interracial solidarity have been sacrificed at the altar of identity politics. Although members of the race-reductionist establishment fancy themselves the leaders of the resistance, they are in fact the reinforcements charged with upholding the floundering regime of racial capitalism in the post–Civil Rights Movement era. Ethnopolitical entrepreneurs on the neoliberal left share common ground with tiki torch–wielding white nationalist sycophants on the "alt-right," as champions of racialization in contemporary American discourse.[9] While legal scholar Nancy Leong encourages a sympathetic approach to those she calls "identity entrepreneurs," I take a less charitable view.[10] Contemporary purveyors of identity politics have been showered with popular acclaim, media platforms, and lavish funding from corporate- and billionaire-sponsored foundations and media conglomerates. They aren't just selling out; they're cashing in.

There is certainly no shortage of contemporary scholarship on "racial relations" and "racial conflict," including enmity among communities of color in the United States. Much of that scholarship is cited in this book. However, conventional race scholarship suffers from two fundamental flaws. First, too many scholars too often assume the salience of the racial categories they examine in failing to consider the deeper historical foundations and fundamental labor management and social control functions that racial division serves in the capitalist economy, thereby reifying rather than dismantling the categories that make such division possible.[11] As legal scholar Ian Haney-Lopez admonishes, "When we uncritically rely on racial ideas, we often, in turn, practice racism. We treat people according to their place in the racial hierarchies created by society and, by doing so, perpetuate those hierarchies."[12] The essentialist perspective is exemplified by the positivist wing of race scholarship, which claims independent effects of racial categories only by ignoring the essential labor management role the race concept

---

9. I borrow the very apt term *ethnopolitical entrepreneurs* from Brubaker 2004.
10. Leong 2021, chap. 4.
11. Darder and Torres 1999, 2004; Haney-Lopez 2003.
12. Haney-Lopez 2003, 7.

plays in the capitalist economy. Essentially, these perspectives err in conflating the analytical coherence of racial categories with their practice, treating race as an independent rather than a dependent variable. Race and capitalism are one system in the American context, not two perhaps related but distinct concepts of equal analytic value. As critical ethnicity scholars Antonia Darder and Rodolfo Torres state unequivocally, "Class and 'race' do not occupy the same analytical space and thus cannot constitute explanatory alternatives to one another."[13] However, even where scholars do pay lip service to the inherent relationship between capitalism and the race concept, they too often fail to state explicitly what, exactly, the basis of that relationship is. I make no bones about it. Racism exists as a material reality *because* it serves an essential function in the capitalist economy: labor management and social control. As Brubaker cautions, "We must, of course, take vernacular categories and participants' understandings seriously, for they are partly constitutive of our objects of study. But we should not uncritically adopt *categories of ethnopolitical practice* as our *categories of social analysis*."[14]

Second, because of their reticence to acknowledge that the capitalist system of labor extraction is itself the genesis of racial divisions and disparities in our society, too many contemporary scholars suffer a preoccupation with policy reforms within the existing system rather than encouraging resistance to the capitalist system in its entirety. Too many of my otherwise brilliant colleagues have unfortunately dedicated too much of their careers to the victimology of crafting sympathetic pity pets out of marginalized and criminalized populations to satisfy the voyeuristic curiosity of well-meaning liberals. For that reason, the sympathetic narratives, tepid analyses, and pandering policy recommendations they offer do not represent an existential threat to the capitalist system. Rather, they threaten only palatable incremental reforms that can be easily implemented within the framework of the existing system, and even more easily dismantled. That is exactly why race-reductive, reformist perspectives are so celebrated by mainstream media, pundits, politicians, scholars, and grant-funding institutions: they serve a supporting role for capital, distracting from the material reality of capitalist labor exploitation, runaway wealth stratification, burgeoning neofascist movements, and impending ecological collapse, while feigning outrage at the symptoms of racial division—as if they occur in a vacuum.

In 2021, the theme of the annual meeting of the American Sociological Association was "emancipatory sociology" and that of its sister organization, the Society for the Study of Social Problems, was "revolutionary sociology." If my colleagues in the academy intend to be true to the imperatives of

---

13. Darder and Torres 2004, 128.
14. Brubaker 2004, 10, author's emphasis.

emancipation and revolution, then we need to reimagine our role as intellectuals and the purpose our academic careers serve. The sociological imagination cannot be limited to boundaries imposed by the capitalist economy and representative governance.[15] Exploitation and oligarchy are not the limit of human social, political, and economic organization. We need to use our intellectual leadership not to encourage reform and retrenchment of the terms on which our present civilization is predicated but, rather, as revolutionary catechism, culminating in a complete reimagination and reorganization of human civilization. Our role in the social revolution that offers perhaps the only hope of escape from impending calamity at this critical juncture in human history is to dismantle the conceptual frameworks that present barriers to the solidarity of the proletariat and provide frameworks for praxis that present the greatest possible threat to the status quo. That is exactly what I intend to do in the pages that follow.

While existing academic critiques have fleshed out the theoretical shortcomings of nationalist ideology and identity politics, racialized conflict between predominantly African American Crip- and Blood-affiliated gangs and predominantly Chicano *Sureño*-affiliated gangs in Los Angeles provides a particularly intriguing case study in how the race concept and nationalist identities operate in practice to undermine solidarity and perpetuate sectarian conflict among subordinate labor populations. Gangs have become perhaps the most ubiquitous form of grassroots social organization in working-class communities throughout much of the capitalist world, filling the void left by systematic deindustrialization and the dramatic expansion of discarded labor populations in late modernity.[16] As critical criminologist David Brotherton suggests, "Gangs are invariably tied to the race, class and gender history of the community. . . . [T]he organizational, ideological and stylistic characteristics of gangs reflect the subcultural histories of a particular community and its subaltern strata."[17] Gang members' conceptualization of their own and others' identities is a direct reflection of the identity politics that achieved hegemony in the academy and, by extension, in the imagination of the African American and Chicano proletariat, in the post–Civil Rights Movement era. Racialized gang identities in Los Angeles are both a reflection of these hegemonic perspectives espoused and disseminated by professional ethnopolitical entrepreneurs in academia and the media, and a harbinger of the sectarian conflict and violence that such divisions can and do engender.

In the modern era, gang members are perhaps the most marginalized, demonized, and criminalized population in America and throughout much

---

15. Mills (1959) 2000.
16. Alonso 2010; Brotherton 2015; Vigil 1988.
17. Brotherton 2015, 16.

of the capitalist world. They are the progeny of labor populations whose labor is no longer useful to capital. It is no accident that the prior use of the word *gang* in the English language was in reference to a group of workers, whereas by the turn of the twentieth century the word had been transformed into a negativistic slur used to demonize and criminalize workers whose labor is no longer useful to capital. Gang members represent not just the lower class but, moreover, the permanent underclass of American society—what Karl Marx and Friedrich Engels called the lumpenproletariat, unable to identify the cause of their material deprivation and therefore unable to focus their rage against those whose unimaginable wealth is possible only at their expense. Rather than threaten the continued reproduction of the American oligarchy, they instead turn the frustration of their material deprivation against one another, with devastating effect for themselves and their communities.

In doing so, gang members have become the instruments of their own oppression, dividing themselves according to groupist identities defined by ethnoracial categories and gang affiliation, therein undermining potential for solidarity among them and instead turning them against one another in protracted blood feuds across gang lines and racial lines that span generations. It isn't difficult to understand why gang members are so inclined to latch onto groupist identities, when the material circumstances of their lives provide the most marginalized, demonized, and criminalized members of our society so little of substance in their personal lives to take pride in. Identity is the consolation prize offered by capital to those for whom the capitalist economy cannot provide material circumstances or a meaningful existence worth taking pride in.

While I hope this book provides some nuance to the existing literature on race, gangs, identity, and sectarian conflict that my academic colleagues can appreciate, and perhaps even some insight that can help practitioners and policy makers be part of the solution rather than the problem, if they are so inclined, my foremost ambition is for this book to trigger an epiphany in gang members themselves. Ultimately, they are the only ones who can build the solidarity that has been denied them by the race concept, nationalist ideology, identity politics, and sectarian conflict. Although the context for this book is based on a case study of gangs in Los Angeles, my aspiration is for the analysis contained herein potentially to apply to sectarian conflicts among subordinate populations throughout the world, conflicts that are almost always fought across boundaries of groupist identity, whether racial, ethnic, religious, tribal, or otherwise, that have been provoked and perpetuated, if not entirely fabricated, by colonial powers. Only by realizing the commonality of their material circumstances vis-à-vis the oligarchy and the irrelevance, if not illusion, of their differences can the discarded labor populations of capitalist modernity redirect their animosity away from one another and against those who are directly responsible for the intractability of their collective subordination. Realizing that potential for social revolution from below is ultimately the aspiration of this book.

The Research Project

The empirical basis for *Divide & Conquer* is a mixed-methods research project that began formal fieldwork in 2012 and continued through 2021. Two primary research methodologies were employed—ethnographic observation and formal interviews—supplemented with rather simple descriptive statistics used to replicate existing research. Ethnographic observation is when researchers join the communities they intend to study in their own context and observe and participate in their daily lives. Having associated with gangs since primary school, the idea of doing an ethnography of my own lifestyle seems a bit contrived. Thus, the portion of the ethnography that involved the *Sureño*-affiliated gangs I grew up with could be considered a species of what sociologists call an insider participant observation ethnography.[18] Although I haven't directly participated in any criminal activity with gang members for decades, they perceive me as a peer rather than an outsider because of the lifestyle I used to live.

As a result of my extensive criminal career as a younger man, most of the *Sureño*-affiliated gang members I observed and interviewed during the fieldwork for this book knew my street identity, and I was acquainted with many of them before I began formal ethnographic research. Thus, my primary status in the minds of most subjects during the formal fieldwork portion of this research project was that of homeboy rather than researcher. As a common mantra in our culture goes, "You can take the homeboy out the hood, but you can't take the hood out the homeboy."

My own prior criminal career not only provided a reference point for respondents to feel as if they already had some intrinsic connection to me, but it also tended to dispel any suspicions that I might use what I know to assist law enforcement. My outstanding reputation for breaking the law with abandon as a younger man certainly shields me from any credible accusation that I might assist law enforcement. My insider status also was a tremendous resource in that many subjects were willing to discuss taboo subjects such as prison and gang politics with me that are generally off-limits to outsiders. In addition to simple ethnographic access, my positionality confers on me an inherent understanding of all the minutiae of gang culture in Los Angeles. I know all the slang, and I can employ the appropriate ver-

---

18. Adler and Adler 1987.

naculars in different contexts as a fluent native speaker. I recognize and understand all of the various cultural identifiers and am capable of authentically displaying them appropriately, depending on context. I am aware of and understand the intricacies of gang politics, and I am capable of navigating them. I have done these things my whole life in a diversity of criminalized contexts from coast to coast. These are, of course, tangible advantages conferred by my own positionality.

While I share political scientist Adolph Reed Jr.'s skepticism about the incontestable authority of positionality, my positionality in terms of my own racial identity surely also had something to do with the analysis I've arrived at for this book.[19] Although I am often racialized as white in certain contexts, presumably because of my government name, I have always been excluded from whiteness by those who enforce its boundaries. My father is an ethnic Kurd of Iranian birth, and my mother is of half-Russian and half-Prussian descent.[20] Yet, like other Americans of Middle Eastern and North African descent, whiteness has always remained out of reach for me.[21] To extend the gender metaphor, my racial identity is elusive in that I don't really have one, something cis-race people take for granted, in the American context especially. While many Americans have a number of "ethnic options" available to them to perform as a symbolic ethnicity, whether real or imagined, there really is no intrinsic ethnoracial identity available to me.[22] I'm not unproblematically accepted by the cis-race members of any ethnoracial category in any context. While no one can be raceless in a racialized society, because we are all perpetually subjected to the racializing gaze of others, there is no ethnoracial category from which I am not excluded. I have always experienced the race concept throughout my life as exclusion and never as belonging. I am the perpetual *other* to everyone in every context. Thus, since I have always been excluded from every ethnoracial category and unable to make a credible claim to any, it should be understandable that nationalist ideology and ethnoracial taxonomies don't appeal to me.

While some people of color cannot escape their racial identity because of their phenotypic appearance, my phenotypic appearance is sufficiently ambiguous that assumptions about my ethnoracial identity vary by context. In the U.S. context, people of Middle Eastern origin are nominally considered white but are not socially accepted by Americans of European origin

---

19. A. Reed 2000, xviii–xix.
20. My birth name is Robert Farshid Pajuhesh, and my Iranian name is Bobak Farshid Pajuhesh Sanjabi, reflecting both the Iranian surname chosen by my grandfather and our Kurdish tribal affiliation. Weide is my maternal grandfather's surname of Prussian origin.
21. Maghbouleh 2017; Maghbouleh et al. 2022.
22. On symbolic ethnicity, see Gans 1973; Waters 1990.

as white.[23] I am unambiguously nonwhite in the European context, where people of Middle Eastern origin like me occupy roughly the same marginalized status of racially excluded outsider that African Americans and Latinos suffer in the U.S. context. In the Spanish-speaking world, people always address me in Spanish first, assuming I am one of them, whoever they may be—that is, until they hear my broken Spanish in response. Thus, if one were to use a gender analogy, one might say that I am *race-nonconforming* in that I do not have a category from which I am not excluded and, for that reason, I refuse to acknowledge the salience of racial categories beyond their role as a vehicle for material oppression and labor division. After failing to assimilate into Ronald Reagan's America as a child in the 1980s, I unconsciously rejected any attempt at whiteness once and for all as a teenager and was instead absorbed into a transracial Chicano ethnocultural identity as a result of my association with *Sureño*-affiliated gangs as a teenager and young adult.

However, my anomalous ethnoracial and street identities were at times an impediment in the second facet of my fieldwork, which consisted of a more traditional participant observer methodology. Because my associations were exclusively with *Sureño*-affiliated gangs, my ethnographic fieldwork with predominantly African American Crip- and Blood-affiliated gangs could not achieve the same level of insider access and perspective that my fieldwork with *Sureño*-affiliated gangs did. However, while I had rarely associated with Crip- and Blood-affiliated gang members prior to starting my fieldwork for this book, I made every effort to embed myself with Crip- and Blood-affiliated gang members wherever possible during the course of my fieldwork. Given the racial animosity that I discuss between *Sureño*-affiliated and Crip- and Blood-affiliated gang members, I was often initially received with some trepidation. However, over the years I've become closely acquainted with a wide cohort of Crip- and Blood-affiliated gang members throughout Los Angeles, some of whom I now count among my closest friends. The fieldwork for this book also contributed to my personal growth, forcing me to overcome my own apprehensions about crossing racial boundaries. In doing so, I arrived at the epiphany that I hope this book triggers in others: *there's no us and them, there's just us.* At the very least, the Crip- and Blood-affiliated gang members I observed and interviewed know that I am a homeboy myself. Some of them even nicknamed me the "*Ese* Professor" or the "Cholo Professor," which I appreciate as titles of endearment.

Despite the barriers to my fieldwork with Crip- and Blood-affiliated gang members, the portion of my fieldwork that required the greatest degree of acumen as a professionally trained ethnographer was my ethnography of

23. Maghbouleh 2017; Maghbouleh et al. 2022.

and interviews with law enforcement officers (LEOs) charged with gang enforcement in various agencies throughout Los Angeles County. Law enforcement is a very insular culture, and, of course, I am not, and I have never been, a sworn officer myself. However, to the best of my ability I socialized extensively with LEOs and was able to earn their trust to such a degree that I was often treated as if I was one myself. To penetrate the very opaque culture of LEOs, I pursued a unique strategy to gain ethnographic access: I became a competitive marksman. In the years before I commenced the formal fieldwork for this project, I had the foresight to anticipate that I would need to develop relationships with LEOs throughout Los Angeles. It dawned on me that shooting sports is the one endeavor I could pursue that would garner me a wide range of contacts from law enforcement agencies throughout Southern California.

My prowess as a competitive shooter has earned the (perhaps grudging) respect of my fellow sportsmen, many of whom work in law enforcement. Over the years I have become well acquainted with quite a few LEOs. Almost every ride-along I went on; LEO interview I conducted, formally and informally; and LEO I came to know personally came out of my participation in shooting sports, one way or another. Having access to LEOs in their own social milieu was invaluable in terms of informal interviewing and observation in that I was able to garner their perspectives in contexts where they were completely at ease and could speak freely in ways they never would in the presence of a stranger or ephemeral acquaintance. My success in this endeavor was apparent during a ride-along I did with a highly experienced gang enforcement officer. He showed me where he kept a backup firearm in the glove compartment of his cruiser and told me, "If the shit hits the fan, I know you know what to do with this." While I have extensive inside knowledge of crimes committed by both gang members and LEOs, I have an ethical obligation to take that knowledge to my grave. As a professionally trained ethnographer, I cannot and will not allow any incriminating information I am privy to as a result of my fieldwork to be used against anyone.

In addition to the nearly ten years of formal ethnographic fieldwork I conducted for this book, I formally interviewed sixty-seven *Sureño*-affiliated gang members and thirty Crip- and Blood-affiliated gang members. However, I should note that, for various reasons, not every respondent provided a response to every interview question, so there are a number of missing values for various results reported throughout the book. Gang members who were interviewed ranged in age from their late teens to their late fifties. The duration of interviews was anywhere from an hour to two-and-a-half hours, depending on the extent of experiences each respondent had to offer.

All interviews were conducted in the contextually appropriate vernacular, whether African American Vernacular English or *Caló* vernacular, or some combination of the two. My subject pool included at least a dozen respondents who had been validated as prison gang associates during their incarceration in California prisons. A half-dozen of my respondents had been charged in various Racketeer Influenced and Corrupt Organizations Act (RICO) cases by the federal government, and, to my knowledge, five respondents were murdered during the course of my fieldwork.

Because I am an accepted member of the community in which I conducted my fieldwork, my interview protocol differs from the type of colonial qualitative research strategy that is too often employed by my academic contemporaries, infiltrating marginalized communities from the outside and subjecting respondents to a structured and measured formal research interview protocol. As excerpts from my interviews reflect, my interviews are more a conversation between two familiar parties, both of whom have firsthand experience with the issues being discussed, rather than an interrogation of an insider by an outsider. This often comes out in my interview quotes, as both my respondents and I already know the answers to various questions being asked, possibly giving the reader who is not personally acquainted with our experiences the impression that I am intentionally leading or excessively sympathizing with my respondents. Nothing could be further from the truth. While no scholarship is entirely objective, I have made every effort possible to check my own inherent biases, including having respondents from *Sureño*-affiliated gangs and Crip- and Blood-affiliated gangs read and provide comments on my research materials and manuscripts throughout the research and writing process prior to publication of this book. Significant revisions were made at their request, even in the final stages of prepublication editing.

Respondents were sampled using three different strategies. Most interview respondents were recruited at gang intervention and prisoner reentry organizations in different parts of Los Angeles. I was not previously acquainted with these respondents, who were recruited in a semi-random pattern in that I merely interviewed whoever happened to be present at the organization on any given day. I also snowball sampled from these respondents to acquire additional respondents. In some cases, after an interview with one respondent concluded, they would insist that I interview someone else to whom they would introduce me. I also did some selective sampling to interview respondents who were members of gangs that I had been unable to interview by random sample to make the sample population as representative as possible of gangs in Los Angeles County. I'm confident that this sample population is as representative of gangs in Los Angeles County as I could hope to have collected.

I should note that location markers such as WS (West Side), ES (East Side), and SS (South Side) generally refer to regional location within Los Angeles County or Los Angeles City. The line of demarcation differs, however, for *Sureño*-affiliated gangs and Crip- and Blood-affiliated gangs. *Sureño*-affiliated gangs typically draw the line between the West Side and the East Side at the Los Angeles River. Crip- and Blood-affiliated gangs typically draw the line along Central Boulevard or the 110 Freeway. However, these area indicators can also refer to more local regional location. For example, East Side Longos refers to the East Side of Long Beach, not Los Angeles.

SUREÑO-AFFILIATED GANGS INTERVIEWED

Downtown Los Angeles/West Side (WS)

Dog Town	Rockwood Street
Drifters	Trece Locos
Easy Riders	Varrio Salifa Rifa
18 Street	Varrio Vista Rifa
Inglewood	Venice
La Mirada Locos	WS White Fence

East Side (ES)

Big Hazard	El Monte Flores
Clarence Street	Primera Flats
Clover Street	2nd Street
Cuatro Flats	El Sereno
Evergreen Locos	State Street
Ghetto Style Criminals	Stoners
Indiana Dukes	3rd Street
Little Valley	Varrio Nueva Estrada
The Lot	ES White Fence

South Side (SS)/South Central (SC)

Barrio Mojados	Neighborhood Norwalk
Clanton 14 Street	Niños Sureños
Florencia	ES Paramount
42nd Street Lil Criminals	ES 13 Street
46 Street Tokers	36 Street Maple Locos
Kansas Street	38 Street Locos
ES Longos	39 Street
La Mirada	Las Tres Palmas

SUREÑO-AFFILIATED GANGS INTERVIEWED (*continued*)

Northeastern Los Angeles (NELA)/
San Fernando Valley (SFV)

Avenues
Frogtown
Toonerville
Vineland Boys

CRIP-AFFILIATED GANGS INTERVIEWED

Neighborhood (Deuces)

Bastard Crips East Coast
East Coast Crips
East Coast Crips 1st Street
Rolling 30s Harlem Crips
Rolling 60s Neighborhood Crips
Rolling 90s Neighborhood Crips
Rolling 100s Underground Crips

Gangsters (Treys)

Avalon Gangster Crips
43 Gangster Crips[24]
Hawthorne 118 Gangster Crips[25]
Lynwood Palm n' Oak Gangster Crips
97 Gangster Crips[26]

Others

51 Trouble Crips[27]
Hoover Criminals
97 Young Nigga Crips[28]
PJ Watts Crips

---

24. Pronounced "Four-Trey Gangster Crips."
25. Pronounced "Hawthorne One-One-Eight Gangster Crips."
26. Pronounced "Nine-Seven Gangster Crips.
27. Pronounced "Five-One Trouble Crips."
28. Pronounced "Nine-Seven Young Nigga Crips."

BLOOD-AFFILIATED GANGS INTERVIEWED

Bloods

Black P Stones
Blood Stone Villains
Bounty Hunters
Inglewood Families
Pasadena Denver Lane
Rolling 20s Neighborhood Bloods

Pirus

Compton Mob Piru
Inglewood Neighborhood Piru
235th Street Scottsdale Piru

I also interviewed seven gang enforcement officers representing five different jurisdictions and four different law enforcement agencies, including the Los Angeles Police Department (LAPD) South Bureau, Los Angeles Sheriff's Department's Compton and Century stations, Huntington Park Police Department, and Long Beach Police Department. In each case, the individuals I interviewed were either commanding officers of gang units or among the units' most experienced member(s). These respondents were recruited through my contacts in shooting sports, with the exception of those of the LAPD South Bureau, and were conducted either immediately before or after a ride-along.

I regularly use extended quotes from both formal and informal interviews, as I believe strongly that it is of the utmost importance to describe phenomena in the words of those who live them. I also identify respondents by the actual gangs of which they are members rather than use fictitious pseudonyms, as is too often the needless practice in scholarship on gangs. There is a great deal of significance to the affiliation of various respondents because of the racial dynamics and conflicts among specific gangs in particular communities. Without considering the affiliation of respondents, their statements would be meaningless precisely because it is the specific conflicts particular gangs have engaged in across racial lines that confer the significance of their perceptions.

In addition to identifying the gang affiliation of respondents, I often include the general location of the specific clique or set with which the respondent is affiliated. This is important as a geographical referent because there are significant cultural, social, and demographic differences among different regions of Los Angeles. It is also important to include the rough location of each respondent's clique or set, because some large gangs have

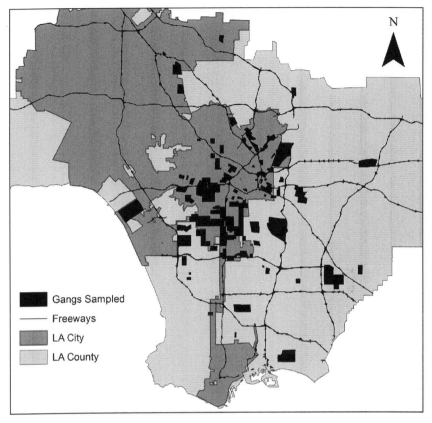

Figure I.1. Map of gangs sampled. (Courtesy of Alex A. Alonso.)

semiautonomous cliques in different regions of Los Angeles. I also include the rough age of respondents, as there are also significant generational differences in the perspectives of gang members, even within the same gang in the same community. However, there are a number of cases in which I interviewed multiple respondents from the same gang, in the same area, within the same age range, so I must offer the caveat that the reader ought not assume that two quotes with the same age, affiliation, and region are necessarily from the same respondent.

There are only two exceptions to this protocol. The first are quotes from transracial gang members used in Chapter 6, as identifying their gang affiliation and age could narrow down who they are to potential readers who are acquainted with them personally, thereby betraying the anonymity I am ethically obliged to guarantee respondents. The second are references to specific individuals named in Chapter 7 who have either published their names in a public document or given their explicit permission to be identified by name to shed light on the critical roles they have played in making peace between opposing racialized gang factions.

I should also make some comments about racial and gang terminology before proceeding. I prefer the term *African American* because of its specificity in reference to people of modern Sub-Saharan African origin in the United States. However, I do use the term *black* as an adjective, and as is common use in lay vernacular, both my respondents and I use *black* as a noun in interview exchanges. Likewise, I prefer the term *Chicano* for its specificity in referring to people of Mexican descent who grew up in the United States. I don't use the term *Mexican American*, because it implies willing assimilation, and I don't use the term *Hispanic*, because it both gives primacy to colonial Spanish identity and is the term used by punitive state institutions. At times I use the term *Latino* when I am referring to both Chicanos and other people of Latin American descent. Likewise, respondents and I use the term *brown* as an adjective to refer to the same population in lay vernacular. Following Cedric Johnson,

> I do not capitalize "black" and "white" when they are used as racial descriptors. Such racial markers are not transhistorical, nor are they rooted in some biological essence. Instead, my usage reflects the view that racial identity is the product of historically unique power configurations and material conditions. This view contradicts the literary practice common to much Black Power radicalism, where racial descriptors are capitalized to denote a distinctive, coherent political community and assert an affirmative racial identity.[29]

By their very nature, these terms are imprecise, owing to the inherently irrational basis of racialized identities, a point I hope is clear by the conclusion of the book. Nonetheless, I want to be as clear as I can about who I am referring to with such terms. Furthermore, I want to emphasize that when I use racialized terms in reference to people in the text, I am using them *not as a category of analysis* but, rather, in an attempt to faithfully reflect the perceptions of the populations I study.

I use the term *ethnoracial* to describe these categories because, in the Los Angeles context, they exhibit the qualities of both ethnicity and the race concept, as understood by contemporary sociologists.[30] Chicano and African American identity categories are assumed to be determined by ascription, phenotype, and primordial origin, as well as by self-identification and

---

29. Johnson 2007, xvii.
30. Cornell and Hartmann 2007, 19–24.

cultural praxis. They are simultaneously imposed on members of marginalized populations and embraced by them. Membership in each category is determined by pseudobiological indicators such as phenotypic appearance and bloodline descent (whether real or imagined), but it is also, as I demonstrate, determined by shared cultural praxis.

The N-word comes up often in my interviews, and where it appears as a racial epithet, I elide it by inserting dashes between the "n" and the "er" so as not to inflict any more trauma and incite more division than is unavoidable in presenting the narratives I share. However, where the word *nigga* is used as a term of endearment rather than a racial epithet, I do not elide it. I explain the linguistic significance of the difference between these two words in both Chapter 3 and Chapter 6, where it is germane to the discussion at hand.

I refer to gangs and gang members in Los Angeles as either *Sureño*-affiliated or Crip- or Blood-affiliated. The term *Sureño* specifically refers to members of predominantly Chicano gangs from Southern California who have drawn blood in prison. Not all *Sureño*-affiliated gang members have. Those who have not are called *South Siders* by *Sureño*-affiliated gang members. However, using the term *South Sider* to describe these gangs and their members may cause some confusion with regional descriptors for the reader who is not intimately acquainted with gang and prison politics in Los Angeles and California. Therefore, I use the term *Sureño-affiliated* because, while not every *Sureño*-affiliated gang member has been to prison and drawn blood there, all are affiliated with gangs that identify as *Sureño*-affiliated in carceral contexts. In contrast, the terms *Crip* and *Blood* are not exclusive of any members of Crip- or Blood-affiliated gangs. These terms apply to all affiliates equally.

I also want to acknowledge my use of the term *gang* in reference to members of street and inmate organizations. The word *gang* is a negativistic term that is employed by law enforcement, media, politicians, and academics sympathetic to law enforcement, with the intent to demonize and criminalize members of marginalized communities. Nonetheless, I use the terms *gang* and *gang member* to refer to street and inmate organizations and their members to avoid confusion for readers who are accustomed to this terminology because, frankly, its use is ubiquitous in lay vernacular. *My intent is not to reify the negative implications of this term for the populations who are the subject of this book by using it as such.* I also recognize that some gang members use this term to describe themselves, for the same reason that some African Americans have appropriated the N-word and recast it as a term of endearment, albeit with a slightly different vernacular pronunciation and spelling. Marginalized populations recognize that these negativistic terms are employed to demean, degrade, and dehumanize them. Recognizing and asserting their humanity, they resist their demonization by appropriating terms that they themselves recognize, either explicitly or implicitly, are used as rhetorical weapons against them.

I also should make clear that I often use the terms *identitarian* and *nationalist* almost interchangeably in the text. While the lay public—and some scholars, perhaps—may think of nationalism in the nation-state sense, the object of critique in this book is the ethnonationalism of subordinate stateless populations in the United States. As I describe at length in Chapter 1, state nationalism is itself predicated on ethnoracial identity and has had a significant influence on the emergence of ethnonationalism and identity politics more broadly among subordinate populations here in the United States and throughout the world. While I focus exclusively on ethnonationalist/identitarian ideology in this book, the terms *nationalist* and *identitarian* can certainly be applied to other sectarian groupist identities in the United States and abroad.

Chapter Outline

Following this Introduction, I begin the book by presenting both a historical background and a theoretical framework for analysis. In Chapter 1, I provide a brief history of the chronological development of the concepts, ideas, and ideologies that inform contemporary racialized gang identities, what I consider the three pillars of modern society: capitalism, the race concept, and nationalist ideology—in that chronological order. I trace the development of these ideas and systems of economic, social, and political organization and demonstrate how they laid the foundation for the identity politics of the modern era. Discussing the historical formation of capitalism, the race concept, and nationalist ideology is imperative not only for the lay reader to have a historically grounded foundation to embark from, but also to demonstrate that contemporary African American and Chicano identities are, ironically, a mirror image of the white nationalism they emerged as a reaction against, conceptually constructed on the basis of dubious historical and pseudobiological race perspectives, and outright mythology.

In Chapter 2, I trace the theoretical development of critiques of ethnonationalism and identity politics, starting with anarchist critiques of ethnonationalism in the late nineteenth and early twentieth centuries, followed by critiques of cultural nationalism made by the Black Panther Party revolutionaries during the Civil Rights Movement era, and finally to modern academic critiques of identity politics from the left. These critiques have not previously been assembled in one work, so I provide a modest catalogue of them not only as a coherent body of literature offering a sophisticated critique of identity politics but, moreover, to provide a theoretical framework for deconstructing the concepts, ideas, and ideologies that make racialized gang identities possible in the first place.

In Chapter 3, I provide what ethnographers describe as a thick description of the myriad cultural elements that define and divide racialized *Sureño*-affiliated and Crip- and Blood-affiliated gang identities from the perspectives of gang members. In the chapter I examine various facets of *Sureño*, Crip, and Blood culture and where boundaries among them are enforced, including clothing, hairstyles, vernacular, music, and car culture. Most important, I examine how the policing of these boundaries enforces and reinforces the salience of racialized gang identities.

In Chapter 4, I examine the extent of explicit racial bias among *Sureño*-affiliated and Crip- and Blood-affiliated gang members to demonstrate the divisive progeny of ethnonationalist ideology and identity politics. I examine racial bias between *Sureño*-affiliated and Crip- and Blood-affiliated gang members in relation to amorous relationships across racial lines, competition for employment and housing, socializing, and collaboration in the underground economy. While I demonstrate that interracial bias is pervasive among gang members in Los Angeles, I consider how those biases manifest themselves on each side of the color line and how they function to conceptually divide *Sureño*-affiliated and Crip- and Blood-affiliated gang members.

In Chapter 5, I provide detailed case studies of racialized conflicts between specific *Sureño*-affiliated gangs and Crip- and Blood-affiliated gangs in different regions of Los Angeles County to demonstrate the kind of violent conflicts that result when ethnonationalist ideology is taken to its logical conclusion. I consider how race thinking informs the perceptions of gang members and the trajectories of racialized conflicts between *Sureño*-affiliated gangs and Crip- and Blood-affiliated gangs, with particular focus on how the media and law enforcement reinforce these racialized interpretations of interracial gang conflicts as they evolve, thereby exacerbating rather than mitigating the racial animosity that drives them.

In Chapter 6, I describe a phenomenon that defies the race-thinking logic of racialized gang identity in Los Angeles: the prevalence of transracial gang members. By *transracial* I mean gang members whose racial identity in a primordial or phenotypic sense does not match their racialized gang identity. I examine both the indicators of the prevalence of transracial gang membership and the experiences of transracial gang members who stand on opposing sides of the black-brown binary. The prevalence of gang members who break the mold of racialized gang identity represents not just an anomaly but, moreover, a gaping crack in the façade of essentializing ethnonationalist ideology that informs racialized gang identities in Los Angeles.

Finally, I conclude with encouraging developments that have occurred as this book was being written. After decades of racialized sectarian conflict that has cost countless lives, gang members themselves have intervened to negotiate a cessation of hostilities across racial lines between and among themselves, both in prison and on the streets of Los Angeles. For the first time in generations, gang members are bringing racialized sectarian conflicts to an end of their own volition. This is an encouraging development that has emerged in spite of, not with the assistance of, state actors, who have never failed to punish those who dare to bring peace and solidarity to the streets of Los Angeles.

1

THE THREE PILLARS

*Historical Foundations of Ethnonationalism
and Identity Politics*

Part of the mechanics of oppressing people is to pervert them
to the extent that they become the instruments of their own
oppression.

—KUMASI[1]

This chapter examines the historical foundations of the ethnonational-
ist ideologies that inform racialized gang identities in the modern era.
Historical perspective is critical to scholarship on gangs because, as
David Brotherton argues,

Disregarding history's importance in making gangs leads to a failure
to understand the multiple contours of development through which
a community must emerge, particularly along the fault lines of race
and class and the political economy of space. . . . [W]ithout the historical lens, we will reproduce representations of the gang that serve
the hegemony rather than a critical reading or deconstruction of the
phenomenon that allows us to see how that hegemony is achieved in
the first place.[2]

With that in mind, the three major concepts I examine in this chapter—
what I consider the three pillars of modern civilization—are capitalism, the
race concept, and nationalism, in that chronological order. The race concept
and nationalist ideology as we know them today emerged and developed to
serve very specific and necessary functions for developing capitalist economic, social, and political organization in the last few hundred years—

---

1. Kumasi, in Peralta 2008.
2. Brotherton 2015, 8–9.

labor management, state formation, and social control.[3] While, for the sake of brevity, I cannot address all of the various academic debates concerning the origins of these concepts, the purpose of this chapter is to provide a baseline historical background for the reader. While I recognize that some of the canonical scholars in the field of race studies project the race concept farther into the past than I believe is warranted, this short chapter is hardly the place to critique scholars whose work is foundational to the study of the race concept.[4] Rather, I favor the economic determinist perspective of the late Birmingham School sociologist Stuart Hall:

> Again, the common assumption that it was attitudes of racial superiority which precipitated the introduction of plantation slavery needs to be challenged. It might be better to start from the opposite end: by seeing how slavery (the product of specific problems of labor shortage and the organization of plantation agriculture, supplied, in the first instance, by non-black, indigenous labor, and then by white indentured labor) produced those forms of juridical racism which distinguish the epoch of plantation slavery.[5]

In any case, I admit I harbor little optimism of persuading contemporary ideologues and ethnopolitical entrepreneurs in academia whose careers are predicated on promoting ethnonationalism. As historian Eric Hobsbawm admonishes:

> No serious historian of nations and nationalism can be a committed political nationalist. . . . Nationalism requires too much belief in what is patently not so. As Renan said: "Getting history wrong is part of being a nation." Historians are professionally obliged not to get it wrong, or at least to make an effort not to.[6]

Oftentimes, scholars overlook the inherent connection among capitalism, the race concept, and nationalist ideology and instead focus on European colonialism and black chattel slavery as the defining historical foundations of modern society. However, there is nothing new in human history about either colonialism or slavery, and while white supremacy has certainly been formative to American institutions, colonialism and slavery

---

3. Allen (1997) 2012; Anderson 1983; Du Bois (1935) 1992; Hobsbawm 1990; Roediger and Esch 2012; Smedley 2007.
4. Fredrickson 2002; Patterson (1982) 2018; C. Robinson (1983) 2000.
5. Hall (1980) 2019, 212.
6. Hobsbawm 1990, 12–13.

alike have global origins and legacies that span millennia. Since ancient times, humans have colonized territory and enslaved one another, usually as prisoners of war, sometimes as debt slaves, and at times to supply a market for slave labor. The ancient empires of both Egypt and Rome, as well as the medieval empires of the Islamic caliphates, Ottoman Turks, and Mongol hordes, among others, engaged in all three types of slavery and conquered vast empires, colonizing disparate populations and enslaving them in vast numbers. Such practices were the norm for empires throughout ancient and medieval times in every part of the world from the advent of sedentary agriculture. Indeed, the etymology of the word *slave* in the modern English, Spanish, and Italian languages traces back to Roman/Byzantine Latin-speaking populations for whom *Slav* and *slave* were linguistically, if not conceptually, synonymous.[7]

In fact, the medieval societies in Africa and the Americas that are commonly claimed as the ancestors of contemporary black and Chicano nationalist projects in the United States were themselves slavers and colonizers. While many contemporary African Americans have adopted Islam under the presumption that their (unknown) ancestors were of Muslim origin, in fact the Trans-Saharan slave trade from the Sudanian savanna to the Maghreb was established by Muslims around the turn of the eighth century.[8] Whether slaves should be exported to foreign markets was a recurring source of conflict between Muslim and pagan Africans throughout medieval times, with Muslims regularly raiding pagan communities to procure slaves for export.[9] The Muslim Kingdom of Mali in West Africa, for example, itself colonized the pagan *Sosso* civilization. The principal point of contention between the *Sosso* and *Malinke* was whether slaves should be subject to foreign export.[10] Colonial empires also existed in the Americas prior to European colonization. While contemporary Chicano nationalists lay claim to the American Southwest by virtue of the *Aztlán* myth of origin, the historical Aztecs (*Mexica* hereafter) colonized a wide swath of Mesoamerica, starting with the Valley of Mexico, east to the Gulf Coast, west to the Pacific Ocean, and south all the way to modern-day Guatemala or perhaps even the isthmus of Panama, taking captive those they had conquered along the way either for labor or for human sacrifice as part of their belief system.[11]

This is not at all to suggest that anyone anywhere deserved to be colonized and enslaved by Europeans. Rather, it is to illustrate that colonization

---

7. Allen (1997) 2012, 8; Wright 2007, 3.
8. Wright 2007, 16–21.
9. Ibid.
10. Bauer 2013, 207–209.
11. León-Portilla (1962) 1992, xxxvii–xli; Soustelle (1962) 1970, 204–215.

and slavery existed prior to the turn of the sixteenth century, but in forms distinct from the particular mode of exploitation that would follow. What was new about the sixteenth century in human history was the invention of agrarian capitalism and the establishment of the foundation for the race concept as we know it today. Capitalism emerged as a new system of labor extraction and wealth accumulation, theretofore unknown in human history. The race concept was then invented as a self-regulating system of labor management and social control within the fledgling colonial capitalist economy. The race concept would not have emerged as we know it, if at all, without the prior invention of capitalism. Capitalism came first, and then came the race concept, in that chronological order. The race concept is a totalizing edifice that permeates every aspect of our society. While facets of what became the race concept can be found earlier, the totalizing institution of the race concept in our society did not fully manifest until around the turn of the eighteenth century, when lifelong chattel slavery and exclusion were codified into law on the basis of race rather than religion, permanently relegating every member of American society to inexorable legal categories defined by racial identity.

As a result of these crucial socioeconomic developments in human history, nationalist ideology proliferated in the late eighteenth and nineteenth centuries. With the first modern nation-states carved out of colonial administrative territories by the revolt of colonial creole elites defending their property interests, nationalist ideology provided a racialized framework for state formation in the postmedieval world, first in the colonies and then in Continental Europe through the turn of the twentieth century. The amalgamation of the race concept and nationalist ideology in the minds of subordinate stateless populations, which is the primary object of critique in this book, was completed in the twentieth century, consolidated in the United States during the Civil Rights Movement era of the 1960s and 1970s. To provide a historical foundation for the critiques of ethnonationalist ideology that follow, this chapter traces the historical and conceptual development of these three pillars of modern society—capitalism, the race concept, and nationalist ideology—from the sixteenth century to their consolidation in the twentieth century.

Origins of Capitalism

The capitalist system of labor extraction and wealth accumulation emerged as a result of very specific socioeconomic and political circumstances that were unique to England in the sixteenth century, collectively known as the enclosure movement. If there is one thing scholars agree on, it is that the capitalist system was anything but an inevitable development in human history. However, before delving into the history of the enclosure movement and the emergence of agrarian capitalism, it is worth first defining what capitalism is and how previous systems of economic organization were qualitatively different and distinct from the capitalist system that emerged first in England and then the Netherlands in the sixteenth century.

In proposing a working definition of *capitalism*, I draw on the work of scholars whose expertise in this area far outweighs my own.[12] However, the definition that I propose is my own synthesis of the perspectives of various scholars, because scholars have substantial disagreements among themselves on the matter. This synthesis that I propose recognizes two basic elements to the capitalist system, both of which are unquestionably unique in human history. First, capitalism introduced a system of labor extraction that is unique in human history: wage slavery. In a capitalist economy, labor populations are compelled to work for a wage because, having been separated from the land en masse, they have no other means of providing for their sustenance. As Karl Marx's classic critique in *Wage Labor and Capital* suggests, in a capitalist economy, laborers don't freely choose to work for a wage; rather, they accept wage labor "in order to live."[13] Wage slavery is, of course, distinct from chattel slavery, which has existed for millennia.

Second, for the first time in human history, wealth began to be accumulated for the express purpose of being reinvested to produce more wealth, ad infinitum. In a capitalist system, accumulated wealth is used to acquire additional assets and productive capacity, which are then used to produce even more wealth, which is then used to acquire even more assets and productive capacity, and so on. The expansion of the capitalist economy, then, is like a cancer that multiplies exponentially until it eventually ends up undermining its own existence by creating the conditions that threaten its own survival.

These two essential qualities of the capitalist system are qualitatively distinct from all other forms of socioeconomic organization previously known in human history and particularly distinct from the feudal system from which capitalism emerged. Prior to the emergence of capitalism, efficiency of agricultural production had stagnated for millennia. Providing for the nutritional necessities of any sedentary agricultural population required the employment of about 80 percent of the population in medieval and ancient times, leaving little surplus to support the parasitic ruling classes. To make matters worse, production cycles were plagued by regular intervals of famine years wherein food production failed to fully support the population.[14]

---

12. Appleby 2010; Kocka 2016; Perelman 2000; E. Wood (1999) 2017.
13. Marx (1849), in Tucker 1978.
14. Appleby 2010.

Most important, production of the food and most of the commodities used and consumed by the vast majority of the population occurred within the community itself. Rulers and aristocrats simply skimmed off the top whatever was produced in excess of that required for reproduction of the population—and, in some cases, more, leading to famine and revolt. The only way to increase one's wealth was to conquer new lands from which surplus production could be skimmed or travel vast distances to bring commodities that were not available in one regional market from another.[15] With the perpetual threat of famine, any surplus production and wealth was either horded by rulers or accumulated as insurance against lean years, when it would be required to purchase foodstuffs to supplement local production to stave off famine and popular revolt.

The transition to capitalism was essentially an accident of history that occurred because of the specific theological and political circumstances in England in the sixteenth century. While England was in no position to conquer any additional lands in the sixteenth century, it watched as both Spain and Portugal reaped theretofore unimaginable wealth from their colonies in the Americas. Needless to say, this spurred a spirit of competition and a motive to increase domestic agricultural production throughout England. England had one export commodity for which there was significant demand: textiles. The demand for English textiles compelled landowners to enclose portions of the countryside for exclusive use in sheep husbandry to produce the wool needed to supply the market for textiles. Lands that until that time had been held in common usage by all members of a community were enclosed by physical fences and legal property lines, denying access to those who had worked them for generations, thereby permanently separating labor populations from the land.

As a result of these developments, the population of landless peasants—vagrants—exploded in mid- to late sixteenth-century England. The only recourse for such landless peasants was to work for a wage, with which they could purchase the necessities of life to provide for their own sustenance or, if they could find no work, resort to begging and stealing.[16] To provide a check on this population of useless labor, the English system of land enclosure preserved a thin intermediate stratum of yeoman tenant farmers who were able to provide for their own sustenance and thus had a stake in defending the emerging system of agrarian capitalism. This early precursor to the middle class provided a stalwart social-control mechanism to regulate the burgeoning population of the destitute and landless pauper class.[17]

---

15. Kocka 2016; E. Wood (1999) 2017.
16. Perelman 2000; E. Wood (1999) 2017.
17. Allen (1997) 2012.

Origins of the Race Concept

Disappointed to find only indigenous populations not conducive to labor extraction and no trace of precious metals in their colonial forays, as the Spanish had, the English turned to tobacco cultivation as an alternative source of profit extraction in the Jamestown colony, established in 1607. As a solution to the labor shortage in the colonies, English authorities and middlemen compelled, conned, and outright kidnapped thousands upon thousands of persons from England's undesirable classes of beggars, paupers, bastards, convicts, and otherwise unattached people known as "duty boys" and shipped them off as indentured bond slaves to English plantation colonies in North America and the Caribbean.[18] According to the headright land grant system, each indentured laborer delivered to the Virginia colony entitled the master to fifty acres of land—whether the bond slave lived to see their freedom or not. Five out of six did not.[19] This policy of forced emigration killed two birds with one stone for the English ruling class, simultaneously providing a captive labor force for profit-seeking ventures in the Americas and a strategy for social control of discarded labor populations in England, what the historian Nancy Isenberg aptly describes as "taking out the trash."[20]

Calamities compiled on the fledgling colony in the early 1620s, beginning with an extremely high mortality rate. The vast majority of bond laborers died before they ever saw a day of the freedom that had been promised them at the conclusion of their servitude. To add murder to misery, on March 22, 1622, the colony was brutally—and, I think it would be fair to say, deservedly—attacked by the indigenous Powhatan Confederacy in a last-ditch effort to evict the Jamestown colony and reclaim their way of life. One third of the colony's residents were killed in the attack in a single day.[21] Finally, and certainly the greatest threat to the prosperity of Jamestown's planter class, was a self-induced crash in tobacco prices as a result of that persistent inevitability of capitalist profit seeking: overproduction. The collapse in tobacco prices that continued to cascade throughout the seventeenth century compelled the colonial ruling class to innovate modifications to the terms of service to which indentured laborers were bound. In thousands of individual cases and hundreds of court cases, planters sought by force and by fraud to deny their indentured labor force their freedom in due time, or, as it were to be, at all.[22]

---

18. Ibid.; Coldham 1992; Isenberg 2016; Jordan and Marsh 2008; Morris 1946; Smedley 2007; Vaver 2011.
19. Allen (1997) 2012.
20. Isenberg 2016, 17.
21. Allen (1997) 2012, 84–87; Morgan 1975, 98–100.
22. Allen (1997) 2012; Morgan 1975; Smedley 2007.

The transition from indentured servitude to the racialized chattel slavery most contemporary Americans are conscious of unfolded in stages throughout the seventeenth century. However, it is important to recognize that throughout the seventeenth century, English bond slaves outnumbered African bond slaves by a wide margin. Indicative of the absence of the modern race concept in the mid-seventeenth century was a legal dispute in 1654 that was the first legal ruling to relegate an African bond slave to a condition of permanent servitude. Tellingly, the plaintiff in the case, Anthony Johnson, was a planter of entirely Angolan origin, having arrived in 1619 with the first bond slaves of African origin to set foot in the fledgling colony. After gaining his freedom at the conclusion of his own term of servitude, Johnson had become a successful planter in his own right. Johnson had purchased the contract for an African bond slave by the name of John Casar (or Casor), who insisted that he had been brought to Virginia in 1638 to serve a seven-year bondage and should have been released rather than sold to Johnson. When Casar went to work for a neighboring white planter, Johnson sued for possession of Casar. The court denied Casar's freedom, and Johnson was awarded his bondage indefinitely. Thus, the first person of African origin to be relegated to lifetime servitude in the absence of any crime having been committed was sentenced to a lifetime in service to a master who himself was entirely of African origin. The planter class in mid-seventeenth-century Virginia was attempting to impose lifetime bondage on its captive labor force to maximize profits rather than out of anything approaching a modern racial consciousness. Their motivations were quite clearly capitalist and not racist in nature, a bigotry that did not yet exist in the mid-seventeenth century.

If there is a moment in time that many scholars agree on as the catalyst for the emergence of the race concept as we know it today, it has to be Bacon's Rebellion in 1676.[23] The circumstances and trajectory of Bacon's Rebellion was a convoluted mess of posturing and miscommunication on all sides of the conflict throughout the life of the affair, but there can be no dispute as to the cause or the effect. Small landowners and recently arrived planters, such as Nathaniel Bacon, found their prospects limited by vast tracts of land held by wealthy colonial elites. At the same time, the boundaries of the colony determined by treaty proscribed the possibility of acquiring additional land to cultivate outside the colony, putting the small landowners, propertyless freemen, and newly arrived speculators in the intolerable position of having no opportunity to extract their own fortunes from the colony. Far from a deliberate attempt at revolution, Bacon's Rebellion can best be

---

23. Allen (1997) 2012; Breen and Innes (1980) 2005; Horne 2018; Morgan 1975; Roediger and Esch 2012; Smedley 2007; Washburn 1957; S. Webb 1984.

described as a breakdown in the social order of the colony, which was necessary to keep the less fortunate freemen and, most important, the bonded labor population in check.[24]

After having slaughtered numerous indigenous communities on the periphery of the colony, Bacon marched his rabble army composed of men of virtually every station and origin that the colony had to offer, freeman and bonded laborer, English, Irish, and African alike, to Jamestown, occupied the capital, looted the estates of the wealthy elite, and burned much of the town to the ground. Governor William Berkeley was forced to flee for his life and regained control of the colony only after Bacon unexpectedly died of dysentery and the mob lost its zeal and simply disbanded, returning to their own homes and families.[25] Bacon's Rebellion was a turning point in history not because of the impact or aspirations of the rebels, which, it's fair to say, were rather ignominious, but because it represented an existential threat to the ruling elite of the colony. With colonists of all stations and origins joining together against their rulers, the system of social control dividing the bonded labor population and the landless free population had broken down completely. The ruling elite of the colony needed to invent a new dividing line among the labor population to prevent the possibility of future rebellions. *The race concept was the panacea that was conceived for this purpose.*

The race concept was invented as a legal category in the late seventeenth and early eighteenth centuries for the express purpose of serving as a self-regulating system of labor management and social control, thereafter dividing white and nonwhite populations socially, legally, economically, and conceptually into exclusive, insular, and oppositional racial categories and relegating even black freemen to a subordinate position as a matter of law.[26] Therein lies the birth of racial oppression as we know it. Over the ensuing decades a steady stream of new laws were passed, culminating in the Virginia Slave Codes of 1705, with the express intent of dividing white and black labor populations in opposition to each other, relegating the status of lifetime chattel bondage exclusively to the black labor population.[27]

Racism, the pseudoscientific racial bias we associate with the race concept, was likewise invented and developed conceptually over the course of the eighteenth and nineteenth centuries as a justification for the racialized system of labor management and social control that had been invented to

---

24. Allen (1997) 2012, 210–217; Horne 2018; Morgan 1975, 250–270; Washburn 1957; S. Webb 1984, 3–163.

25. Ibid.

26. Allen (1997) 2012; Morgan 1975; Roediger and Esch 2012; Smedley 2007.

27. Allen (1997) 2012; Breen and Innes (1980) 2005; Morgan 1975.

divide and exploit black and white labor populations in North America. At first, white workers had to be taught and convinced by a deliberate propaganda campaign that they were fundamentally different from and should disdain black workers.[28] This was necessary to turn white labor populations against black labor populations, creating a self-regulating system of labor management wherein the labor population polices itself across racial lines. Over the course of the eighteenth and nineteenth centuries, the race concept took on a life of its own, drawing the attention and efforts of some of the most renowned European minds of the time, essentially trying to provide a rationalization for the racialized legal categories that had already been invented as a system of labor management and social control.[29]

The culmination of these two centuries of speculation and theorizing on the race concept is what the anthropologist Audrey Smedley calls the modern "racial worldview." She articulates the core conceptual components of the modern race concept as we know it today. First, it is *universal*, which means that, according to race ideology, all human beings can be categorized as one race or another. No one is raceless. Second, racial categories are *exclusive*, which means that they divide every human being on the planet into separate categories that do not overlap. Third, these exclusive categories are *hierarchical*, with the white or European category always at the pinnacle of the hierarchy and the black or African category always at the bottom. Fourth, membership in one category or another is acquired by accident of birth as a matter of inheritance from one's parents and is *immutable*. Fifth, racial categories are determined by *divine will* or, from a scientific perspective, are a fact of *human nature*. Finally, and of particular significance for the analysis presented in this book, there is

> the belief that the outer physical characteristics of different human populations were but surface manifestations of inner realities, for example the cognitive linking of physical features with behavioral, intellectual, temperamental, moral, and other qualities. Thus, what today most scholars recognize as cultural (learned) behavior was seen then as an innate concomitant of biophysical form.[30]

That is to say that racial identity denotes not just superficial phenotypic appearance but, moreover, dictates behavior, disposition, attitude, and, most important, *cultural praxis*. Race thinking conceives culture as a form of

28. Allen (1997) 2012, 248–252; Roediger (1991) 2007.
29. Hannaford 1996; Marks (1995) 2008; Smedley 2007.
30. Smedley 2007, 28.

intellectual property exclusive to each ethnoracial category and its bona fide members, however defined.

Origins of Nationalist Ideology

As the race concept coalesced in the eighteenth century, the final pillar of modern civilization proliferated: nationalist ideology. Nationalist identities were invented as a vehicle for state formation on the basis of the racialized identities made possible by the prior invention of the race concept. The emergence of the first modern nation-states, carved out of colonial administrative territories in the Americas in the late eighteenth century, brought the initial era of European colonialism to a gradual close and ushered in the modern era. The first modern nation-states that emerged and those that followed were, and remain, qualitatively distinct from all prior forms of political organization.[31] Brief consideration of historical examples prior to the emergence of modern nation-states is instructive in differentiating modern states from medieval forms of political organization.

The Normans were a people of mixed Danish, Norwegian, and Frankish ethnic origins who built their identity as a people as the descendants of the Norwegian raider-turned-aristocrat Rollo, who was granted dominion over the region subsequently known as Normandy by Frankish King Charles the Simple in the year 911.[32] Rollo's descendants came to conquer and rule over far-flung regions from one end of the medieval world to the other, including France, England, Sicily, Southern Italy, and the crusader city-state of Antioch in modern-day Syria. The Norman King Henry VII was the king of England and France at the same time.[33] The people who lived under Norman rule represented a wide range of ethnic origins, from Franks and Normans in France to Celts, Britons, and Anglo-Saxons in England; Arabs, Berbers, Greeks, Lombards, and Latins in Sicily and Calabria; and Arabs, Armenians, Greeks, and Latins in Antioch. The range of languages and dialects spoken by people under Norman rule in the eleventh, twelfth, and thirteenth centuries was even more diverse.

The Habsburg Empire of the sixteenth century also provides an example of the heterogeneous nature of medieval states and their subjects. Holy Roman Emperor Charles V, in whose name the Aztec and Incan empires were annihilated, ruled over disparate territories so far and wide that his domain

---

31. Calhoun 1994, 316–317.
32. The date 911 is traditionally given by the chronicler Dudo, who wrote the first history of the Normans in the early eleventh century at the behest of Norman King Richard II.
33. Chibnall (2000) 2006; Crouch 2002.

was dubbed "the empire on which the sun never sets." It included modern-day Spain and Portugal, the Netherlands, Germany and Austria, Italy, and much of Eastern Europe, as well as all of Mesoamerica, the Caribbean, and the northern portion of the South American continent.[34] The full range of languages, dialects, and vernaculars spoken by the subjects of the Habsburg Empire in the early sixteenth century is nearly unimaginable.

I emphasize the eclectic diversity of ethnic and linguistic groups in premodern states, as well as the geographical dispersion of their territories, because these are the elements that differentiate them from modern nation-states of the nationalist era. Modern nation-states, unlike their predecessors, consist of five key conceptual components.[35] First, they purport to represent a *homogeneous*—or, at least, dominant majority—ethnonationalist identity as the normative identity category represented by the state itself. Second, modern nation-states in the nationalist era possess a single written and spoken *standardized language* that purportedly correlates with the ethnoracial identity of the state and is the sole lingua franca for purposes of communication and commerce within the state. Third, modern nation-states in the nationalist era are composed primarily of a single *contiguous territory* that encompasses the putative ancestral "homeland" of the citizens of the nationalist state. Fourth, modern nation-states in the nationalist era assume a *myth of origin* as a narrative construction that justifies the claim to the territory occupied by the state and claimed by the corresponding identity group. Fifth, modern nation-states invent and appropriate *cultural practices* and anoint them with the symbolism of the state and the nationalist identity that corresponds with the state. No ancient or medieval form of political organization in any part of the world reflected all five of these core conceptual components of nationalist identity and ideology.

Political scientist Benedict Anderson of Cornell University suggested in his magnum opus, *Imagined Communities*, that modern nation-states in the nationalist era require three institutions for their maintenance: the census, the map, and the museum.[36] To this short list I would venture to add the flag and the ubiquitous use of surnames as integral artifices of both nationalist identity and state authority. Aside from its function as an instrument of bureaucratic authority, the census serves the purpose of sorting the population of the state into natives and foreigners, those who share the purported common descent of the bona fide members of the nation-state and those who do not. The map is necessary as a vehicle for defining the boundaries of the state and, therefore, of the population it purportedly represents. The

---

34. Elliot 2002.
35. Anderson (1983) 2016; Calhoun 1997; Hobsbawm 1990.
36. Anderson (1983) 2016, 163–185.

museum—or, as Anderson implies, the academy—is necessary to invent the pseudohistorical narratives that define the purported ancestry of the putative population the nation-state represents. I add the flag to this list as a necessary accoutrement of any nationalist identity, a visible visceral symbol of the ethnonationalist identity the nation-state represents. I also include the universal use of surnames, not only as a bureaucratic invention of the nationalist state for means of population identification and sorting, but, moreover, as a means of denoting the ethnoracial identities nationalism is predicated on, differentiating citizen from foreigner.

Historically, the idea that there is such a thing as a coherent national identity and that all those who share that identity share a national language, common names, symbols, and cultural inheritance is an artifice that owes the possibility of its existence in large part to the introduction of the movable-type printing press in Europe in the mid-fifteenth century. To sell more books to publics not educated in Latin, printing houses began printing books in local vernaculars. Wherever movable-type printing presses first appeared in various countries and printing industries emerged, the local vernacular became the standard vernacular by virtue of being printed and then distributed throughout the region to localities that employed other dialects and vernaculars in their common parlance.[37] The proliferation of printed material in standardized languages made the emergence of nationalist ideology and identities possible by encouraging the twin fiction that all members of the modern nation-state share not only a political union but also a common cultural inheritance and corresponding racial identity. There can be no serious debate that such fictions are of entirely European invention during the colonial era.

The first modern nation-states that were explicitly predicated on a nationalist framework of state and identity formation emerged from bourgeois revolutions of creole elites who rebelled against economic and political limitations imposed by monarchs in Europe. The first of these creole nation-states carved out of colonial administrative territories that ushered in the modern nationalist era was, of course, the United States of America, which won its independence from England in 1776. While the mythology of the American state fetishizes this "revolution" as one fought for freedom and self-determination, as the critical historian Gerald Horne admonishes, this star-spangled propaganda is far from the truth. The so-called revolution was declared by wealthy creole elites in the American colonies, many of whom were slavers, to protect their property interests. The founding fathers were not the heralds of freedom, as we Americans were raised to believe; quite the contrary. They were the reaction of vested colonial interests to the pos-

---

37. Anderson (1983) 2016; Eisenstein (1983) 2016; Febvre and Martin (1958) 2010.

sibility that the English crown might threaten their estates, many of which were made possible only by the holocaust of black chattel slavery.[38] Rather than drawing on distant history, the creole nation-states of the nationalist era created their own mythologies and concurrent cultural practices as an artifice to consolidate political control over a disparate population explicitly divided by class, race, and gender.

The tension and conflict between European-born *peninsulares* and Mexican-born *criollos* also provided the initial impetus for the protracted struggle for Mexican independence from Spain in the wake of the Napoleonic conquest of Spain in 1808, culminating in a peasant uprising in 1810 that ultimately was crushed by royalist forces.[39] What was unique about the independence of Mexico from Spain was that, while Spanish remained the lingua franca, starting with the *Plan de Iguala* in 1821, the emergence of the Mexican nation-state was predicated on dismantling the complicated racial caste legal system imposed by Spanish colonial rule, with Spanish-born *peninsulares* at the top and *Indigenas* and *Afro-Mexicano/a* populations at the bottom of the colonial stratification hierarchy. The fledgling Mexican nation-state replaced the Spanish colonial caste system with a single racial identity for all Mexicans to embrace: *Mestizaje*. The Myth of Mestizaje (also known as the mestizo myth) behind this invented identity was that, as a result of colonialism, the Mexican population was mixed to such a degree that it was impossible for anyone to know what particular racial admixture they were.[40] However, this wasn't an abolition of the race concept but, rather, the invention of a new racial identity as an instrument of state formation, ostensibly shared by all citizens of the fledgling Mexican nation-state, whether or not they were actually direct descendants of the historical *Mexica*.

These early modern nation-states in the late eighteenth and early nineteenth centuries were followed by the emergence of the prototypical modern nation-states in Europe in the second half of the nineteenth century. The twin paragons of the modern nation-state in the nationalist tradition, from my perspective, are Italy (1861) and Germany (1871). The invention of these nations and corresponding identities over the course of the nineteenth century are instructive not merely to continue the chronological progression of the historical narrative thus far provided but, moreover, because they represent the archetype models for the modern ethnonationalist ideology of the late twentieth and early twenty-first centuries that is ultimately the object of critique in this book. They also are instructive not only because they are explicitly ethnonationalist states predicated on demonstrably contrived eth-

---

38. Horne 2014.
39. Altman et al. 2002; Van Young 2002.
40. Altman et al. 2002; Vinson 2017.

noracial identities, but also because both took ethnonationalist ideology to its logical conclusion in the mid-twentieth century, perpetrating unthinkable atrocities on the basis of ethnonationalist identity and racist pseudoscience. In contrast to the formation of the prior modern nation-states out of colonial administrative territories, the modern nation-states invented in the second half of the nineteenth century wove elaborate and long-reaching myths of origin stretching back millennia to validate the political unification of territories inhabited by culturally disparate populations speaking a panoply of languages, dialects, and vernaculars. In the interest of brevity, I limit my review to the invention of the German state and corresponding identity.

Like that of Italy, the invention of Germany was made possible by the fracturing of the Habsburg Empire, which resulted from the military conquests of France's Emperor Napoleon I in the early nineteenth century. In the wake of Napoleon's defeat, Continental Europe was carved up by the major powers at the Congress of Vienna in 1815, with roughly outlined regions of influence divided among France, the Netherlands, Prussia, and Austria. The panoply of regions that make up modern Germany had been loosely affiliated under the Holy Roman Empire for a millennium prior to the invention of Germany. However, even as late as the turn of the nineteenth century, there was no Pan-German identity that united them politically, culturally, linguistically, or conceptually. Populations that spoke various Germanic dialects and vernaculars, roughly grouped into High and Low German, conceived of their identities in terms of the region and regime in which they lived, whether under the domain of a king, duke, prince, or ecclesiastic authority. In the nineteenth century, a wave of nationalist propaganda swept across Germanic language–speaking populations in what would become Germany and Austria.

While German nationalists advocated the unification of all these regions with the Austrian Empire into one Pan-German political entity, the Kingdom of Prussia that had emerged in the wake of the Napoleonic Wars had its own ambition to unify Germany under a Prussian king, rather than a Habsburg. Prussia's Chancellor Otto von Bismarck's pragmatic strategy of *realpolitik*, combined with the resounding victory of Prussian armies in three consecutive wars against Denmark, Austria, and France, gave nationalists the opportunity to unite all of present-day Germany into one single political entity under the rule of the Prussian Kaiser Wilhelm I in 1871, dubbed the First German Reich.[41] German nationalist ideology was, of course, taken to its logical conclusion in the twentieth century by Nazi Führer Adolf Hitler's genocidal Third Reich.

---

41. Barraclough 1984; Stern 1979.

The Italian and German unification movements are of particular significance because they succeeded in creating modern nation-states out of territories that had not theretofore been politically unified on the basis of ethnoracial identities. It is important to recognize that these identities did not exist prior to the nineteenth century. They were inventions of the nationalist movements, made possible by the standardization of a lingua franca in print combined with a contrived cultural unity and purportedly shared myth of origin. These explicitly nationalist states employed all five of the conceptual components essential to the modern nation-state in the nationalist era. They divided their populations into in-group and out-group members based on their ethnoracial identities. They established a standardized lingua franca for communication and commerce. They established the boundaries of these ethnoracial identities in geographic terms ostensibly on the basis of a putative "homeland." And they manipulated historical narratives to invent myths of origin and encouraged the myth of a common cultural inheritance shared by all members of society who could make a legitimate claim to membership in the ethnoracial identity that defined citizenship.

It was these core features of modern nationalist ideology that were adopted by subordinate labor populations in the twentieth century to invent their own nationalist identities in the United States and elsewhere in the postcolonial world. This reactionary ethnonationalism, ironically often referred to as "revolutionary nationalism" (an oxymoron if there ever was one), is what I now turn to in concluding this chapter on the historical foundations of contemporary racialized gang conflict in Los Angeles.

From Cultural Nationalism to Identity Politics

The origins of the black nationalist ideology that informs contemporary African American gang identities and served as a model for Chicano nationalism emerged in the aftermath of hundreds of years of racialized chattel slavery, European colonialism, and the apocalypse of mass genocide on an intercontinental scale.[42] In the period leading up to the American Civil War, the Abolitionist Movement in northern states employed educated African Americans who had experienced chattel slavery firsthand, such as Frederick Douglass and Solomon Northrup, to share their experiences, both in public lectures and in print, to demonstrate not only the moral corruption of slavery but also, to white Americans, the outstanding intellectual and moral quality of African Americans in response to the racist pseudoscience of the

---

42. Horne 2018.

era.[43] This integrationist movement to gain the respect and acceptance of white Americans would continue with the first generation of African American racial spokespersonship: Booker T. Washington and Harvard's first African American doctor of philosophy, the sociologist W. E. B. Du Bois. Adolph Reed Jr. provides an accurate summary of Washington's career:

> More than Douglass had ever been, Washington became the singular, trusted informant to communicate to whites what the Negro thought, felt, wanted, needed. Washington's stature derived from skill at soothing white liberals' *retreat* from the Reconstruction era's relatively progressive racial politics. He became the first purely freelance race spokesman; his status depended on designation by white elites rather than by any black electorate or social movement. To that extent he originated a new model of the generic Black Leader—the Racial Voice accountable to no clearly identifiable constituency among the spoken for.[44]

Du Bois, a true intellectual, however, implicitly recognized the inherently divisive role of the race concept as a vehicle for labor management and social control in his magnum opus, *Black Reconstruction in America*, writing:

> The political success of the doctrine of racial separation, which overthrew Reconstruction by uniting planter and the poor white, was far exceeded by its astonishing economic results. The theory of laboring class unity rests upon the assumption that laborers, despite internal jealousies, will unite because of their opposition to exploitation by the capitalists. According to this, even after a part of the poor white laboring class becomes identified with the planters, and eventually displaced them, their interests would be diametrically opposed to those of the mass white labor, and of course to those of the black laborers. This would throw white and black labor into one class, and precipitate a united fight for higher wage and better working conditions.
>
> Most persons do not realize how far this failed to work in the South, and it failed to work because the theory of race was supplemented by a carefully planned and slowly evolved method, which drove such a wedge between the white and black workers that there are probably not today in the world two groups of workers with prac-

43. Northrup (1853) 2014; Trotman 2011.
44. A. Reed 2000, 79, author's emphasis.

tically identical interests who hate and fear each other so deeply and persistently and who are kept so far apart that neither sees anything of common interest.[45]

Ironically, perhaps, Du Bois had also entertained nationalist perspectives earlier in his career.[46]

Thirty-five years prior to the publication of *Black Reconstruction*, Du Bois was an attendee of the first Pan-African Conference (later Congress) in London in 1900, which was organized by Henry Sylvester Williams, a prominent early black nationalist and attorney from Trinidad who was living in London at the time.[47] The conference was conceived, organized, and overwhelmingly attended by notable members of the African diaspora from the United States, the Caribbean, and Europe, with only a handful of attendees who were actually from Africa.[48] That all people of African descent shared a common identity was, of course, an idea derived specifically from an African diaspora perspective by those who could not trace their ancestry to any specific region or linguistic/ethnic community within Africa. Stemming from their inability to imagine a more complex notion of heritage beyond the conceptual boundaries of the colonial societies that hosted them, these men were embracing all of the facets of the race concept invented by racist (white) European and American theorists, theologians, and pseudoscientists over the eighteenth and nineteenth centuries, subsuming the entire range of variety of human societies and cultures in an entire continent and diaspora population into a single racialized identity. The only facet of the race concept discussed previously that Pan-African nationalists did not embrace is the idea that Africans are inferior to Europeans.

This racial worldview matured into an explicitly nationalist ideology with the first bona fide black nationalist demagogue of the early twentieth century, Marcus Garvey. While Garvey must have looked like the messiah of black liberation compared with the likes of Booker T. Washington, the black nationalist ideology Garvey espoused was a flagrant mimicry of the white nationalism with which he found common cause. A native of Jamaica known for his pompous outfits, Garvey often dressed as if he were the dictator of an imaginary Pan-African nation-state in the European model. While in Kingston, Garvey established the Universal Negro Improvement Association and African Communities League (UNIA-ACL) in 1914. The stated objective of the UNIA was "to establish a brotherhood among the black race,

---

45. Du Bois (1935) 1992, 700.
46. Bracey et al. 1970, 246–298.
47. Mathurin 1976; Sherwood 2011.
48. Mathurin 1976.

to promote a spirit of race pride, to reclaim the fallen and to assist in civiliz-ing the backward tribes of Africa."[49] Of course, the idea that indigenous Africans were backward and in need of "civilization" is at the core of Euro-pean colonial perspectives. That irony was lost on Garvey and his acolytes, both then and now.

Garvey's explicitly black nationalist political platform did not catch on in his native Kingston. Following accusations that he had embezzled UNIA funds, Garvey fled and took his hustle to New York City in 1917. Despite the accusations of financial impropriety that followed him, membership in the UNIA increased dramatically in the years after he arrived in the United States, with branches established across half the country. Despite his affin-ity for the British Empire; his Roman Catholic faith; his attempt to enlist in the U.S. Army during World War I; his enthusiastic collaboration with the Ku Klux Klan, with which he found common cause in pursuit of a racially segregated society; and his proud association with the Italian fascist dictator Benito Mussolini, Garvey's explicitly black nationalist rhetoric denounced those assimilationists he accused of being allies of white America, such as the National Association for the Advancement of Colored People (NAACP), led by none other than W. E. B. Du Bois.[50] At a UNIA rally at Madison Square Garden in 1920 that drew an estimated audience of twenty-five thou-sand, Garvey was declared the "President of Africa," putative leader of a continent he had never set foot in and of whose thousands of languages he spoke not a one. Garvey also was the inventor of another essential facet of black nationalist identity, the *tricolour* red, black, and green Pan-African flag, the symbolic representation of a Pan-African nation-state not only imagined in the European model but represented symbolically by a flag that bears an uncanny similarity in design to those of numerous European co-lonial powers.

After surviving a wide range of accusations of impropriety connected to the many capitalist enterprises associated with the UNIA, Garvey was even-tually convicted of mail fraud in 1923 as a result of a scheme involving a UNIA-affiliated business, the Black Star Line. The company had appropri-ated its name from the British maritime company the White Star Line, per-haps best known today for the sinking of the *RMS Titanic* in 1912. The fi-nances of the Black Star Line sank almost as fast, perhaps compelling Garvey to offer for sale shares of stock in a ship the company did not actually own, the crime for which he was convicted. Sentenced to five years in prison, he was generously released with a presidential pardon after only two years, under the condition that he be deported back to Jamaica. Enjoying some

---

49. Grant 2008, 54.
50. Cronon 1969; Gilroy 2000; Grant 2008.

popularity in Kingston upon his arrival, he quickly set about rebuilding the UNIA there but managed to get himself thoroughly ostracized and ultimately left, a broken and dejected man, for London, where he died in 1940.[51]

Garvey railed against miscegenation and integration, proposing instead that people of Sub-Saharan African descent in the Americas return to Africa in a mass migration and establish colonies there. It was an ambition that never came to fruition; nor did his dream of a black nationalist regime that would rule all of Africa, with him as president for life. Having never set foot in Africa and being utterly ignorant of the incredible diversity of cultures, societies, and linguistic communities throughout the continent, Garvey held a perception of Africa as uncivilized that was decidedly Eurocentric. Garvey's ideas were essentially a mirror image of the nationalism of white supremacy. Despite the rank hypocrisy and almost comical irony of his rhetoric and praxis, Garvey was lionized after his death, both in the United States and in his native Jamaica, and was elevated in death to the cult-like figure that he could never quite achieve in life. His reactionary nationalist ideology would have a tremendous influence on the black power movement in the second half of the twentieth century.

Garvey's brand of reactionary nationalism crystallized during the Civil Rights Movement era in the 1960s and 1970s, with ardent black nationalists such as Stokely Carmichael (a.k.a. Kwame Ture), who is credited with popularizing the term *Black Power*, and Ron (Maulana) Karenga, both of whom had denounced the Black Panther Party (BPP) for organizing across racial lines. Certainly, the BPP was not distinguished from its ethnonationalist contemporaries by any less concern with black liberation and racial oppression. Rather, it was distinguished by its greater concern with the material and institutional inequalities rooted in the capitalist economy that could be addressed only through international pan-racial solidarity and revolution, not the merely symbolic cultural machinations preferred by its ethnonationalist opponents within the black community. Whereas the political scientist Cedric Johnson focused his analysis on Harold Cruse and Amiri Baraka (LeRoi Jones), both of whom were significant figures in the black nationalist movement of the Civil Rights Movement era, I focus my analysis on the career of Karenga, both because he was a critical figure in the black nationalist Pan-African movement and because his career was crucial to the proliferation of ethnonationalist ideology in the Los Angeles context specifically. Karenga advocated an ideology he explicitly termed *cultural nationalism*: the idea that African Americans could achieve liberation by appropriating the cultural practices of African cultures with which they had

---

51. Cronon 1969; Grant 2008.

no material indigenous connection aside from an assumption of ancestry, a reactionary species of what the sociologist Herbert Gans called *symbolic identity.*[52]

Karenga is an especially significant figure in the evolution of black nationalist ideology in the United States because it was he who added the remaining essential conceptual components of the Pan-African nationalist identity championed by Garvey: a lingua franca, Africanized names of various origins, and a myth of common cultural inheritance. Karenga and the US organization he founded (as in, us versus them) made a conscious attempt to appropriate aspects of various African cultures by assuming names of African origin; adopting the Swahili language indigenous to the East African coast; wearing clothing appropriated from West African cultures, such as the dashikis of the Yoruba and boubous of the Hausa-Fulani communities of modern-day Nigeria; and inventing a religion Karenga called Kawaida. Karenga had no qualms about his use of invention to supplement and repackage ideas, history, and culture he appropriated from various African societies, pronouncing mythology as the first of the seven "criteria of a culture" he theorized as the basis for Pan-African civilization.[53]

Karenga was much more knowledgeable than Garvey had ever been about Africa and its incredible diversity of cultures and linguistic communities. However, Karenga's education in African language and cultures was acquired not directly in indigenous contexts but, rather, through his studies at Los Angeles City College and the University of California, Los Angeles (UCLA), in the early 1960s. He was influenced by the work of Western anthropologists, such as Eileen Krige's exhaustive study of the Zulu society in southeastern Africa, *The Social System of the Zulus.*[54] Karenga was also influenced by leaders of anticolonial independence movements that employed nationalist ideology as a framework for independence and state formation, such as Jomo Kenyatta, Kenya's first president (for life).[55]

The US organization was ostensibly founded with the objective of carrying on the legacy of Malcolm X after his assassination, with US members wearing shirts bearing Malcolm's likeness. After splitting with cofounder Hakim Jamal, who had been personally acquainted with Malcolm X, Karenga changed the image on the shirts to his own likeness, reflecting the cult of personality that the US organization became under his leadership. The parallel to Garveyism should be apparent. Karenga's US organization clashed

---

52. Gans 1973.
53. Brown 2003.
54. Krige (1936) 1974.
55. Brown 2003.

regularly with the BPP across ideological lines over the issue of ethnonationalism in the Civil Rights Movement. Following in Garvey's footsteps, Karenga railed against organizing across racial lines and denounced the BPP for doing so, while Karenga himself met with both LAPD Chief Thomas Reddin and Governor Ronald Reagan on separate occasions to advise them on how to quell unrest in the black community in the wake of the assassination of Martin Luther King Jr.[56]

Karenga was accused by Louis E. Tackwood, a Federal Bureau of Investigation (FBI) asset-turned-whistleblower, of knowingly receiving weapons from the FBI in his explosive exposé of the Counter Intelligence Program (COINTELPRO) operation published as the book *The Glasshouse Tapes*.[57] A total of four BPP members in Southern California were murdered by members of Karenga's US organization as part of FBI-orchestrated COINTELPRO assassination operations.[58] On January 17, 1969, President Alprentice "Bunchy" Carter and Vice President John Huggins of the BPP's Los Angeles chapter were assassinated by US organization members during a meeting of the Black Student Union at UCLA. Karenga was conveniently not present, but a fight reportedly broke out between Carter and Huggins on one side and US organization members Harold Jones (Tawala) and the brothers George and Larry (Watani) Stiner on the other.[59] According to multiple sources, including retired FBI whistleblower Wesley Swearingen, who was assigned to the bureau's Los Angeles COINTELPRO unit at the time, both of the Stiner brothers were FBI assets.[60] US organization member Claude Hubert (Chuchessa Haidi), also reportedly an FBI asset, allegedly shot both Huggins and Carter dead on the spot, according to witnesses.[61] As BPP cofounder Bobby Seale recounted the following year in his memoir, *Seize the Time* (1970):

Alprentice "Bunchy" Carter was killed because a group of blacks— black racists and cultural nationalists from Ron Karenga's US organization—became the enemies of the people and, in essence, sided with the capitalist power structure. These pig, black racists really work with the power structure against their own people and do it

---

56. Ibid.
57. Tackwood 1973, 106.
58. Bloom and Martin 2013, 218–222; Churchill and Vander Wall 1988, 42–43; Swearingen 1995, 82–83.
59. Brown 2003; Churchill and Vander Wall 1988; Swearingen 1995.
60. Churchill and Vander Wall 1988, 42–43; Swearingen 1995, 82–83.
61. Bloom and Martin 2013; Churchill and Vander Wall 1988; Drummond 2015; Fleischer 2007; Pool 2008.

out of a psychological need to hate white people just because of the color of their skin.[62]

Claude Hubert mysteriously vanished from the face of the earth that day and has never been seen or heard from again, save for Larry (Watani) Stiner's claim to have been in contact with him in Guyana.[63] The Stiner brothers were convicted of the murders in 1969 and sentenced to life in prison but miraculously escaped in 1974 from San Quentin State Prison.[64] That was the same prison where George Jackson, founder of the Black Guerrilla Family, was gunned down in a purported escape attempt three years earlier, in 1971.[65] Both Stiner brothers also vanished from the face of the earth, but Larry (Watani) Stiner reemerged twenty years later, in 1994, and turned himself in to U.S. authorities after (according to him) falling on hard times in Suriname, where he claimed to have been living since 1978. After having been on the lam for twenty years having escaped prison to avoid a life sentence for murder (for which he inexplicably received no time added to his sentence), Stiner was released from San Quentin in 2015. This was a curiously generous parole decision compared with that of Bunchy Carter's surviving brother, Kenneth "Fati" Carter, who has been incarcerated in California's maximum security prisons continuously since 1973 and has been denied parole consistently since he first became eligible in 1978.[66] For what it's worth, Stiner has emphatically denied being involved in any assassination conspiracy, with his own account of events as evidence supporting his denial.[67]

The BPP assassinations at UCLA were followed by the assassinations of two other BPP leaders by members of the US organization in San Diego, at the FBI's behest, later in 1969.[68] The US organization member Jerry Horne shot and killed BPP San Diego member John Savage on May 23, 1969. Then, on August 15, 1969, BPP San Diego member Sylvester Bell was murdered, and two other members were wounded, by US organization members whom Swearingen also identified as FBI assets.[69] The incredible hypocrisy of four Black Panthers being murdered by members of the US organization, the foremost proponents of black nationalism in Southern California at the time, obviously undermines the dubious claim that nationalist frameworks

---

62. Seale (1970) 1991, 271.
63. Fleischer 2007.
64. Drummond 2015; Fleischer 2007; Swearingen 1995.
65. Berger 2014; Cummins 1994; Durden-Smith 1976; Weide 2020.
66. Bunchy's brother Glen Carter was shot dead by a police officer in 1968.
67. Stiner 2021.
68. Swearingen 1995, 84.
69. Churchill and Vander Wall 1988, 42; Swearingen 1995, 84.

serve as a vehicle for internal unity around racialized identities. No member of the US organization was ever murdered or even shot at by any member of the BPP.

The assassinations orchestrated by the FBI of BPP leaders and opponents of cultural nationalism in Los Angeles and San Diego by members of the US organization were followed by the FBI-orchestrated assassination of Chicago's BPP Chairman Fred Hampton later that year, on December 4, 1969.[70] Hampton was a fearless critic of cultural nationalism and, like Alprentice "Bunchy" Carter, was attempting to politicize and organize black and brown street gangs in Chicago at the time of his assassination.[71] An FBI informant who had infiltrated the Chicago chapter of the BPP, William O'Neal, not only provided detailed maps of the apartment to aid the Chicago Police Department's assassination team but ate dinner with Hampton, his wife, and victim Mark Clark, drugging them all and then leaving the apartment.[72] Hampton was executed as he slept in a fusillade of gunfire that erupted as soon as the police kicked the door in. The FBI's obvious choice as to which framework for black liberation it found most threatening to the institutionalized order it was charged with defending ought to be instructive.

After being released from prison for orchestrating the kidnapping and torture of two black women who had attempted to leave the US organization, Karenga has enjoyed a prolific academic career, becoming the chair of the Department of Africana Studies at California State University, Long Beach, a position he retains as of the time of this writing. He has published extensively in Pan-African studies journals and is the author of numerous books, including the most widely used introductory textbook in the academic field of Pan-African studies. Karenga is also the inventor of the Pan-African holiday Kwanzaa (named for the river in Angola), a black nationalist alternative to Christmas that is practiced by millions of African Americans, many of whom know little about its origins or inventor.

The Civil Rights Movement was a crossroads in American history for black and brown liberation, but not for the reasons we are taught in secondary school. In the wake of the FBI-orchestrated assassinations of the most outspoken critics of cultural nationalism, Bunchy Carter and Fred Hampton, in 1969, and the criminalization, incarceration, and exile of BPP revolutionaries nationwide, law enforcement intent on maintaining the status quo made sure that black nationalist frameworks emerged from the collapse of the Civil Rights Movement as the hegemonic ideological foundation for ensuing generations in the black community. These assassinations paved the

---

70. Churchill and Vander Wall 1988, 65–66; Haas 2010.
71. Churchill and Vander Wall 1988, 65–66.
72. Ibid.; Haas 2010, 173–192.

way for the proliferation of ethnonationalist ideology by removing the principal critics of black nationalism and champions of an alternative vision of black liberation from the field of discourse. With those martyrs died the class-consciousness and pan-racial solidarity that they championed.

While the Black Panther Party is better known to the lay public, it was the cultural nationalist ideology of its adversaries in the US organization that became hegemonic in the wake of the collapse of the Civil Rights Movement. By positioning themselves in the academy, professional ethnopolitical entrepreneurs such as Karenga have situated themselves to write history in their image, as the victors in any war inevitably do, and that is exactly what they have done. There is a direct line between Karenga and contemporary Pan-African leaders, academics, and activists, such as Melina Abdullah (formerly Melina Rachel Reimann), my colleague at California State University, Los Angeles, the cofounder and putative leader of Black Lives Matter–Los Angeles, who has publicly claimed Karenga as her mentor on numerous occasions. Karenga was even invited to give the keynote speech at the fiftieth anniversary of the Pan-African Studies Department on our campus. (Of course I attended.) As the propaganda from Abdullah's recent campaign to be named the inaugural dean of ethnic studies at Cal State LA stated emphatically, "Ethnic studies is the most enduring victory of the black power movement." I couldn't agree more.

The Chicano nationalism that informs the identities of contemporary *Sureño*-affiliated gang members in Los Angeles is rooted in the nationalist ideology that informed the mestizo myth, which was invented as an instrument of Mexican state formation to bind the disparate populations of Mesoamerica into one national racialized identity. This myth of origin, predicated on the presumption of shared *Mexica* descent, is at the core of both Mexican national identity and, by extension, Chicano identity in the American Southwest. As the University of California, Berkeley, legal scholar Ian Haney-Lopez writes:

> It bears emphasizing that the Chicano conception of mestizaje depended upon understanding race as a matter of descent. To this extent, nature determined racial identity, making one Chicano by birth, not by choice. It was nature, and not a common history of religion or language, that most firmly bound Mexicans to one another. Mestizaje—the biology of race—made all Mexicans the same.[73]

---

73. Haney-Lopez 2003, 220.

However, the idea that all Mexicans, much less Chicanos, are the direct descendants of the historical *Mexica* is patently absurd. Prior to the arrival of the *conquistadores*, there were dozens of different societies and at least half a dozen major language families, not counting isolates, indigenous to Mesoamerica, of which Uto-Aztecan is only one. Even today, *Indigenas* Mayan communities speaking a panoply of different languages and dialects persist throughout much of the Yucatán Peninsula and Chiapas. However, not all people of modern Mexican origin can trace their ancestry hundreds of years to precolonial times to know exactly which of these disparate populations they are descended from. It should be obvious that not everyone of Mexican origin today is descended from the historical *Mexica*. Many, if not most, are likely descendants of precolonial populations who either avoided, resisted, or were victims of *Mexica* colonization.

In addition to the *Indigenas* population of Mesoamerica, more than 200,000 African slaves were brought to colonial New Spain.[74] While many contemporary Chicanos are loathe to identify with their Iberian descent, they ought not neglect that many of the *conquistadores* who settled in the Americas were actually *conversos*—Jews and Spanish Moors of North African, West African, and Middle Eastern origin—who had been forced to convert to Catholicism in the late fifteenth century in the wake of the *Reconquista*, such as the famous explorer Estevan el Morro (Steven the Moor). With such a diverse range of populations constituting the heritage of contemporary Mexican and Chicano populations, how can anyone know from whom they are descended exactly? And what does it matter? From a nationalist perspective, it doesn't, because the Mexican myth of origin assumes that all contemporary Mexican and Chicano populations are descended from the historical *Mexica*. Whether that is historically accurate for any individual, and whatever other ethnic, linguistic, and cultural identities are erased by this myth of origin, is immaterial from a nationalist perspective. What matters is that contemporary Chicanos *think* they are descended from the *Mexica*, an aspect of their myth of origin that figures prominently in *Sureño* iconography.

Whatever anyone's precise ethnolinguistic origin, surely the most significant historical juncture in the development of a distinctively Chicano ethnoracial identity has to be the sacrifice of half the territory controlled by the fledgling Mexican nation-state at the altar of Manifest Destiny. As the U.S. Marine Corps hymn preserves for posterity in its opening line, "From the Halls of Montezuma," the unprovoked invasion of Mexico by the United States and the subsequent collapse of the unstable Mexican government

---

74. Boyd-Bowman 1969; Palmer 1976; Sue 2013; Vinson 2017; P. Wood 1996.

compelled the surrender of California and what is now the entire American Southwest to the United States in the lopsided Treaty of Guadalupe Hidalgo in 1848. In the wake of the transfer of half of Mexico's territory to the United States and the conveniently timed discovery of gold by Anglo settlers at Sutter's Mill the same year, the first of several massive waves of immigration brought hordes of Anglo prospectors and settlers to California.[75]

With the arrival of Anglos in California came the Anglo-American system of racial categorization, discrimination, and subordination, which rendered all nonwhite populations subordinate to the newly arrived Anglo-American population. Anthropologist Martha Menchaca characterizes the historical experience of the Chicano population of the American Southwest as "double colonization," whereby the *Indigenas* populations of the American Southwest had to endure first Spanish and then Anglo colonization within a period of less than two centuries, each with its own unique racial caste system of labor management and social control.[76] Many Mexicans in the late nineteenth century, particularly those of lighter complexion and with greater financial resources, attempted to elude the imposition of the North American racial order by asserting that they were of Iberian descent and therefore not Mexican.[77] Despite these last-ditch attempts to maintain their status and property by claiming European heritage, even the elite of the Mexican population of Los Angeles had been relieved of all significant property holdings by the turn of the twentieth century, finding themselves reduced to the lowest level of social status in Anglo-American society, situated similarly to the African Americans who began to arrive with the influx of Anglo settlers in California in the late nineteenth century. Upon their arrival in California, African American labor populations were intentionally played off against Mexican labor populations by employers to maintain the racial division and animosity necessary to facilitate labor exploitation. As historians David Roediger and Elizabeth Esch recount, "Black and Mexican workers competed for jobs in a system of concentrated race management designed to divide and drive them."[78]

The consolidation of contemporary Chicano identity in Los Angeles was also made possible by the geographical isolation of Mexican American populations in the first half of the twentieth century. Racially exclusive housing laws, policies, and practices, such as racially restrictive housing covenants

---

75. In the colonial context of the American Southwest, *Anglo* refers to English-speaking settler populations of European heritage.

76. Menchaca 2001.

77. Gomez 2007.

78. Roediger and Esch 2012, 204.

and redlining, separated the Mexican American population in Los Angeles not only from the Anglo population, but also from the African American community. Prior to being ruled unconstitutional by the U.S. Supreme Court in 1948, racially restrictive housing covenants and redlining schemes were commonly employed and enforced to confine nonwhite populations in tightly circumscribed communities that were geographically isolated from the Anglo community and from one another, condemning African American and Chicano communities to generations of marginalization and criminalization.[79] By establishing these racial enclaves, the Anglo Angeleno establishment succeeded in establishing them as a common destination for generations of black and Latino immigrants to Los Angeles, long after the covenants themselves were legally dissolved, with the vast majority of African Americans settling in the Central Avenue corridor in South Los Angeles, and the vast majority of Chicanos settling in the low-lying hills and flood-prone flatlands of East Los Angeles. This geographical isolation was not chosen by the African American and Chicano communities of their own volition; rather, it was imposed on them by racist housing covenants and redlining schemes that forbade them from settling in most areas of the city, which were reserved for Anglos, and concentrated them instead in areas that placed them in close proximity to labor needs so their labor could be exploited conveniently.

In addition to deliberate government policies that enforced racial segregation, it's important to consider how law enforcement efforts to undermine the Civil Rights Movement provoked the emergence of racialized identities in the Chicano community. In his analysis of the Chicano movement in Los Angeles during the Civil Rights Movement era, Haney-Lopez argues that formal arrest and prosecution, and extralegal violence and intimidation by law enforcement—what he collectively calls "legal violence"—led to the radicalization of the Chicano movement and the crystallization of an exclusive, insular, oppositional racial identity among Chicano youth. Haney-Lopez suggests that the Chicano identity that crystallized in this period embraced rather than challenged the foundations on which racial categories and racial oppression are predicated:

> Indigenous descent allowed Chicanos to lay special claim to the Southwest. It also provided a source for a Chicano culture presumably untainted by Anglo norms. Both claims were supremely racial in nature. Consider first the assertion that Chicanos deserved the Southwest by right of prior possession; this claim resurrected the worn belief that divine provenance allocated the world's continents

---

79. Darden 1995; P. Robinson 2010; Bloch and Phillips 2022.

to different races. . . . When Chicanos claimed the Southwest by descent, they did so on the ground of racial entitlement.[80]

Haney-Lopez argues that legal violence perpetrated against Chicano activists by law enforcement transformed the Chicano movement from a movement that denounced the race concept as a vehicle for disparate treatment into one that embraced the race concept as a nationalist identity exclusive to Chicanos and in opposition to all other races, as epitomized by the nationalist slogan *Viva la Raza!* Haney-Lopez suggests that this paradigmatic shift fundamentally undermined solidarity between the African American and Chicano communities by dividing them into exclusive, insular, oppositional racial identities:

> As Chicano activists moved to distinguish themselves from blacks, they analogized their identity to that of Native Americans. . . . Mexicans stressed their native ties partly in order to distance themselves from the black experience in the United States. . . . Though Chicanos did not want to be white, neither did they want to be black.[81]

The formation of an exclusively Chicano ethnonationalist identity took on an increasingly significant role as a conceptual boundary, not only between Chicano and Anglo populations in Los Angeles, but also between African American and Chicano communities starting in the late 1960s and early 1970s. As Haney-Lopez states in no uncertain terms, "Chicano nationalism was at root an insistence on racial division."[82]

Echoing the prior institutionalization of black nationalism in the academy, Chicano nationalism was consecrated in the American academy with the proliferation of Chicano/Latino studies departments in the 1970s and 1980s. As Antonia Darder and Rodolfo Torres recount,

> Since the 1960s, Latino studies scholars have tended overwhelmingly to focus on notions of "race" in ways that draw directly on the intellectual and political tradition of many African American scholars. Hence, the use of the concept of "race" became the new orthodoxy among Chicano scholars. . . . In turn, this literature has reinforced a racialized politics of identity and representation, with its problematic emphasis on "racial" identity as the overwhelming impulse for political action. Thus, identity politics has become the bat-

---

80. Haney-Lopez 2003, 212–213.
81. Ibid., 211–212.
82. Ibid., 216.

tlefield for efforts to construct a coherent social movement among Latinos in the United States.[83]

Such explicitly ethnonationalist fields of study—whether Pan-African, Chicano/Latino, or otherwise, collectively known as ethnic studies—are now deeply entrenched in the American university system. Just as "intelligentsias were central to the rise of nationalism in the colonial territories," they have likewise been integral to the consecration and proliferation of contemporary identity politics in American society through the academy.[84] *Identity politics*, a term that was coined by the black feminist Combahee River Collective Statement in 1977, is essentially the reactionary nationalism of the likes of Garvey and Karenga repackaged, minus the explicit misogyny:

> The focusing on our own oppression is embodied in the concept of identity politics. We believe that the most profound and potentially radical politics come directly out of our own identity, as opposed to working to end somebody else's oppression.[85]

In other words, identity politics has essentially "two main characteristics: first, an emphasis on difference rather than commonality; second, the local or particular community of identity—such as lesbianism or the African American community—was intended as the central point of identification for the self."[86] As Adolf Reed Jr. suggests, identity politics is not merely a passive form of identification and social organization but a political project that overtly aims to impose its worldview as an alternative to class analysis:

> The term refers most generally to a political approach that gives priority to advancing the perspectives and interests of specific groups defined in ethnic, racial, or cultural terms—that is, as explicit alternatives to class. And it implies a belief that asserting and demanding recognition of the distinctiveness and independent cultural legitimacy of one's group is a crucial political objective in its own right.[87]

This politics of identity and division became scripture in American academia in the post–Civil Rights Movement era. Using the academy as a ve-

---

83. Darder and Torres 2004, 124–125.
84. Anderson (1983) 2016, 116.
85. Cohambee River Collective (1977) 2017, 19.
86. Zaretsky 1994, 198.
87. A. Reed 2000, 133.

hicle, professional ethnopolitical entrepreneurs have indoctrinated generations of students—and, through them, entire communities—with racial pride, nationalist ideology, and identity politics. As the late iconoclast activist intellectual Todd Gitlin observed more than a quarter-century ago:

> The appeal of identity politics to an incoming student is easy to understand. Identity politics is already a tradition in its second generation, transmitted, modified, and transmitted again, institutionalized in departments and courses, supported by a critical mass of faculty and a surrounding, permissive ambivalence, embedded in living units, jargons, mentors, gurus, conferences, associations, journals, publishing subfields, bookstore sections, and jokes. By the time they arrive on campus . . . . many students—particularly the political activists—have already absorbed the spirit of hard-edged identity politics from the media, secondary school, or home. Awaiting the perplexed is an identity package—academic studies, perspectivist theory, identity politics, social networks, "diversity" workshops—a whole world organized around identity culture.[88]

It is this legacy that informs contemporary notions of identity in the late twentieth and early twenty-first centuries and, likewise, provides the conceptual foundation for the racialized gang identities that are the subject of this book.

In August 2021, I gave an impromptu campus tour to an incoming transfer student, a *Sureño*-affiliated gang member who had been recently released after serving a quarter-century in prison. I led him around, pointing out different spaces on campus: "This is the Student Union. This is the black student space. This is the Latinx student space." He immediately cut me off: "Whoa! Trip out! College is just like prison!" He didn't realize how prescient his observation was. It is no mere coincidence that the emergence of the modern racialized inmate factions in California, and the conflicts between them, perfectly coincides with the proliferation of ethnonationalist ideology and identity politics in the academy in the wake of the collapse of the Civil Rights Movement.[89] This coincidence is not mere correlation.

In the wake of the suppression of Chicano and African American attempts to resist their collective subordination in American society, racialized street and prison gangs filled the void by providing a sense of identity

---

88. Gitlin 1995, 148–149.
89. Weide 2020.

and a raison d'être for disaffected, dispossessed, discarded labor populations in Los Angeles and California's prisons, turning their rage against the ruling classes responsible for their subjugation onto one another instead.[90] In a single generation, the Chicano and African American proletariat was transformed from the vanguard of class resistance into the instruments of its own oppression, embracing exactly the kind of division the race concept was invented to provoke. As a result, contemporary gang members, both Chicano and African American, perceive themselves as the vanguard of diametrically opposed racialized communities, thus turning their frustrations and fury on one another rather than against those responsible for the subjugation they endure at the bottom of America's racialized stratification hierarchy. Racial pride and identity politics came at the cost of class-consciousness and interracial solidarity—a deal with the devil if ever there was one (pun intended).

The perceptions of difference, bias, and conflict discussed through the remainder of this book did not manifest out of thin air. Contemporary members of *Sureño*-affiliated and Crip- and Blood- affiliated gangs in Los Angeles are the inheritors, not the inventors, of the ethnonationalist ideologies that divide them. The ethnonationalist identities that contemporary gang members and their communities take for granted are a colonial construct invented with the express intent of serving as vehicles for labor management and social control by division. Thus, the ethnonationalist identities of subordinate populations in the U.S. context reflect an unconscious mimicry of the nationalist ideology of their colonizers. They are not just dreaming in the Pilgrim's tongue: they are imagining themselves in the image of their oppressors, dividing themselves according to categories explicitly invented with the intent of colonizing both their bodies and their minds. White supremacy was the first identity politics. The rest are just imitators.

---

90. Alonso 2004, 2010; Hagedorn 1988, 2008; Vigil 1988, 2002a, 2002b, 2007.

2

Deconstructing Identity

*Theoretical Foundations for Critiques
of Ethnonationalism and Identity Politics*

The theoretical foundation for the analysis this book presents represents a synthesis of classical Marxist critiques of the capitalist system and anarchist critiques of ethnonationalism that originated in the second half of the nineteenth century. While Marxist critiques of capitalism have informed subsequent analysis for generations since, anarchist critiques of ethnonationalism were largely discarded and forgotten over the course of the twentieth century. My intention in this chapter is to revive those classical critiques and demonstrate how subsequent critiques of cultural nationalism in the Civil Rights Movement era, and contemporary critiques of identity politics more broadly, represent an unconscious reflection of the critiques that are at the core of classical anarchist analyses of race, identity, and nationalist ideology.

I begin the chapter by reflecting on Marxist analyses of the surplus labor population to establish the theoretical critique of capitalism that is germane to the divisive role the race concept plays in dividing labor populations along ethnoracial lines. The discussion of Karl Marx's classical analysis of the management of surplus labor populations is followed by an examination of some of the most influential anarchist critics of ethnonationalism of the late nineteenth and early twentieth century. I include as a late classical critique in this second section a discussion of the critique of cultural nationalism that was employed by Black Panther Party (BPP) leaders such as Fred Hampton, Huey P. Newton, and Assata Shakur, although we have no reason to believe that they had read or were aware of the prior anarchist critiques. I conclude with a summary of contemporary academic critiques of ethno-nationalism and identity politics. While the contemporary critiques likewise ignore the classical anarchist critiques, I explore not only how they echo those critiques, but also how they expand on them to analyze contemporary manifestations of ethnonationalism and identity politics in the twenty-first century.

The Capitalist Conundrum

In his magnum opus, *Das Kapital*, Karl Marx provided an analysis of the role of the surplus labor population in the capitalist economy. The surplus labor population is the "industrial reserve army" of laborers who are unemployed, marginally employed, or underemployed in the production of capital, particularly in the manufacture of goods for consumption.[1] This "relative surplus labor population," as Marx termed it, serves an essential purpose for the capitalist system in wage suppression. Under the perpetual threat of being replaced by an "industrial reserve army" of surplus labor, actively employed workers in any industry are limited in their leverage to make demands on their employers. The surplus labor population is to capital, as Marx puts it, "a mass of human material always ready for exploitation."[2]

Capitalist accumulation also requires increasing efficiency of production, either by increasing production at a higher rate than wages or by technological innovation. However, increasing efficiency inevitably renders a greater proportion of the labor population superfluous to the process of production, thereby persistently inflating the size of the surplus labor population relative to the active labor population. In Marx's words, "Capital increases its supply of labor more quickly than its demand for workers. The overwork of the employed part of the working class swells the ranks of the reserve, while conversely the greater pressure that the latter by its competition exerts on the former, forces these to submit to overwork and to subjugation under the dictates of capital."[3] The conundrum presented for the capitalist system by the ever expanding surplus labor population is that, while the surplus labor population is necessary to suppress wages, it also presents an existential threat to the capitalist system in that members of the surplus labor population, such as gang members, have little material interest in the capitalist system to which their labor—and, therefore, existence—is super-fluous. While they cannot overthrow capital by withholding their labor and

---

1. Marx (1867) 1976, chap. 25, secs. 3–4.
2. Ibid., 784.
3. Ibid., 789.

seizing the means of production as the active labor population can, the surplus labor population can potentially present an existential threat to the personal security of oligarchs and their families.

Marx's analysis was borne out in the late nineteenth and early twentieth centuries when anarchist militants carried out a campaign that spanned decades to assassinate heads of state and capitalist magnates around the world in retaliation for the violent subjugation and ruthless exploitation the ruling elite perpetrated against the working classes. These self-sacrificing martyrs always emerged from the surplus labor population: Leon Czolgosz, who assassinated President William McKinley in 1901; Gaetano Bresci, who assassinated King Umberto I of Italy in 1900; Alexander Berkman, who attempted to assassinate Henry Clay Frick, chairman of the Carnegie Steel Company, in 1892; and Nikolai Rysakov and Ignacy Hryniewiecki, who assassinated Czar Alexander II of Russia in 1881.[4] More than any other segment of capitalist society, it is the surplus labor population that has the most potential to present an immediate and direct threat to the lives of the ruling classes, whether heads of state or heads of industry.

Marx's classic analysis of the surplus labor population was picked up a century later, in the mid-1970s, by a trio of criminologists who employed it to formulate a theory of criminalization and deviance production. According to William Chambliss, Steven Spitzer, and Richard Quinney, the concept of crime is a tool of social control.[5] They suggest that the concept of crime can be employed directly on the people of the surplus labor population by criminalizing, arresting, and incarcerating them when they present a direct threat to the capitalist system. However, as direct suppression is costly, the invention of crime provides for a more insidious and subtle method of surplus labor population management by turning members of the surplus labor population against one another. As both law enforcement and criminals come from the same surplus labor populations, the same communities, even the same families in many cases, the invention of crime serves to orient members of the surplus labor population in opposition to one another, with lawbreakers on one side and law enforcers on the other—*divide and conquer.*

While some deviants do not present an imminent threat to the capitalist class, what Spitzer called "social junk"—the homeless, drug users, prostitutes, and so on—other members of the criminalized surplus labor population have the potential to present an existential threat to both the capitalist system and the personal security of the ruling elite specifically. Spitzer calls these deviants "social dynamite"—revolutionaries, terrorists, narco-

---

4. Goldman (1931) 2006; Kemp 2018.
5. Chambliss 1975; Quinney 1977; Spitzer 1975.

traffickers, and, especially, gang members. There are many contemporary discarded labor populations for whom the capitalist economy has little of material substance to offer, but gang members represent, perhaps, a greater existential threat to the personal security of the ruling classes than any other population in capitalist society. Gang members outnumber law enforcement and military personnel in most American cities by a wide margin, are armed and experienced in violence, are generally not intimidated by the threat of death or incarceration, are distributed throughout virtually every urban community in the country, and, most important, are already organized into decentralized units and lines of command that could serve as the basis for an armed guerrilla insurrection that has the potential to present a direct threat to the personal safety and security of the American oligarchy, the likes of which they have never known.

Anarchist Critiques of Ethnonationalism

Since the beginning of the eighteenth century, the race concept has consistently served the capitalist system as the primary axis of division that operates to undermine solidarity and provoke conflict between similarly situated subordinate labor populations.[6] The function of the race concept in dividing labor populations in opposition to one another has been foundational to anarchist theoretical frameworks almost from their inception, beginning with Mikhail Bakunin's blistering critique of the emergence of German nationalism in the nineteenth century and its purported antithesis, Pan-Slavic nationalism.[7] The Pan-Slavic movement emerged, as nationalist movements among subordinate populations inevitably do, out of the oppression experienced by ethnic Slavs as a result of the German nationalist unification movement, which culminated in the establishment of an explicitly ethno-German state in 1871, as described in the previous chapter.[8]

Bakunin suggested that this ethnoracial hubris inherent in the German nationalist movement provoked a reactionary Pan-Slavic nationalist movement in response:

> Like all conquerors of a foreign land and subjugators of an alien people, the Germans with consummate injustice hate and scorn the Slavs simultaneously. We have already said why they hate them, they scorn them because the Slavs have been unable and unwilling to be Germanized. . . . Threatened, or, more accurately, persecuted from

---

6. Allen (1994) 2012, (1997) 2012; Isenberg 2016; Roediger and Esch 2012; Smedley 2007.
7. Bakunin (1873) 1990.
8. Barraclough 1985; Stern 1979.

all sides but not completely crushed by this Pan-Germanism, the Austrian Slavs, with the exception of the Poles, have countered it with another highly repugnant absurdity, another ideal that is no less opposed to freedom and lethal for the people—Pan-Slavism.[9]

Ironically, Bakunin himself was a proponent of Pan-Slavism earlier in his revolutionary career, after the failed Austrian Revolution of 1848 that led to his extradition to Russia, where he spent more than a decade in the most draconian prison on the planet at the time, the Peter and Paul Fortress in St. Petersburg. In the wake of this devastating turn of events, Bakunin wrote a desperate plea for a revolutionary nationalist Pan-Slavic movement later that year, entitled *Appeal to the Slavs*, wherein he made the first call in history for the establishment of a grand Pan-Slavic ethnostate in the Slavic-inhabited regions of what was then the Austrian Empire.[10]

Given the incredible range of his experiences in the quarter-century between these conflicting publications, Bakunin, by the end of his life, had reconsidered his analysis in regard to revolutionary nationalism when he published his magnum opus, *Statism and Anarchy*, in 1873.[11] While the bulk of the book is dedicated to a dual-pronged attack on German nationalism, on one hand, and Marxist authoritarian communism, on the other, there is a foundational critique of ethnonationalism in Bakunin's devastating condemnation of his prior revolutionary nationalist perspective. He chastised the "Slavophiles," as he mocked them, for choosing as their vehicle for resistance to German nationalism, nationalism itself, a concept they themselves learned from their German oppressors. Reversing his earlier call for Slavic nationalism as a vehicle for revolution, Bakunin implored the Slavic populations of all countries to reject ethnonationalism as a false panacea:

It is remarkable to what degree that accursed German civilization, intrinsically bourgeois and therefore statist, has succeeded in penetrating the souls of even Slavic patriots. They were born into a German bourgeois society, they studied in German schools and universities, they grew accustomed to thinking, feeling and aspiring in German, and they would have become perfect Germans had not the goal they are pursuing been anti-German: by German ways and means they want to liberate the Slavic people from the German yoke. Prevented by their German education from comprehending any other method of liberation than the formation of Slavic states or of

---

9. Bakunin (1873) 1990, 36–37.
10. Bakunin 1848.
11. Bakunin (1873) 1990.

a single mighty Slavic state, they are setting themselves a thoroughly German objective.[12]

Bakunin's analysis explicitly recognizes ethnonationalist identity and
ideology as an intrinsic barrier to working-class solidarity. Worse yet, as nationalist identities are inherently exclusive of out-group members, nationalist ideology orients the population of every nationalist identity in seemingly
natural opposition to one another, thereby provoking division and conflict
between them. A world of nationalist identities, from Bakunin's perspective,
is a world of all against all—the absolute antithesis of solidarity. The alternative to nationalism as a framework for revolution that Bakunin advocated
was to discard ethnonationalist identities in favor of class solidarity, based
on the material conditions of the working classes relative to the ruling classes in every country on earth. Bakunin advocated class war as opposed to race
war, imploring the German people, the Slavic people, and all other people
around the world to join together in solidarity to overthrow the kaiser, the
czar, and all other forms of state authority the world over:

> On the Pan-German banner is written: *Maintain and strengthen the
> state at all costs.* On the social-revolutionary (anarchist) banner, our
> banner, in letters of fire and blood, is inscribed: *Abolish all states,
> destroy bourgeois civilization, organize freely from below upward, by
> means of free association—organize the unshackled laboring hordes,
> the whole of liberated humanity, create a new world for all man-
> kind.*[13]

The significance of Bakunin's critique of ethnonationalism continued to
prove its salience in the early twentieth century, as nations across Europe
appealed to their citizens' racial vanity and nationalist hubris in mobilizing
tens of millions of men to fight a brutal world war of attrition that cost millions upon millions of lives. In 1914, at the outset of World War I, the anarchist revolutionary Errico Malatesta reiterated his mentor Bakunin's critique of the race concept as a vehicle for exploitation and division in his
appeal for the European working classes of every country to refuse to participate in the war on any side:

> Today we hear Socialists speak, just like any bourgeois, of "France,"
> or "Germany," and of other political and national agglomerations—
> results of historical struggles—as of homogeneous ethnographic

---

12. Ibid., 38.
13. Ibid., 197, author's emphasis.

units, each having its proper interests, aspirations, and mission, in opposition to the interests, aspirations and a mission of rival units. This may be true relatively, so long as the oppressed, and chiefly the workers, have no self-consciousness, fail to recognize the injustice of their oppressors. There is, then, the dominating class only that counts; and this class, owing to its desire to conserve and to enlarge its power, even its prejudices and its own ideas, may find it convenient to excite racial ambitions and hatred, and send its nation, its flock, against "foreign" countries, with a view to releasing them from their present oppressors, and submitting them to its own political economical domination.[14]

Malatesta reiterated that the true enemies of the working classes are the ruling classes who exploit them by employing their racial vanity to manipulate them into hostilities against one another across racial lines and national boundaries. His solution is the same offered by Bakunin: solidarity across racial lines, across national boundaries, among all the working classes of the world, without regard to race, ethnicity, nationality, or any other lines of division based on identity, affinity, or origin. Malatesta extolled his contemporaries, as world war broke out and young men flocked to sacrifice their lives on the altar of nationalism, to choose sides instead on the basis of common material interests and the ideas to which they adhere rather than the canard of ethnonationalist identity:

But the mission of those who, like us, wish the end of all oppression and of all exploitation of man by man, is to awaken a consciousness of the antagonism of interests between dominators and dominated, between exploiters and workers, and to develop the class struggle inside each country, and the solidarity among all workers across the frontiers, as against any prejudice and any passion of either race or nationality.

And this we have always done. We have always preached that the workers of all countries are brothers, and that the enemy—the "foreigner"—is the exploiter, whether born near us or in a far-off country, whether speaking the same language or any other. We have always chosen our friends, our companions-in-arms, as well as our enemies, because of the ideas they profess and of the position they occupy in the social struggle, and never for reasons of race or nationality. We have always fought against patriotism, which is a survival of the past, and serves well the interest of the oppressors; and we

---

14. Malatesta 1914.

were proud of being internationalists, not only in words, but by the deep feelings of our souls.[15]

This incipient critique of ethnonationalism as essentially divisive formed the foundation of anarchist thinking not just on state nationalism, but also on racial and ethnic identity more broadly throughout the late nineteenth century and into the twentieth century in the United States. The anarchist firebrand and Haymarket widow, Lucy Parsons, reflected the anarchist perspective on race not only in her writing, but in her presentation of self, as well. In 1885, she was quoted by the *Chicago Tribune*: "Let every dirty, lousy tramp arm himself with a revolver or a knife and lay in wait on the steps of the palaces of the rich and stab or shoot the owners as they come out. Let us kill them without mercy, and let it be a war of extermination."[16] She was reputed by the Chicago Police Department, even in her golden years, to be "more dangerous than 1000 rioters."[17]

The most explicit enunciation of the anarchist perspective on race in Parsons's writing is from her article "The Negro: Let him Leave Politics to the Politician and Prayers to the Preacher," published on April 3, 1886, in *The Alarm*, less than a month before the Haymarket riot, as a result of which her husband, Albert Parsons, was martyred. Parsons both denounced the idea of racial identity as a vehicle for resistance and, at the same time, acknowledged the common brotherhood and material position of all working-class people relative to the ruling classes, without regard to racial identity:

> Are there any so stupid as to believe these outrages have been heaped upon the Negro because he is black? Not at all. It is because he is poor. It is because he is dependent. Because he is poorer as a class than his white wage-slave brother of the North.[18]

The enigma of Lucy Parsons's personal life has been all the more perplexing to her many aficionados and biographers.[19] A less than sympathetic biography published in 2017 by the historian Jacqueline Jones created some buzz because it purported to have documented Parsons's origins and "true" racial identity—as if there is such a thing. Although she enjoyed a somewhat ambiguous phenotypic appearance, it was apparent that she had at least some descent of Sub-Saharan African origin. However, over the course of

---

15. Ibid.
16. Hochschartner 2012.
17. Rosenthal 2011.
18. Parsons (1886) 2003, 54.
19. Ahrens 2004; Ashbaugh (1976) 2012; Jones 2017; Katz 2012; Rosenthal 2011.

her life she was intentionally and defiantly evasive about what her racial origins were exactly. Born Lucia Carter, according to Jones, Parsons had used a multiplicity of surnames on official documents that suggested various ethnic and racial identities over the course of her life, including Carter, Diaz, Gonzalez, Gaithings, Hull, Markstall, and Parsons, demonstrating her utter contempt for state bureaucracy.[20] Despite her phenotypic appearance, she always denied any Sub-Saharan African descent. Instead, she oscillated between claiming combinations of Mexican and indigenous American heritage, though the details always seemed to change.[21] Parsons's death certificate even listed her parents as the Mexican nationals Pedro Diez and Maries Gonzalez, variations of names she had used at various times in her life.[22]

My interpretation of Parsons's presentation of self is that her evasive and conflicting accounts of her heritage and racial identity, when she did acknowledge any, was a comical and amusing form of self-entertainment for her, mocking those who pestered her with an unhealthy obsession to categorize human beings according to contrived racial taxonomies. She cast herself as essentially *race-nonconforming*. That is to say, over the course of her long life, she consistently refused to acknowledge the salience of any racial identity for herself or anyone else, for that matter. Parsons didn't just advocate for the anarchist theoretical framework established by Bakunin that rejects the salience of racial identities outright; she lived it. The contemporary irony is that in the identitarian environment of the post–Civil Rights Movement era we live in, Parsons is often invoked by modern black and Chicana nationalist projects and discourses that attempt to co-opt her legacy on the grounds of shared ethnoracial identity, an endeavor at which Parsons surely would have scoffed.[23] The obvious irony in this, other than the fact that she actually possessed no Mexican heritage whatsoever, is that she thought the idea of racial identity a ridiculous distraction from class solidarity. Parsons was far from alone in her perspective among the anarchist theorists and militants who were her contemporaries.

Parsons was also a founding member of the revolutionary trade union established on anarchist principles in 1905, the Industrial Workers of the World (IWW). Recognition of the race concept as a vehicle for labor management and social control was a foundational principle of the IWW, the only trade union of its time to openly welcome and organize workers across racial lines. The IWW's bylaws open with Article I, Section I, which states,

---

20. Ahrens 2004; Ashbaugh (1976) 2012; Jones 2017; Katz 2012; Meier and Gutierrez 2000; Rosenthal 2011.

21. Jones 2017.

22. Ibid.

23. Hemming 2015; Meier and Gutierrez 2000.

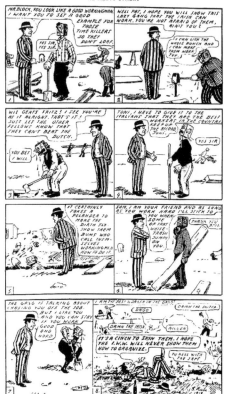

Figure 2.1. Mr. Block "He Meets
the Others." (Courtesy of the IWW.)

"No working man or woman shall be excluded from membership Unions because of creed or color."[24] The purpose of such a statement first and foremost in the union's bylaws is to acknowledge an explicit recognition of the labor management function that racial division serves in the capitalist economy. Perhaps there is no more iconic representation of this explicit recognition of the role of race as an axis of labor division than a Mr. Block cartoon entitled "He Meets Others," the invention of IWW member Ernest Riebe, that was published in 1912 in an issue of the IWW-affiliated periodical *Industrial Worker*. The comic depicts a foreman or owner appealing to the racial pride of his workers to manipulate them into working harder and turn them against one another in the process.

The role of the race concept as a vehicle for labor division was also explicitly stated in various articles and pamphlets published by the IWW and

---

24. Heideman 2018, 154.

its members. Perhaps the best example is from a 1919 IWW pamphlet written by an unnamed African American member:

> As we are both wage workers, we have a common interest in improving conditions of the wage working class. Understanding this, the employing class seeks to engender race hatred between the two. He sets the black worker against the white worker and white worker against the black, and keeps them divided and enslaved. Our change from chattel slaves to wage slaves has benefitted no one but the masters of industry. They have used us as wage slaves to beat down the wages of white wage slaves, and by a continual talk of "race problems," "Negro questions," "segregation," etc., make an artificial race hatred and division by poisoning the minds of both whites and blacks in an effort to stop any movement of labor that threatens the dividends of the industrial kinds.[25]

Panthers and Pork Chops

While there is no evidence that any of the most prominent leaders of the radical Civil Rights Movement era had read or were aware of the prior classical anarchist theoretical frameworks, in an apparent case of theoretical polygenesis, BPP leaders came to the same epiphany based on their own experiences and analysis, explicitly recognizing ethnonationalism as an inherently divisive and counterrevolutionary ideology. Surely the most profound of these critiques delivered by BPP leaders that has survived for posterity is the last recorded speech given by Fred Hampton, chairman of the BPP's Chicago chapter, at Northern Illinois University in November 1969, less than a year after the Federal Bureau of Investigation (FBI) orchestrated the Counter Intelligence Program (COINTELPRO) assassination of Bunchy Carter and John Huggins and less than a month before his own assassination in a joint FBI–Chicago Police Department COINTELPRO operation.[26] In the speech, Hampton denounced black nationalists such as Stokely Carmichael (a.k.a. Kwame Ture) and Ron Karenga and defended the BPP's interracial alliances with like-minded white, Latino, and Asian revolutionaries:

> People talking about the Party co-opted by white folks. That's what that mini-fascist, Stokely Carmichael said. He's nothing but a jacka-

25. Ibid.
26. Austin 2008; Bloom and Martin 2013; Haas 2010; Hampton 1969; Murch 2010; Swearingen 1995.

napes. As far as I'm concerned, he's a jackanapes, cause I've been knowing him for years, and that's all he could be, if he go around murder-mouthin' the Black Panther Party.[27]

In Hampton's view—as in that of Bakunin, Parsons, and Malatesta before him—revolution requires working-class solidarity without preference for racialized identities or geographic origin. While Bakunin appealed to change the perspective of those who informed their praxis with an ethno-nationalist ideology by ridiculing his Pan-Slavic contemporaries, Hampton outright denounced his cultural nationalist contemporaries in the strongest terms possible and rejected them with a mocking disdain even more contemptuous than Bakunin's for the Slavophiles. From Hampton's perspective, his cultural nationalist ethnopolitical entrepreneur contemporaries, whom he and other BPP leaders derided as "pork chops," were clearly in the counterrevolutionary camp—a rib off the pig, so to say.

Echoing Bakunin's analysis, Hampton cited miseducation in the American academy as the cradle of cultural nationalism. From Hampton's perspective, the cultural appropriations and accoutrements of the cultural nationalist movement were indicative of little more than a counterfeit symbolic ethnicity. Hampton's fierce oratory left no doubt as to his utter contempt for cultural nationalists such as Karenga:

> Anybody that doesn't admit that is showing through their non-admittance and their non-participation in the struggle that all they are, are people who fail to make a commitment; and the only thing that they have going for them is the education that they receive in these institutions—education enough to teach them some alibis and teach them that you've gotta be black, and you've gotta change you name. And that's crazy. . . .
>
> And any n—er that runs around here tellin' you that when your hair's long and you got a dashiki on, and you got boubous and all these sandals, and all this type of action, then you're a revolutionary, and anybody that doesn't look like you, he's not—that man has to be out of his mind. Because we know that political power doesn't flow from the sleeve of a dashiki. We know that political power flows from the barrel of a gun. . . .
>
> Changing your name is not gonna change our set of arrangements. The only thing that's gonna change our set of arrangements is what's gotten us into this set of arrangements and that's the oppressor. And it's on three stages, we call it the three-in-one: avari-

27. Hampton 1969.

cious greedy businessmen, demagogic lying politicians, and racist pig-fascist reactionary cops. Until you deal with those three things, then your set of arrangements will remain the same. The only difference will be that you're still under fascism, but instead of Fred being under fascism, I'll be Oogabooga under fascism.[28]

Along with numerous other BPP members, Hampton, prior to his assassination, had harbored suspicions that proponents of cultural nationalism such as the US organization were FBI assets created to neutralize the BPP and the "class war, not race war" analysis it advocated. Hampton's speech at Northern Illinois University alludes to the possibility that cultural nationalists such as Karenga were operating with the tacit approval of law enforcement, as he invoked the assassinations of Bunchy Carter and John Huggins:

Check the people who went back to 11th century culture. Check the people that are wearing dashikis and boubous and think that that's going to free them. Check all of these people, find out where they're located, find out the addresses of their office, write them a letter and ask them if in the last year how many times their office been attacked. And then write any Black Panther Party, anywhere in the United States of America, anywhere in Babylon, and ask them how many times the pigs have attacked them. Then when you get your estimation of both of them, then you figure out what the pigs don't like. That's when you figure out what the pigs don't like. We've been attacked three times since June. We know what pigs don't like. We've got people run out of the country by the hundreds. We know what pigs don't like. Our Minister of Defense is in jail, our Chairman is in jail, our Minister of Information's in exile, our Treasurer, the first member of the Party, is dead. The Deputy Minister of Defense and the Deputy Minister of Information, Bunchy, Alprentice Bunchy Carter, and John Huggins from Southern California, murdered by some pork chops, talking about a BSU [Black Student Union] program. We know what the pigs don't like. . . .

Mamalama Karangatang Karenga, a big bald-headed bazoomba as far as we're concerned. That's what he is. And we think that if he's gonna continue to wear dashikis, that he ought to stop wearing pants cause he look a lot better in miniskirts. That's all a motherfuckin' man needs in Babylon that ain't got no gun, and that's a miniskirt. And maybe he can trick his way out of something, cause he not gonna shoot his way outta nothing. He won't fight temptation, but

---

28. Ibid.

he never killed anybody but the Black Panther member. Name some-body. Name me a time you read about Karangatang's office being attacked. The only time he ever had the occasion to use a gun was on Alprentice Bunchy Carter, a revolutionary. This brother had more revolutionary poetry for a motherfucker than anybody, revolution-ary culture, John Huggins, the only time they lifted a gun was against these people. As Huey says in prison, when they lifted their hands against Bunchy and when they lifted their hands against John, they lifted their hands against the best that Babylon possesses. And you should say that. You should feel any time when revolutionary brothers die. You never heard about the Party going around murder-ing people. You dig what I'm saying? Think about it. I'm not even gonna tell you. You think about it for yourself.[29]

Perhaps most significant for both the historical and theoretical frame-work presented in this book, Hampton pushed the analysis that preceded him even further than his anarchist predecessors, historically situating racism and the race concept as an unambiguous invention of the capitalist system:

We never negated the fact that there was racism in America, but we said that the by-product, what comes off of racism, that capitalism comes first and next is racism. That when they brought slaves over here, it was to make money. So first the idea came that we want to make money, then the slaves came in order to make that money. That means that capitalism had to, through historical fact, racism had to come from capitalism. It had to be capitalism first and racism was a by-product of that.[30]

Huey P. Newton, in his 1972 essay "On Pan-Africanism or Commu-nism," assumed a very similar position to Hampton's, identifying racial op-pression as a function of economic exploitation: "We must agree, for ex-ample, that black people inside the United States live in an oppressed state. Furthermore, the primary characteristic of this oppression is economic with racism at its base."[31] Taking on Pan-Africanism directly, Newton argues that Pan-Africanism serves as a vehicle for exploitation rather than liberation, providing for the perpetuation of the capitalist economy in the guise of black capitalism, which does nothing to ameliorate the circumstances of the vast majority of African Americans:

---

29. Ibid.
30. Ibid.
31. Newton 1972, 248.

Pan-Africanism . . . is hardly the issue. It is not only outdated, it sets back the liberation of all oppressed people. It leaves room for exploitative endeavor by men. It suggests both an all-Africanized version of capitalist economic distribution in a world where capital and its power lie tightly in the hands of the U.S. rulers, and it fails to encompass the unique situation of black Americans.[32]

In her autobiography, Assata Shakur makes a similar point, outright dismissing the idea that race was the sole source of oppression for African Americans. She explicitly recognized that the subordination of African Americans was the result of both racial oppression and class subordination, which combined to keep the vast majority of the African American population at the bottom of the socioeconomic stratification distribution. That a small proportion of African Americans were able to climb up the ladder and acquire financial assets and interests did nothing for those who were left behind, and the interests of the haves and the have-nots were diametrically opposed, despite their shared racial identity:

I got into heated arguments with sisters and brothers who claimed that the oppression of Black people was only a question of race. I argued that there were Black oppressors as well as white ones. That's why you've got Blacks who support Nixon and Reagan or other conservatives. Black folks with money have always tended to support candidates who they believed would protect their financial interests. As far as i was concerned, it didn't take too much brains to figure out that Black people are oppressed because of class as well as race, because we are poor and because we are Black. It would burn me up every time somebody talked about Black people climbing the ladder of success. Anytime you're talking about a ladder, you're talking about a top and a bottom, Black people are always going to wind up at the bottom, because we're the easiest to discriminate against. That's why i couldn't see fighting within the system. Both the democratic party and the republican party are controlled by millionaires. They are interested in holding onto their power, while i was interested in taking it away.[33]

Newton's solution to the predicament of not just African Americans, but all oppressed populations the world over, was essentially the same as Bakunin's:

---

32. Newton 1972, 253–254.
33. Shakur 1987, 190.

If it is agreed that the fundamental nature of oppression is economic, the first assault by the oppressed must be to wrest economic control from the hands of the oppressors. If we define the prime character of the oppression of blacks as racial, then the situation of economic exploitation of human being by human being can be continued if performed by blacks against blacks or blacks against whites. If, however, we are speaking of eliminating exploitation and oppression, then the oppressed must begin with a united, worldwide thrust along the lines of oppressed versus oppressor.[34]

Against the Grain

A growing cadre of contemporary scholars on the left have dared to challenge the hegemony of identity politics, approaching their critiques from a wide range of theoretical perspectives and academic fields of study. While contemporary scholars unfortunately ignore the classical critiques of ethnonationalism and cultural nationalism, contemporary left critiques of identity politics often share a great deal with the classical critiques and, in many ways, push the analysis further than the classical theorists, into the twenty-first century. Here I present a modest catalogue of notable works in this line of contemporary scholarship.

Perhaps the most significant among them is the firebrand political scientist and activist Adolf Reed Jr., whose collection of essays *Class Notes* (2000) presented a foundation of critiques that would resonate in the ensuing decades. Reed roundly denounced the vacuous notion that identity automatically confers authority to speak on behalf of others who presumably share the same identity category, as if there is some essential essence to that shared identity:

> At bottom, identity politics rests on problematic ideas of political authenticity and representation. These derive from the faulty premise that membership in a group gives access to a shared perspective and an intuitive understanding of the group's collective interests. This leads to two related beliefs that are wrong-headed and politically counterproductive: that only a group member can know or articulate the interests of the group, and that any group member can know or articulate the interests of the group, and that any group member can do so automatically by virtue of his or her identity.[35]

---

34. Newton 1972, 254–255.
35. Reed 2000, 136.

Reed charged those who make lucrative careers out of perpetuating the racial worldview with manipulating themselves into positions of racial spokespersonship, purportedly speaking on behalf of those with whom they do not actually share the material deprivation and hypercriminalization that results from racial oppression. Their spokespersonship is predicated not on the actual oppression they have personally experienced but, rather, like that of Booker T. Washington before them, on the patron-client relationship they have established with the ruling classes:

> The interest-group model depends on a form of elite brokerage, centered on a relation between governing elites and entities or individuals recognized as representatives of designated groups. The heart of the relation is negotiation of policies, programs, and patterns of distribution of resources that presumably protect and advance the interests of the pertinent groups, but safely—in ways that harmonize them with the governing elite's priorities. . . . This is what the "politics of recognition" that arises from the postmodernist/poststructuralist sensibility boils down to—a call to accept the authority of cultural theorists as articulators of the voices of populations who are presumed by the theory to be incapable of speaking clearly for themselves in public, explicit ways.[36]

Ethnopolitical entrepreneurs champion identity politics not as a vehicle to defend the interests of populations that suffer from material deprivation, oppression, and criminalization. They do so as a strategy to elevate themselves into the halls of power, no matter who they have to throw under the bus to get there:

> This is a politics motivated by the desire for proximity to the ruling class and a belief in the basic legitimacy of its power and prerogative. It is a politics which, despite all its idealist puffery and feigned nobility, will sell out any allies or egalitarian objectives in pursuit of gaining the Prince's ear.[37]

Another critique of ethnonationalism from a left perspective, published the same year, is British-born sociologist Paul Gilroy's *Against Race*.[38] Gilroy takes a rather principled position, advocating what I would characterize as a racial abolitionist perspective, which endeavors to dismantle the race con-

---

36. Ibid., xxi–xxii.
37. Ibid., 112.
38. Gilroy 2000.

cept and remove it from our collective consciousness entirely. He states as much in unambiguous terms:

> I am suggesting that the only appropriate response to this uncertainty is to demand liberation not from white supremacy alone, however urgently that is required, but from all racializing and raciological thought, from racialized seeing, racialized thinking, and racialized thinking about thinking.[39]

In his view, the solution to racial division necessitates not just a renouncement of race thinking on the part of dominant populations who enjoy racial privilege, but, moreover, a repudiation of the race concept by the subordinate populations who suffer the ignominy of its material consequences. At the same time, Gilroy recognizes that convincing those who have internalized their oppression to such a degree that it defines them is a daunting task:

> People who have been subordinated by race-thinking and its distinctive social structures (not all of which come tidily color-coded) have for centuries employed the concepts and categories of their rulers, owners, and persecutors to resist the destiny that "race" has allocated to them and to dissent from the lowly value it placed upon their lives. Under the most difficult of conditions and from the imperfect materials that they surely would not have selected if they had been able to choose, these oppressed groups have built complex traditions of politics, ethics, identity, and culture. . . . But they have gone far beyond merely affording protection and reversed the polarities of insult, brutality, and contempt, which are unexpectedly turned into important sources of solidarity, joy, and collective strength. When ideas of racial particularity are inverted in this defensive manner so that they provide sources of pride rather than shame and humiliation, they become difficult to relinquish. For many racialized populations, "race" and the hard-won, oppositional identities it supports are not to be lightly or prematurely given up.[40]

While the kind of contrived cultural nationalist aesthetic that Hampton denounced was just in its infancy in 1969, the commodification of ethnonationalist identities was so pervasive by the time Gilroy wrote his book, at the turn of the millennium, that racial identities themselves had become

---

39. Ibid., 40.
40. Ibid., 12.

commodified. Gilroy argues that racial identity has become "a thing to be possessed and displayed."[41] However, in staking claims to exclusive racialized identities, ethnonationalists align themselves in opposition to all those who cannot make a credible claim to share in their racial inheritance:

It is a silent sign that closes down the possibility of communication across the gulf between one heavily defended island of particularity and its equally well fortified neighbors. . . . When identity refers to an indelible mark or code somehow written into the bodies of its carriers, otherness can only be a threat. Identity is latent destiny. Seen or unseen, on the surface of the body of buried deep in its cells, identity forever sets one group apart from others who lack the particular, chosen traits that become the basis of typology and comparative evaluation.[42]

The commodification of racialized identities also takes a more conventional form in the marketing of cultural and aesthetic accoutrements that identify consumers as members of a racially exclusive cultural community:

Style and fashion offer something of the same forms of mechanical solidarity conferred by the uniform of the bourgeois male, which works a different racial magic for the Nation of Islam. In both cases, the unclothed body is not considered sufficient to confer either authenticity or identity. Clothing, objects, things, and commodities provide the only entry ticket into stylish solidarities powerful enough to foster the novel forms of nationality found in collectivities like the Gangsta Nation, the Hip Hop Nation, and, of course, the Nation of Islam. This is no nihilism, for there is an axiology here— the axiology of the market.[43]

The marketing of racial identities is a theme taken up by a cadre of scholars who have documented how nationalist identities are employed in advertising, marketing, and commodity fetishism to simultaneously market commodities to racially defined consumer populations and to create and encourage the racially defined markets that drive demand for commodities that are used to display a racialized presentation of self in the first place.[44] The culture indus-

---

41. Ibid., 103.
42. Ibid.
43. Ibid., 268.
44. Davila 2001; Pitcher 2014; Widdowson and Howard 2008.

try supplies the demand created by ethnonationalist identities, but it also creates and reifies those identities, thereby generating the demand it supplies.

While the classical Frankfurt School theorists critiqued the culture industry as a diversion from the politics of resistance, it's actually much more pernicious than that.[45] The culture industry isn't merely a distraction from the vicissitudes of capitalism; it is a vehicle for ethnonationalist indoctrination, consecrating the divisive identities that are necessary to maintain the status quo. Following the Frankfurt analysis, the seemingly diverse identities peddled by the contemporary culture industry are in fact varieties of the same ideology: ethnonationalism.

Literary theorist Walter Benn Michaels further argues in his book *The Trouble with Diversity* that diversity itself has become a commodity to be marketed and coveted as a resource not just for individuals, but also for universities, corporations, and government entities. They tout the kind of diversity exalted by identity politics as an accomplishment in and of itself—irrespective of how they actually treat any of the ostensibly diverse populations they use as a kente cloth to the drape over the institution:

> Among the most enthusiastic proponents of diversity, needless to say, are the thousands of companies providing "diversity products," from diversity training (currently estimated to be a $10-billion-a-year industry) to diversity newsletters (I subscribe to *Diversity Inc*, but there are dozens of them) to diversity rankings (my university's in the top ten) to diversity gifts and clothing. . . . The "Show Me the Money Diversity Venture Capital Conference" says what needs to be said here. But it's not all about the Benjamins. There's no money for the government in proclaiming Asian Pacific American Heritage Month (it used to be just a week, but the first President Bush upgraded it) or in Women's History Month or National Disability Employment Awareness Month or American Indian Heritage Month. . . . And there's no money for the Asians, Indians, blacks and women whose history gets honored.[46]

Michaels explicitly recognizes that, while the concentration of wealth at the pinnacle of the pyramid scheme that is the American economy has continued unabated, the putative left has neutered any potential for sustained opposition by incessantly feeding its obsession with the identity politics of recognition. As a result, identity politics has become an alternative to actual economic justice on any material level for anyone:

---

45. Adorno and Horkheimer (1944) 1997; Marcuse (1964) 1991.
46. Michaels 2006, 13.

Giving priority to issues like affirmative action and committing itself to the celebration of difference, the intellectual left has responded to the increase in economic inequality by insisting on the importance of cultural identity. So for thirty years, while the gap between the rich and the poor has grown larger, we've been urged to respect people's identities—as if the problem of poverty would be solved if we just appreciated the poor. . . . Celebrating the diversity of American life has become the American left's way of accepting their poverty, of accepting inequality.[47]

The battleground of contemporary politics accepted by both conservatives and liberals is therefore the extent of diversity, rather than the degree of economic stratification. Michaels is therefore not unjustified in his assessment that "the distinction between our conservatives and our liberals is that our conservatives think we've already won that fight while our liberals think we've only just begun."[48]

Antonia Darder and Rodolfo Torres likewise elucidate the function racism serves in the capitalist economy in their book, *After Race* (2004): "There is no question but that racism as an ideology is integral to the process of capital accumulation."[49] They reject the perspective that racial identity is a function of cultural praxis. Rather, they argue that racial identities serve a fundamental function in the capitalist economy rather than merely reflecting intrinsic cultural differences. They likewise critique the framing of the rebellion on the streets of Los Angeles in the wake of the acquittal of four police officers charged with beating motorist Rodney King as inherently divisive, pitting different identity groups against one another:

What was successfully camouflaged in Los Angeles was the fact that racism is not about cultural differences; it is about political economy. By converting racism into a conflict of cultural differences, whether it was between blacks and Latinos, or Latinos and Koreans, or blacks and whites, the commonsense notion of "race" was effectively preserved in Los Angeles and the inequality of class relations normalized. Thus people are socialized to perceive "race" as a matter of cultural (and often individual) differences, when in truth what generally passes under the guise of "race" are deeply entrenched racialized class relations. In the process, the political economy of racism, embedded in capitalism, effectively divides oppressed communities,

---

47. Ibid., 7.
48. Ibid., 76.
49. Darder and Torres 2004, 106.

leaving much of the world's population vulnerable to economic exploitation.[50]

Legal scholar Ian Haney-Lopez critiques the ethnonationalist identities embraced by Chicano nationalists in the Civil Rights Movement era as predicated on the core elements of the race concept discussed in the previous chapter, thereby reifying rather than challenging the categories that make racial oppression possible in the first place:

It bears emphasizing that the Chicano conception of mestizaje depended upon understanding race as a matter of descent. To this extent, nature determined racial identity, making one Chicano by birth, not by choice. It was nature, and not a common history or religion or language, that most firmly bound Mexicans to one another. Mestizaje—the biology of race—made all Mexicans the same.[51]

Sister scholars Karen and Barbara Fields provide a penetrating critique of race thinking, as well, making a telling analogy between witchcraft and modern pseudobiological conceptualizations of the race concept—what Fields and Fields aptly dub *racecraft*. This analogy suggests that racial categories are no more material than witches and warlocks. However, by treating them as if they were coherent categories, their adherents conjure them into seeming reality: "If race lives on today, it does not live on because we have inherited it from our forebearers . . . but because we continue to create it today."[52] In their view, "Race is not an idea but an ideology."[53] Ideology is a fitting description of the impermeability of race-reductionist ontology, which depends on a series of fictions that are seemingly immune to both logic and biological reality:

When virtually the whole of a society, including supposedly thoughtful, educated, intelligent persons, commits itself to belief in propositions that collapse into absurdity upon the slightest examination, the reason is not hallucination or delusion or even simple hypocrisy; rather, it is ideology. And ideology is impossible for anyone to analyze rationally who remains trapped on its terrain.[54]

---

50. Ibid., 19–20.
51. Haney-Lopez 2004, 220.
52. Fields and Fields 2014, 146.
53. Ibid., 121.
54. Ibid., 118–119.

Like Bakunin and Hampton before them, Fields and Fields also locate the academy as a primary setting where racecraft is conjured and cast:

Those who create and re-create race today are not just the mob that killed a young Afro-American man on a street in Brooklyn or the people who join the Klan and the White Order. They are also those academic writers whose invocation of self-propelling "attitudes" and tragic flaws assigns Africans and their descendants to a special category, placing them in a world exclusively theirs and outside history—a form of intellectual apartheid no less ugly or oppressive, despite its righteous (not to say self-righteous) trappings, than that practiced by the bio- and theo-racists; and for which the victims, like slaves of old, are expected to be grateful. They are the academic "liberals" and "progressives" in whose version of race the neutral shibboleths *difference* and *diversity* replace words like *slavery, injustice, oppression*, and *exploitation*, diverting attention from the anything-but-neutral history these words denote.[55]

Fields and Fields remind our colleagues in the academy of the origin and function of the race concept in our society. Virginia was a profit-seeking venture; until race was realized as the preferred vehicle for dividing labor populations, it mattered not to planters who slaved in their fields or where they came from, as long as they converted land into profit. As Fields and Fields state unequivocally: "Slavery was a system for the extortion of labor, not for the management of 'race relations,' whether by segregation or by integration."[56]

While I share Cedric Johnson's skepticism of the value of recuperating the Cohambee River Collective's original iteration of the term *identity politics*, Asad Haider's *Mistaken Identity* (2018) otherwise stands on a firm historical foundation.[57] Haider alone among contemporary scholars invokes the historical precedent of the Black Panthers' opposition to the kind of cultural nationalism espoused by Karenga's US organization.[58] Haider also correctly situates Bacon's Rebellion as the turning point in the invention of the race concept in North America and the inauguration of its role as a means of imposing internal division on labor populations.[59] Haider makes explicit in his analysis the divisive function that the invention of the race concept was intended to accomplish from its inception:

55. Ibid., 146–147, author's emphasis.
56. Ibid., 161.
57. Haider 2018; C. Johnson 2019.
58. Haider 2018, 18.
59. Ibid., 54–55.

Let us be clear on what the invention of the white race meant. It meant that Euro-American laborers were prevented from joining with African American laborers in rebellion, through the form of social control imposed by the Euro-American ruling class. In exchange for white-skin privilege, the Euro-American workers accepted white identity and became active agents in the brutal oppression of African American laborers. But they also fundamentally degraded their own conditions of existence. As a consequence of this bargain with their exploiters, they allowed the conditions of the Southern white laborer to become the most impoverished in the nation, and they generated conditions that blocked the development of a viable mass workers' movement.[60]

Haider's analysis also touches on a familiar theme: *racial tokenism*. As he puts it, "To demand inclusion in the structure of society as it is means forfeiting the possibility of structural change."[61] Thus, from Haider's perspective, tokenism is actually better described as cronyism with a thinly disguised patronage arrangement between the American oligarchy and the token representatives of marginalized populations, whereby anecdotal inclusion is accepted in return for the preservation of the system of economic exploitation and political subjugation of virtually everyone else. Haider argues that the race thinking represented by the identity politics of recognition thus reduces systematic oppression and exploitation to individualized tokens of inclusion and recognition, whose fortunes intersect with those less fortunate than them only in their racial imaginations and certainly not in any material sense.

British-born Ghanaian philosopher Kwame Anthony Appiah likewise builds on previous critiques in his book *The Lies That Bind* (2018).[62] Appiah adds an explicit critique of that Excalibur of identity policing: "cultural appropriation." The identitarian slur "cultural appropriation" weaponizes identity by marshalling its imagined boundaries to exclude from enjoyment of engaging in cultural practices associated with it by any but those who can make a credible claim to membership in the identity category by virtue of birth. Like standardized language on a page, race-reductionist slurs serve as an artificial disruption of the process of cultural diffusion that would otherwise occur between populations as naturally as linguistic morphology. "That's why we should resist the term 'cultural appropriation' as an indictment," Appiah writes. "All cultural practices and objects are mobile; they like

---

60. Ibid., 58.
61. Ibid., 22.
62. Appiah 2018.

to spread, and almost all are themselves creations of intermixture."[63] The debate over who has the racial prerogative to engage in any number of cultural practices is not a debate worth engaging in, from Appiah's perspective. As he suggests, "The real problem isn't that it's difficult to decide who owns culture; it's that the very idea of ownership is the wrong model."[64] Thus, treating cultural praxis as a possession is not only to accept, but to actively reify, racial taxonomies. In participating in the policing of racial boundaries, the victims of racial subordination are themselves appropriated by the racial regime that makes their oppression possible in the first place. As Appiah puts it, "Those who parse these transgressions in terms of ownership have accepted a commercial system that's alien to the traditions they aim to protect. They have allowed one modern regime of property to appropriate *them*."[65]

Recent events have also prompted critiques of ethnonationalism specifically, and identity politics more generally, in regard to issues of transracial identity and police violence. The moral panic that exploded around Nkechi Amare Diallo (formerly Rachel Dolezal), a transracial woman who was born to white parents but assumed a black identity in early adulthood, provided fertile ground to expand the critique of ethnonationalism to include the possibility of transracial or otherwise racially nonconforming existence. Reed and sociologists Ann Morning and Rogers Brubaker approached the issue of transracial identity by comparing it to the gender transition of the Olympic gold medalist and aspiring Republican politician Caitlyn Jenner (formerly Bruce Jenner), which occurred around the same time as the identity policing pandemonium that engulfed Diallo.[66]

Echoing Gilroy, Michaels, and Appiah, Reed also employed the property metaphor to describe the racial boundary policing to which ethnopolitical entrepreneurs subjected Diallo. From Reed's perspective, racial identity is a form of currency to be zealously defended to monopolize its exploitation by those who can make a credible and exclusive claim to it. His choice of vocabulary is apt:

There is a guild-protective agenda underlying racial identitarians' outrage about Dolezal that is also quite revealing. . . . The charge is what those making it want to be true; they assume it's true because they understand black racial classification as a form of capital. . . . When all is said and done, the racial outrage is about protection of the boundaries of racial authenticity as the exclusive property of the

---

63. Ibid., 208.
64. Ibid.
65. Ibid., 210, author's emphasis.
66. Brubaker 2016; A. Reed 2015.

guild of Racial Spokesmanship. . . . Beneath all the puerile cultural studies prattle about "cultural appropriation"—which can only occur if "culture" is essentialized as the property of what is in effect a "race" . . .[67]

Reed makes explicit that, while ethnopolitical entrepreneurship is a career path to be defended for its purveyors, the identitarian ideology they espouse serves an intrinsic role in the capitalist economy by diverting attention away from economic stratification to identity politics:

> Race politics is not an alternative to class politics; it is class politics, the politics of the left-wing of neoliberalism. It is the expression of the active agency of a political order and moral economy in which capitalist market forces are treated as unassailable by nature.[68]

In an intrepid op-ed published in the *Huffington Post* a couple weeks later, Morning cited the work of the demographer Carolyn A. Liebler in pointing out that millions of Americans change their self-reported racial category on the U.S. Census over the course of their lives.[69] Morning furthermore made the very apt comparison between racial identities and astrological signs, neither of which has any basis in objective reality:

> Instead of being a matter of natural, objective facts, race is more like astrology. It's a way of dividing human beings up into different categories, and we are the ones who invent those categories, not Mother Nature. The idea that there are "black" people and "white" people is no different than the belief that there are Geminis and Scorpios. Indeed, astrology and racial classification both claim to be grounded in nature. Race ostensibly reflects our biological constitution, while sun signs are meant to capture planetary forces that imprinted us at birth. But it's not too hard to see that a whole lot of human cultural thinking has gone into both. The reality is that scientists are far from any agreement on what race has to do with genes. And the racial classifications so familiar to Americans today are actually products of the 1700s, when they were forged by Europeans who were trying to explain the physical, social and moral qualities of peoples they had come to colonize across the world.[70]

---

67. A. Reed 2015.
68. Ibid.
69. Liebler and Ortyl 2014; Liebler et al. 2017; Morning 2015.
70. Morning 2015.

The following year, Brubaker's keen critique, *Trans* (2016), picked apart the hypocrisy of policing racial boundaries while simultaneously defending the permeability of gender boundaries. It is a devastating indictment of the seeming abdication of logic on the part of the reactionary identity police who savaged Diallo while heaping praise on Jenner, all without so much as a hint of self-circumspection.[71] In the wake of the hysteria over the racial-boundary crossing perpetrated by Diallo, Brubaker also reminds us that there is nothing novel in American history about transracial identity, or "reverse-passing," from dominant into subordinate racial identities. Brubaker points to musicians of the pre–World War II era such as the jazz clarinet virtuoso Mezz Mezzrow (born Milton Mesirow, of Russian Jewish descent) and the "Godfather of R&B" Johnny Otis (born John Veliotes, of Greek descent), both of whom lived their adults lives as openly and unapologetically black. Tellingly, the identity policing they were subjected to in the mid-twentieth century came from white supremacists, who viewed them variously as race traitors or just plain delusional. In apparent contrast, the identity policing Diallo was subjected to came primarily from the ostensibly anti-racist left. However, the praxis is the same because both white supremacists and contemporary ethnopolitical entrepreneurs on the neoliberal left share the same reactionary nationalist framework of identity as predicated on exclusion.

Brubaker posits the starkly different reactions on the part of ethnopolitical entrepreneurs to Diallo and Jenner as the result of the pseudoscientific biological descent perspective that race is inherited by bloodline descent from one's parents, whereas sex or gender category is not "pre"-determined by virtue of ancestral inheritance. This distinction is significant in that the sincerity of crossing gender boundaries can be truly known only to the individual who chooses to make that transition, whereas the racial identity of purportedly any individual can be determined simply by looking at their immediate ancestry:

A key part of what constitutes racial identity—notably one's ancestry, as well as the classification practices of others—is understood to be located outside the self and open to inspection by others.[72]

While this might seem straightforward on a superficial level for cis-racial people whose racial identity conveniently coincides with one of the available categories in any given context, it denies the very existence of not only transracial people, but also those who are "in-between" races and those people

---

71. Brubaker 2016.
72. Ibid., 141.

incapable of making a credible claim to any racial category in a given taxonomy, an identity conundrum I describe as *race-nonconforming*.

Following the economic determinist perspective I favor, I would suggest that ethnoracial categories are more rigorously policed because gender categories are more evenly distributed across all classes, though by no means perfectly distributed, of course. In sharp contrast, there are wide material disparities in the class position of different ethnoracial groups, not just in the United States, but throughout the world. Crossing boundaries of ethnoracial identity, therefore, can entail the assumption or renouncement of opportunities, privileges, and material advantages inequitably distributed by ethnoracial category.

Reed also took the lead in denouncing the variety of ethnonationalism that has informed the #BlackLivesMatter "branding exercise," as he describes it.[73] While African Americans are killed in police shootings at nearly double the rate that their share of the U.S. population would predict if Americans were murdered by police equally (a hypothetical that epitomizes the race-reductionist perspective of racial justice), they do not constitute a majority of those killed by police in the United States. By "blackwashing" a mosaic of state violence monotone, the Black Lives Matter (BLM) ethnopolitical entrepreneurs both deny us a conceptual vehicle for opposing all police killings and divide our opposition to state violence along racial lines in the process. As Reed writes,

> The shrill insistence that we begin and end with the claim that blacks are victimized worst of all and give ritual obedience to the liturgy of empty slogans is—for all the militant posturing by [DeRay] McKesson, [Alicia] Garza, [Ayo (Opal)] Tometi, [and Patrisse] Cullors et al.—in substance a demand that we *not* pay attention to the deeper roots of the pattern of police violence in enforcement of the neoliberal regime of sharply regressive upward redistribution and its social entailments. It is also a demand that, in insisting that for all intents and purposes police violence must be seen as mainly, if not exclusively, a black thing, we cut ourselves off from the only basis for forging a political alliance that could effectively challenge it. All that could be possible as political intervention, therefore, is tinkering around with administration of neoliberal stress policing in the interest of pursuing racial parity in victimization and providing consultancies for experts in how much black lives matter.[74]

---

73. A. Reed 2016.
74. Ibid.

This is not to deny that well-publicized police violence against African Americans can be the catalyst for the type of urban rebellions we saw in Los Angeles in the 1960s and 1990s and that we've seen again across the nation in the wake of the murder of George Floyd in 2020.

Cedric Johnson picked up the critique in the wake of the Floyd murder. As he rightly recognized, "This moment is a triumph for Black Lives Matter activists."[75] However, the triumph was one of political clout, publicity, fundraising, and career advancement for BLM leaders rather than substantive justice or economic reparations for victims of state violence and their families. Like Reed, Johnson explicitly recognizes that BLM is a fundamentally neoliberal ethnonationalist project, not only dedicated to the careerivist aspirations of its self-proclaimed leaders but also a vehicle to blackwash both state violence and socioeconomic stratification across the board:

> Black Lives Matter is essentially a militant expression of racial liberalism. Such expressions are not a threat but rather a bulwark to the neoliberal project that has obliterated the social wage, gutted public sector employment and worker pensions, undermined collective bargaining and union power, and rolled out an expansive carceral apparatus, all developments that have adversely affected black workers and communities. Sure, some activists are calling for defunding police departments and de-carceration, but as a popular slogan, Black Lives Matter is a cry for full recognition within the established terms of liberal democratic capitalism. And the ruling class agrees.[76]

As Johnson so adroitly points out, this message of racial tokenism absent material redistribution is understandably appealing to corporate America and to its collaborators in government.

There is perhaps no more telling indication of the impotence of BLM than its slogan being painted by the state itself in monumental scale up and down major thoroughfares throughout the nation in a thinly veiled attempt to stave off rebellion in the wake of George Floyd's murder. The billionaire barons of corporate America find the movement a welcome distraction from the runaway wealth stratification accelerated by a pandemic that has simultaneously rendered much of the working population of the world utterly destitute. Even the world's richest man, Amazon's Chief Executive Jeff Bezos, offered penance: "'Black lives matter' doesn't mean other lives don't matter, I have a 20-year-old son, and I simply don't worry that he might be choked to death while being detained one day. It's not something I worry about.

---

75. C. Johnson 2020.
76. Ibid.

Black parents can't say the same."[77] Feigning concern for black lives easily absolves someone like Bezos, even as he denied bathroom breaks and personal protective equipment to his workforce and hired teams of counterintelligence operators to neutralize labor organizing among Amazon employees, all while becoming the first human being in modern history to exceed $200 billion in net worth.[78] As Johnson so adroitly puts it, "Corporate antiracism is the perfect egress from these labor conflicts. Black Lives Matter to the front office, so long as they don't demand a living wage, personal protective equipment and quality healthcare."[79]

Among the most sophisticated of recent critiques of contemporary ethnonationalist ideology are those made by Adolph Reed Jr. in a pair of articles published in the *New Republic* and the *New Labor Forum* in 2019 and 2020, respectively.[80] In the former, Reed quite easily exposes disingenuous accusations of class reduction as not only contrived but also deliberately designed to silence dissent to the identitarian race regime:

> Class reductionism is the supposed view that inequalities apparently attributable to race, gender, or other categories of group identification are either secondary in importance or reducible to generic economic inequality. It thus follows, according to those who hurl the charge, that specifically anti-racist, feminist, or LGBTQ concerns, for example, should be dissolved within demands for economic redistribution.
>
> I know of no one who embraces that position. Like other broadbrush charges that self-styled liberal pragmatists levy against "wishlist economics" and the assault on private health insurance, the class reductionist canard is a bid to shut down debate. Once you summon it, you may safely dismiss your opponents as wild-eyed fomenters of discord without addressing the substance of their disagreements with you. . . . The simple fact is that no serious tendency on the left contends that racial or gender injustices or those affecting LGBTQ people, immigrants, or other groups as such do not exist, are inconsequential, or otherwise should be downplayed or ignored. Nor do any reputable voices on the left seriously argue that racism, sexism, homophobia, and xenophobia are not attitudes and ideologies that persist and cause harm.

---

77. Quoted in ibid.
78. Day 2020.
79. C. Johnson 2020.
80. A. Reed 2019, 2020.

"Class reductionism" is, in other words, a myth. It is a caricature rooted in hoary folk imagery.[81]

In his subsequent article, Reed lays out a theoretical framework for critiquing ethnopolitical entrepreneurs on the putative left, such as the leaders of BLM, who have a vested interest in perpetuating the cult of identity because identity is the only claim to leadership they can make. If one inspects their backgrounds, one finds that none of the founders of BLM—nor the putative leader of Black Lives Matter–Los Angeles, for example—grew up in the core of the African American community in South Los Angeles. None of them has personally experienced the kind of hypercriminalization or state violence for which they claim exclusive spokespersonship. None of them is the mother of a victim of state violence. Nonetheless, they have appropriated for themselves the exclusive authority to speak for communities to which they are not themselves indigenous, on forms of oppression that they themselves have not personally experienced.

This is why the resource that identity represents to them has to be defended at all costs. Identity is the only claim they have to spokespersonship of an issue such as state violence, which they have only experienced as cosplay by getting themselves arrested *on purpose*—the epitome of bourgeois class privilege. By asserting racial identity as the sole qualification in speaking for victims of state violence, ethnopolitical entrepreneurs justify and defend the boundary they draw between themselves and those who actually experience state violence but are not black, as if that boundary were more meaningful than the boundary between themselves and the black victims of state violence who lack the institutional support, material privilege, and media platform that the leaders of BLM clearly enjoy. As Reed suggests, they do not accept the input of anyone else, much less those who in good faith offer their solidarity but cannot make a credible claim to commonality on identitarian grounds. These racialized outsiders are merely "allies," not worthy of contributing to discourse or strategy, bodies to fill the vacancy of space created by the lack of enthusiasm for the Black Lives Matter branding exercise on the part of those who are actually indigenous to the core of black and brown Los Angeles and who have personally experienced the brutality of state violence firsthand throughout their lives as a result. Reed writes:

Ethnic or groupist spokespersons themselves have a material interest in insisting on the primacy of group identity. The claim to represent

---

81. A. Reed 2019.

distinctive group interests or perspectives is a form of capital or professional expertise. Drawing tight boundaries around the group and its supposedly racially distinctive political concerns is in that sense partly a guild-protective move. . . .

Even within supposedly insurgent circles, militant protest of presumed racial outrages is often focused as much on policing access to media recognition as on affecting policy of public attitudes. This narrative discards the notion of solidarity in favor of the demeaning construction that whites should perform only "allyship"—the equivalent of a vampire's human familiar (exchanging John Brown for Bram Stoker's Renfield as a model of interracial alliance)—with no rights to speak or opine because all such opportunities must be preserved for the voices of oppressed communities. Not simply an idiosyncratic political perversity, this phenomenon underscores the degree to which this politics is also a career path. The personalities associated with #BlackLivesMatter are not exceptional in this regard. No matter what its proponents or performers may believe, this putative insurgency is more a hustle within the neoliberal culture industry than a politics.[82]

Reed's critiques are not a matter of mere conjecture, either. As of the time of this writing, more than a dozen BLM chapters around the country have defected from the organization in protest over the centralized control, opaque leadership, lack of accountability, absence of democratic process, collaboration with the Democratic Party, and fiscal misappropriation and financial opacity of the Black Lives Matter Global Network and its preeminent chapter, Black Lives Matter–Los Angeles.[83] As the public statement made by the Black Lives Matter–Inland Empire chapter states unequivocally:

The (BLM) Global Network is a top-down dogmatic organization that promotes certain chapters that choose to align with their direction and sequester the ones that don't. For us locally, that chapter has been Los Angeles. For years, the leadership of the Los Angeles chapter has aligned with the Global Network and One United Bank to impose on various chapters, particularly ours. We believe that while doing this they received substantial donations and funding, despite them continually soliciting the community for donations. Together, the Los

---

82. A. Reed 2020, 40–41.
83. Black Lives Matter–Cincinnati 2018; Black Lives Matter–Inland Empire 2021; BLM10 2020; King 2020.

Angeles Chapter along with the Global Network have consistently tried to strong-arm other groups and have worked to undermine a grassroots movement by capitalizing on unpaid labor, suppressing any internal attempt at democracy, commodifying Black death, and profiting from the same pain and suffering inflicted on Black communities that we're fighting to end.[84]

Black Lives Matter cofounder Patrisse Cullors in particular came under recent criticism after her burgeoning real-estate empire was revealed following the purchase of a $1.4 million estate in the upscale community of Topanga Canyon, in addition to other properties in South Los Angeles and rural Georgia.[85]

Black Lives Matter leaders have also been publicly denounced by the parents of victims of some of the most publicized police murders of young black men, including Michael Brown and Tamir Rice. Michael Brown Sr. demanded to know, "Where is all the money going?"[86] The mothers of Tamir Rice and Richard Risher, victims of police murders, issued a joint public statement denouncing the whole cast of #BlackLivesMatter careerivists:

> Tamika D. Mallory, Shaun King, Benjamin Crump, Lee Merritt, Patrisse Cullors, Melina Abdullah and the Black Lives Matter Global Network need to step down, stand back, and stop monopolizing and capitalizing off our fight for justice and human rights. We never hired them to be the representatives in the fight for justice for our dead loved ones murdered by the police. The "activists" have events in our cities and have not given us anything substantial for using our loved ones' images and names on their flyers. . . .
>
> We don't want or need y'all parading in the streets accumulating donations, platforms, movie-deals, etc. off the death of our loved ones, while the families and communities are left clueless and broken. Don't say our loved ones' names period!
> That's our truth![87]

There is nothing democratic about how decisions are made or resources are distributed in the Black Lives Matter Global Network Foundation (BLMGNF), the primary recipient of the more than $100 million that has been donated to support the BLM movement. There has never been a public

---

84. Black Lives Matter–Inland Empire 2021.
85. H. Alexander 2021.
86. Gunn 2021.
87. Bruce 2021.

account of how much money has been collected and how, exactly, it has been spent. While a 501(c)(3) registered nonprofit organization is required to make its finances public, the BLMGNF finally completed its legal transition to a 501(c)(3) in December 2021, more than five years after the Black Lives Matter Global Network was incorporated in 2016.[88] The process ordinarily takes only a few months to complete; it thereby shielded its finances from public scrutiny for the overwhelming duration of its existence. Patrice Cullors resigned from her position as executive director of the BLMGNF in May 2021, but not before purchasing two six-million-dollar mansions, one in tony Studio City just over the hill from Hollywood and Beverly Hills and the other in her partner Janaya Khan's hometown of Toronto, transacted through a legal entity set up by Khan, rather than through BLM's Canada affiliate.[89]

Upon her resignation, Cullors announced that activists Makani Themba and Monifa Bandele would assume executive control of the BLMGNF, both of whom publicly stated that they never assumed the positions. The BLMGNF revealed in early 2021 that it had about $60 million remaining from 2020, its most lucrative year, though the address used for the most recent tax filing, in 2019, has never been occupied by the BLMGNF.[90] The organization apparently has no physical offices or executive leadership, despite claiming to have spent more than $8 million on overhead in 2020.[91] As of this writing, no funds have been dispersed to the families of black men, women, and children killed by police in whose names the money was raised or to those arrested or injured in nationwide protests that ostensibly have occurred under the BLM banner since 2014. It would take a forensic accounting analysis to unravel how much money has been raised under the BLM banner; what entities and individuals were the recipients of that money; for what purpose they received the funds; and what their connections to one another are exactly. I doubt that such an accounting is forthcoming.

Reed's son, historian Touré Reed, argues in his book *Toward Freedom* (2020) that race-reductionist identity politics betray "corporate Democrats' and a stratum of identitarian progressives' commitment to a class politics—shrouded in a language of identity and attitudes, uncoupled from political economy—that has long failed disproportionately black and brown working people."[92] According to Reed the younger, such race thinking has been di-

---

88. Daniel Funke, "How the Black Live Matter Global Network Is Set Up," June 17, 2020, https://www.politifact.com/factchecks/2020/jun/17/candace-owens/how-black-lives-matter -global-network-set.

89. H. Alexander, 2022; Campbell 2022b.

90. H. Alexander 2022; Campbell 2022a.

91. Campbell 2022a.

92. T. Reed 2020, 10.

sastrous for African Americans particularly, as any opportunity for substantive material improvement of the plight of the vast majority of African Americans has been sacrificed at the altar of identity politics and racial tokenism:

> Liberals' tendency to divorce race from class has had dire consequences for African American and other low-skilled workers. Specifically, race reductionism has obscured the political-economic roots of racial disparities, resulting in policy prescriptions that could have only limited value to poor and working-class blacks.[93]

Rather than narrow racially exclusive reparations, what the Reeds suggest as an alternative is a systematic and comprehensive redistribution of society's resources, which would necessarily benefit the most marginalized segments of the population because it is they who are farthest from parity. Logically, bringing all populations to parity, without regard for identity, would be most advantageous for those who have the least and would threaten those who have the most to lose:

> Pursuing socialist equality and combating racial inequality are not at all incompatible or in conflict. An agenda of egalitarian redistribution on class terms would proportionately benefit blacks and other nonwhites, women, and probably LGBTQ (lesbian, gay, bisexual, transgender and queer) people as well because these populations are disproportionately poor and working class.[94]

Thus far, I have laid out the historical development of the ideas that made ethnonationalist ideology possible and presented a wide range of critiques that have been leveled against ethnonationalist ideology and identity politics. In the chapters that follow, I turn to the empirical outcomes the cult of identity has engendered in Los Angeles. History and theory isn't some metaphysical ephemeral alternate universe; it is the material reality that we live. It defines the terms of our lives. When we divide ourselves conceptually, we invite manipulation, division, and, ultimately, conflict and violence into our lives and communities.

---

93. Ibid., 12.
94. Ibid., 38.

3

AN INVISIBLE WALL

Culture, Identity, and Division

There's a lot of things that— There's an invisible wall there.
—WS Easy Riders 13, forties

Aprogeny of the hegemony identity politics achieved in the wake of the collapse of the Civil Rights Movement, racialized gang identities proliferated in the African American and Chicano communities in Los Angeles in the post–Civil Rights Movement era, each with its own racialized identity, cultural praxis, and presentation of self. Unlike New York and Oakland, where boundaries between historical African American and Latino communities are measured in blocks, not miles, in Los Angeles the historically African American community in South Los Angeles and the historically Chicano community in East Los Angeles, since their inception, have been separated by a distance of multiple miles, numerous train lines, and the Los Angeles River. Because of this physical, geographical, cultural, and conceptual isolation from one another, the core of the African American and Chicano communities in Los Angeles grew even more ostracized from one another over the course of the twentieth century.

The exclusive, insular, oppositional racial identities that crystallized in the wake of the collapse of the Civil Rights Movement provided the conceptual foundation for the proliferation of racialized street and prison gangs in the 1970s and 1980s. Indications of these ethnonationalist identities can be found in various cultural symbolism employed in street and prison gang culture that started in the Civil Rights Movement era. One obvious example is the choice of languages gang members in California prisons have used for clandestine communication since the early 1970s. African American in-

Figure 3.1. *Azteca paño* prison art. (Photograph by the author.)

mates in this period absorbed the black nationalist lingua franca, Swahili, as their chosen vehicle for covert communication. Reflecting a nationalist identity rooted in the *Mexica* myth of origin, Chicano inmates chose the *Mexica* language, *Nahuatl*, as their *lingua secretum*. Another obvious reflection of nationalist identity, particularly among *Sureño*-affiliated gang members, is their art and tattoos. Ornate works of art and tattoos of *Mexica* mythology and archaeological artifacts such as war shields, jaguar warriors, calendars, maidens, and monumental architecture are not only pervasive among Chicano gang members, but also carry symbolic meaning, communicating the status of those who bear them. As this chapter illustrates, an elaborate system of disparate cultural practices and presentation of self emerged in the wake of the collapse of the Civil Rights Movement, reinforcing racialized gang identities and conceptually dividing one from another.

The cultural chasm between predominantly Chicano *Sureño*-affiliated gangs and predominantly African American Crip- and Blood-affiliated gangs in Los Angeles is easily identifiable from individual to individual, regardless of race, if one possesses the *street literacy* necessary to know what to look for.[1] From vernacular to preferences in music and cuisine; aesthetic styles that cultural criminologists remind us not to overlook; and the way that people relate to one another in their everyday lives, *racialized gang identities are expressed and regulated through cultural praxis.* All of the cultural accoutrements of racialized gang identity serve as a repertoire not only to communicate who and what an individual is, but also, and just as important, who and what an individual is *not.* Indeed, as cultural criminologist Jeff Ferrell reminds us, *style matters.*[2] In this way, cultural style and praxis, as Ferrell suggests, serve to denote subcultural affiliation and define the perceived boundaries among racialized gang identities. The cruel irony is that, as the classical Birmingham School suggests, while the subcultural aesthetics and praxis of *Sureño*-affiliated and Crip- and Blood-affiliated gang members represent symbolic resistance to their subordinate position in the capitalist economy, their expression through cultural nationalist identity categories functions fundamentally to divide gang members from one another across racial lines.[3]

Perceptions of these subcultural divisions are almost universally agreed on by members of the *Sureño*-affiliated and Crip- and Blood-affiliated gangs I interviewed in Los Angeles. *Sureño*-affiliated and Crip- and Blood-affiliated respondents were in almost unanimous agreement about what exact cultural practices and artifacts define the boundaries of their identities, as well as where those boundaries overlap. The most fundamental difference between the expression of African American and Chicano gang culture in Los Angeles is that in Crip and Blood gang culture, drawing attention to oneself through ostentatious displays of style, behavior, and discourse is welcomed and encouraged; whereas in *Sureño* gang culture, drawing attention to oneself is fiercely discouraged. Crip- and Blood-affiliated gang members tend to want to stand out from their peers. In Crip and Blood gang culture, everyone wants to be the most stylish and the smoothest-talking in their peer group—the homie with the most "swag," as the contemporary lexicon describes it. Cultural innovations are encouraged by status rewards. In contrast, *Sureño*-affiliated gang members favor a more unassuming presentation of self. Individual innovations in cultural expression are often

---

1. Conquergood 1997.
2. Ferrell 1995.
3. Clarke (1975) 2006a, (1975) 2006b; Hebdige (1975) 2006, 1979.

zealously regulated, and anyone who dares cross the boundaries of acceptable cultural style, behavior, or praxis risks ridicule and social ostracism, at the least, and violent censure, at the worst. The *Sureño* cultural regime is tightly regulated both formally and informally by peer cohorts and *veteranos*, the elder statesmen of *Sureño* gang culture.

Of course, not every gang member uniformly conforms to the cultural expectations of racialized gang identities, but such cultural expectations are nonetheless widely shared among *Sureño*-affiliated and Crip- and Blood-affiliated gang members and their wider Chicano and African American communities in Los Angeles. In fact, the salience of such conceptual correlations between racialized gang identities and cultural praxis requires the kind of zealous identity policing by gang members themselves that professional ethnopolitical entrepreneurs encourage. While the idea that racial identity and cultural praxis are inextricably linked is a centuries-old core facet of the race concept, the zealous enforcement of these boundaries is what maintains their salience in the present. The boundary enforcement in which gang members engage is merely a reflection of the ethnonationalist ideology they have unwittingly inherited.

Another important theme in this chapter is the cultural morphology that naturally occurs over time in any human population, which is artificially repressed by identity policing, just as linguistic morphology is repressed by standardized print language. There are essentially two sources of cultural morphology: *cultural innovation* and *cultural diffusion*. When *cultural innovation* occurs, a new subcultural style or practice is created by members of the subculture through their own imagination, often modifying or expanding on existing styles and practices. When *cultural diffusion* occurs, a new style or practice is adopted from another source, most often either another subculture, media depictions, or a combination thereof.[4] Ethnopolitical entrepreneurs zealously condemn this naturally occurring cultural exchange and diffusion with the nouveau identitarian slur "cultural appropriation," fanatically policing the boundaries of racialized identities they deem sacrosanct. As this chapter illustrates, policing the boundaries between racialized *Sureño* and Crip and Blood identities is also of paramount concern to many gang members. However, there are those gang members who do dare to engage in boundary penetration, enjoying cultural styles and practices that do not coincide with their racialized gang identity. They are often met with stiff disapprobation from their peers for having crossed the sacrosanct cultural boundaries that divide racialized identity communities. The negotiation of these culturally defined boundar-

---

4. Clarke (1975) 2006b.

ies is an ongoing process that is constantly stymied by boundary policing within and between opposing racialized identity communities.

Clothing

The first area of cultural division between *Sureño* and Crip and Blood culture in Los Angeles is clothing styles. It is perhaps the first and most apparent cultural indicator of racialized gang identity, because it is readily visible for all to see. Clothing and aesthetic style is the first cultural indicator by which gang members are judged by their peers and thus sets the frame for identifying and organizing individuals into different racialized gang identities. Following one of the major themes of this chapter, traditional *Sureño* clothing styles are markedly uniform, with relatively little variation in content between individuals, while Crip and Blood clothing styles are much more varied and ostentatious. As one respondent said:

> As South Siders, we try to, appearance is everything to us, you know? Just kinda like a, like a status symbol, you know? Gotta make sure you're nice and pressed; don't sag your pants; keep your shoes clean. You know? (ES Evergreen Locos 13, thirties)[5]

I add to the traditional cholo aesthetic previously described by cultural anthropologist James Diego Vigil a temporal perspective of cultural evolution and diffusion.[6] The early prototypical cholo clothing style was the zoot suit of the 1930s and 1940s.[7] The pachuco-style zoot suit was the popular clothing style in the Chicano community in Los Angeles when the cholo subculture first came to the general public's attention with the "Sleepy Lagoon" murder in 1942 and the Zoot Suit Riots that followed, in 1943.[8] One respondent expressed the connection:

> I believe we still have the same style of dressing, like the zoot suit days back in the '20s and all that, the '40s, whatever. We were the last of the pachucos. We were cholos. (ES White Fence 13, fifties)

---

5. As noted in the Introduction, ES stands for East Side; WS stands for West Side; SS and SC stand for South Side and South Central, respectively; and NELA stands for North East Los Angeles. These are designations used by gang members themselves.

6. See Vigil 1988. *Cholo* is a contemporary term for a Chicano gang member.

7. Alvarez 2008. A zoot suit is a style of suit made with excess material so as to be worn larger than the standard size of the wearer.

8. Pagán 2003. *Pachuco* is a dated term for a Chicano gang member, commonly used in the mid-twentieth century.

However, as the practice of wearing a full suit every day waned in American culture generally, the zoot suit style began to be replaced with a more casual working-class aesthetic in the 1960s and 1970s. Dress slacks began to be replaced with less expensive khaki work pants and corduroy pants, while shoe styles also relaxed from Imperials, a pointy leather dress shoe, to Hush Puppies, a comfortable and casual rough leather shoe with high seams around the front crest. It was in the 1970s that wearing sneakers became commonplace, as well, as the ubiquitous Converse Chuck Taylor All Star canvas shoe with a flat rubber sole became common in both the barrio and the ghetto, due in large part to its affordable price tag. It was also in the 1970s that white T-shirts and Pendleton button-up shirts became popular daily wear in the barrio, replacing the button-up dress shirt and jacket one would wear with a full zoot suit. An African American member of a *Sureño*-affiliated gang in East Los Angeles described to me the styles when he came of age in the 1970s and how the aesthetic popular in his community was received by his African American cousins who lived in South Los Angeles:

> A: My cousins were raised in South Central in Watts. They used to wear Levi's and things like that. In East LA, gang members wore khakis and Pendleton [shirts] and white T-shirts. The white T-shirts didn't get popular in Watts and South Central until later on. When I was incarcerated, we used to talk about those things. I was wearing white T-shirts in the '70s, and only certain companies used to manufacture them: Sears and JCPenneys, Towncraft and Staffords.
>
> Q: What about shoes? What kind of shoes were popular with gang members when you were growing up?
>
> A: Both sides wore Chuck Taylors, or over here we used to wear Imperials or Hush Puppies. They didn't wear Imperials in black areas, 'cause when I wore them to visit my cousins, they'd be like, "You must grow up with Mexicans to be wearing those pointy shoes, right?" [*Laughs*]

The prototypical cholo uniform established in the 1980s and 1990s consists of oversize work pants or Levi's 501 blue jeans, typically much larger than the wearer's standard waist size. Popular brands of work pants are Ben Davis and Frisco Ben's, which are made of a heavy-duty canvas material and are commonly worn by blue-collar workers. The pants and jeans are folded, starched, ironed, and pleated in a particular way to accommodate the extra material around the waist and to achieve a uniform clean, military-pressed aesthetic. Levi's 501 jeans are also very common; those who choose to wear jeans, though, must wear 501s to comply with the *Sureño* cultural canon.

The pants are traditionally worn high at the navel, rather than low around the hips, and are typically held up by military style pull-and-catch belts, which are commonly found at surplus stores. The design enables multiple buckles to be attached to the same belt, so that buckles bearing different letters can spell out an acronym that more precisely identifies the wearer's gang allegiance.

White T-Shirts are ubiquitous in *Sureño* gang culture, available both in prison and on the street. The most popular is the Stafford brand, sold exclusively at JCPenney department stores. It is a thick white T-shirt that is sold in tall sizes so it can be either easily tucked in or worn draped lower below the belt than a typical T-shirt would extend:

> The Ben Davis and Frisco's and, you know, khakis, 501s, all that. White shirts, the JCPenneys, the Staffords—JCPenney first, that's what we used to wear, then they became Stafford. Yeah, so, you know: trying to be clean and, you know, always look sharp. That's how we did it, you know? (ES El Sereno 13, thirties)

Pro Club–brand T-shirts in neutral colors such as blue, brown, black, and gray are acceptable, as well; logos and designs are less acceptable, depending on the content. Other popular shirts are the Ben Davis work shirts, made of a rough canvas material like the pants and with a stiff collar, often in a vertically striped pattern. Also popular are polo shirts commonly sold at swap meets throughout the city made either of cotton or a polyester-cotton blend and often with a thick horizontal-stripe pattern. Another traditional shirt still worn by *Sureño*-affiliated gang members is the Pendleton-brand heavy button-up plaid shirt. Finally, jerseys of Los Angeles area sports teams—particularly the Raiders and the Dodgers—are commonplace. All shirts are worn oversize, in at least a 2XL for an average-size person.

Since the 1980s, the iconic cholo sneaker has been the Nike Cortez. Also popular and universally acceptable is the Nike Air Force 1 in white on white. Every effort is made to keep white shoes white, with constant cleaning and shoe dye being applied to keep the shoes looking clean and new and thus maintain the sharp, clean aesthetic favored by *Sureño*-affiliated gang members. White shoes are typically topped with tall white socks, pulled up to the knees:

> Basically what I would wear everyday would be 501 Levi's, creased up, ironed, you know? Some Nikes—you know, Nike Cortez, the canvas ones, the blue ones, the black ones. And white T-shirts, you know? Maybe a Raider shirt or Dodger shirt. Shit like [that], and that prolly be it. (SC Clanton 14 Street, forties)

Figure 3.2. *Estilo Sureño*: Florencia members dressed down. (Courtesy of Estevan Oriol.)

While we have rather respectable ethnographies of cholo gangs in Los Angeles, there is an unfortunate lack of ethnographic work on Crip and Blood gang culture in Los Angeles in the academic literature.[9] There are respectable historical accounts of the emergence of Crip and Blood gangs in Los Angeles but no real descriptive work on what Crip and Blood culture consists of.[10] Therefore, it is even more worthwhile to present a thick description of Crip and Blood clothing styles, not only as a contribution in itself, but also to show its distinctness when compared with *Sureño* clothing styles.

As my colleague Alex Alonso recounts, the Crip and Blood culture arose from the ashes of the Civil Rights Movement.[11] As a result, early Crip and Blood gang members imitated the aesthetic styles of their predecessors, who had transformed from gang members into political activists in the Black Panther Party (BPP). The black leather jacket, adopted from the dress of BPP members in the late 1960s, was one article of clothing that defined the early Crip and Blood style.[12] However, the Panther style of the early 1970s soon

---

9. On LA cholo gangs, see Moore 1978, 1991; Sánchez-Jankowski 1991; Vigil 1988, 2007; Ward 2013.

10. Alonso 2004, 2010; Davis 1990; Vigil 2002a.

11. Alonso 2004, 2010.

12. Alonso 2010.

gave way to the *Super Fly* style of the Blaxploitation film era. Loud and elaborate "pimp suits" became common in the African American community as media representations glorifying the pimping subculture enthralled a generation of black youth in the ghettos of Los Angeles. Flashy suits were topped off with elaborate jewelry and fancy shoes made of leather or game animals, such as the notorious "gators" (Italian designer shoes made from alligator hide). Of course, some remnant of that subculture still exists, but in the 1970s the flamboyant *Super Fly* style was the dominant aesthetic style favored by African American gang members in South Los Angeles, as one respondent recounted:

A: We used to wear slacks, believe it or not—suits kinda like the Blaxploitation films. Like, I don't know if you've seen *Super Fly*. It would be kinda like along those lines. It's funny: silk shirts and shit.
Q: They were popular back then?
A: That was popular dress.
Q: With the fly shoes and all that?
A: Yes, leather jackets, you know? Hat occasionally. Whatever. And that changed throughout the years. (WS Rolling 20s Neighborhood Bloods, fifties)

In the 1980s, Crips and Bloods gravitated toward a harder aesthetic, borrowed but also modified from their Chicano peers. Khaki work pants became more popular, though Crips and Bloods tended to prefer the Dickies brand and wore them less baggy than cholos would. Black gang members often wear their pants with an exaggerated sag so that their underpants— and even much of their buttocks, in some cases—show above the beltline. This area is typically draped over with a long shirt so that it appears that one's legs are shorter than they really are. It was in the late 1970s that white T-shirts, Pendleton shirts, sports jerseys, and Dickies suits became popular with Crips and Bloods. Matching Dickies suits in blue, red, burgundy, black, and khaki became a popular outfit, often signaling one's Crip or Blood gang identity, depending on the motif.

Wearing tennis shoes also became standard as Chuck Taylors, Pumas, K-Swiss, Reebok, and other brands became popular, often with thick laces, a stylistic innovation borrowed from the emerging hip hop subculture on the East Coast. Multiple accessories also became pervasive, including thick gold chains; blacked-out, square-frame Locs sunglasses; and a common handkerchief, the notorious blue or red rag indicating Crip or Blood gang allegiance. These styles were reinforced by the explosion of the gangster rap genre beginning in the late 1980s. As the gangster rap era waned, the "bling bling" rap era emerged in the 2000s, with its gaudy displays of jewelry such as gold fronts worn on one's teeth. In the past decade, urban aesthetics in the African American community have evolved into a sort of urban hipster culture of the 2010s, with each generation of Crip and Blood gang members keeping pace with the current nationwide streetwear trends of their generation.

Stylistic innovation is one of the hallmarks of African American culture, and it is certainly prominent among Crip and Blood gang members in Los Angeles. Whatever the newest styles that media outlets and urban celebrities portray, Crip and Blood gang members are quick to incorporate and innovate on them. Stylistic innovation is not only tolerated but, indeed, celebrated in the black community in Los Angeles and throughout the nation. Those who are able to display the newest stylistic innovations in their presentation of self are rewarded with high status among their peers. As a result of this constant innovation and evolution in clothing styles by Crip and Blood gang members, there is a wide range of variation in aesthetic presentation among them.

Khaki pants gave way to designer jeans, worn fitted and even tight in some cases. Wearing fitted jeans is now so commonplace among Crip and Blood gang members that, in many cases, they don't "look like gang members" at all:

Well, me, I can tell because blacks are more, we try to keep up with fashion more, you know? And versus the Hispanic gangs, they still dress old school, you know? Like, like gangsters. We kinda dress more casual now, you know what I'm saying? It's not Dickies no more. We wear jeans—like, designer jeans now—you know what I'm saying? But they don't care for that, you know? (WS Rolling 30s Harlem Crips, twenties)

Designer jeans are held up with expensive logo-print belts from high-end European designers such as Louis Vuitton and Gucci. Polo shirts from designer clothing companies are common, as are T-shirts with prominent logos from urban streetwear companies—whichever ones happen to be in vogue from year to year. At times they are bedazzled with rhinestones, faux gold leaf, and other embellishments, with gold chains draped on top and stones in the ears. A kaleidoscope of colors and designs on baseball caps and shoes top off and bottom out the modern urban streetwear style that is popular with Crip and Blood gang members. The availability of shoes and hats in a variety of designs, patterns, and colors has exploded in the past twenty years as corporations such as Nike and New Era have responded to increasing demand for stylistic innovation in the urban streetwear market.

Go to any gang function in the ghettos of Los Angeles and one will find Crip- and Blood-affiliated gang members dressed down and "turned up" in

Figure 3.3. Blood style: Rolling 20s Neighborhood Bloods members flamed up from the feet up. (Courtesy of Estevan Oriol.)

outfits with designer jeans and matching shoes, shirts, hats, and accessories, often with subtle signifiers that identify their gang affiliation. Those on the cutting edge of stylistic innovation enjoy a significant boost to their status among their peers:

> In Watts, everybody's kinda dressed, like, hip, you know? Like hip hop ways or very urban. That's how we dress. Current styles, you know? We're like trendsetters. We also follow trends, but you have some people who are, um, who are stuck in the ways of the '90s and '80s, and there's nothing wrong with that. They stick to their heritage and their culture. Umm, those cholos wear their pants to their navel or higher, you know? And most Black gang members, we probably let our pants sag a little bit. (Watts Bounty Hunter Bloods, thirties)

Aesthetic presentation of self is quite different in the *Sureño* cholo culture, however, where innovations in clothing styles are often a source of significant angst and occasional conflict across generational divides. Many young *Sureño*-affiliated gang members are adopting contemporary urban streetwear in their clothing styles as a result of cultural diffusion, particularly those who grow up in the racially heterogeneous neighborhoods of South and West Los Angeles. Crip- and Blood-affiliated gang members are free to follow stylistic innovations wherever they go, but *Sureño*-affiliated gang members' forays across stylistic boundaries are often met with sharp rebuke from their peers and elders.

Some youngsters conform and display the traditional *Sureño* aesthetic by choice. Others resist peer pressure and test the limits of stylistic expression by adopting aspects of the urban streetwear that are commonly associated with an African American cultural identity. Some of the more common items to cross over are accessories such as flashy Nike sneakers and New Era hats. Limited edition Nike Air Jordans and Air Force 1s that span the rainbow in color and design, for example, are popular with some *Sureño*-affiliated gang members. Urban streetwear brands such as Lifted Research Group (LRG), Diamond Supply Co., The Hundreds, Supreme, and Ecko, while common among Crip and Blood gang members, are occasionally worn by *Sureño*-affiliated gang members, as are urban streetwear brands marketed specifically to the cholo consumer, such as the timeless Joker Brand, the brainchild of cultural icons Estevan Oriol and Mister Cartoon. In some cases, *Sureño*-affiliated gang members even break strict cultural conventions by sagging their pants or wearing a hat cocked sideways.

Stylistic transgressions are often met with disapprobation, threats, or even violence. However, in each case the enforcer makes a decision about whether it's worth policing stylistic boundaries and to what extent. Some *veteranos*, particularly those who have spent extensive time incarcerated in the California prison system, where they literally went to war with black gang members, are adamantly opposed to any blurring of the boundaries between *Sureño*-affiliated and Crip- and Blood-affiliated gang members. They are entirely contemptuous of clothing styles associated with a black gang identity:

> Wow, they [black gang members] dress way out, man. They like to be the center of attention. How can I say it? They're entertainers, aye? With their big mouths, with their loud-ass clothes. They need to always have attention. They have some kind of malfunction in their genes or something. (ES Clover Street 13, fifties)

The most basic and innocuous method of enforcing these boundaries is by "clowning" someone, or undermining their status by ridiculing their aesthetic presentation of self. However, confronting transgressors of these boundaries can be much more direct, as youngsters are often "checked" by *veteranos* for their excessive use of styles associated with a black presentation of self. These boundaries are vigorously enforced because culture is the crux upon which racialized gang identities are imagined. Cultural diffusion is perceived as a threat because it blurs the boundaries that divide racialized *Sureño* and Crip and Blood gang identities. It is in gang members' accounts of these differences that one can comprehend the importance of these cultural indicators in defining who is what:

> They mainly like to sag. Like, you see how they wear it: their clothes are, like, halfway; you can see their whole fuckin' ass, you know? Like, we don't get down like that. We don't do that. So when you see some one that's Mexican do that shit, we fuckin' tell 'em, "Pick up your fucking pants! You ain't black!" You know what I mean? 'Cause that's what they're known for. They fuckin'— How can I start? They wear, like, all these way-off colors. They fucking put those shits on their teeth. They do all that shit like wear those big-ass chains, and we don't do that shit. (ES White Fence 13, twenties)

The other reason for the move toward a more "casual" streetwear style is to avoid attention from law enforcement and to surprise potential rivals. A defense mechanism used by gang members has been to try to pass under the radar by dressing in ways that will not be associated with gangs—as hipsters, skaters, or whatever's clever:

> A: Yeah, back in the day you could tell, but nowadays you can't. Everybody just dress like; everybody trying to just dress like normal now.
> Q: So everyone tries to dress, like, more low-key like a civilian now?
> A: Yeah, more you see alotta more, like, low-key dressing now, like more people trying to be under the table, like, "I'm a gang member but I just don't want people to know." So they dress like skaters or they'll dress like pretty boys. They don't dress like banged-out no more. (SC 38 Street, twenties)

Another advantage of passing is that not only law enforcement has trouble identifying gang members. So do potential rivals. Clever gang members can avoid getting "caught slipping" themselves or might be able to get the drop on potential rivals by approaching them without them being perceived as a potential threat, as one respondent described:[13]

> It's pretty tricky. There's no uniform anymore. Anybody could be a gang member. Two years ago, while I was still active, I had a kid on

---

13. *Caught slipping* means being caught unaware or made a victim of violence.

a fixie ride by me.[14] I used to sell weed at the time, right? And he ride by me [and says], "Wassup man?" And I was like— I thought it was one of the youngsters wanting weed. I'm going to go buy a blunt, and I look, I was like, "What's crackin'?" He's like— He jumps off the bike. He's got on skinny jeans and pulls out a Beretta with a 25 round, you know? I'm a fuckin' gun man. That's always been my thing. That's all I've ever been busted for is weapons. He pulls it out; he's like, "Where the fuck you from?" and I was like, "What the fuck? Like you serious?" And he was like, and he told me where he's from, and I'm like, "I'm from La Mirada Locos." Homie starts dissin' the neighborhood. I'm like, "Oh man, it's easy to diss with a gun pointed at me. Come on. Put the gun down. Wassup?" "Fuck you! Fuck you!" and I was like, "No, fuck you." I turn around back to go grab my shit. I didn't catch up to him, you know? . . . But, I was like, "Wow! I got caught slippin' by a dude in skinny jeans!" [*Laughs*] Well, I don't know where the fuck he pulled the gun out of. Like, where could it fit? Especially when it's a extended clip! [*Laughs*] You know, but, you know what? Right now it's a time of pure caution, and you have to be very tentative, and if you're not, you're going down. . . . Can't put it past nobody, bro. Can't put it past nobody. (WS La Mirada Locos 13, thirties)

Hairstyles

Hairstyles are also a source of cultural division between *Sureño*-affiliated and Crip- and Blood-affiliated gang members. Following the pattern found in clothing styles, cholo hairstyles have changed little from generation to generation, with only one major evolution in half a century, whereas popular hairstyles among Crip and Blood gang members have changed often over different eras, with each generation following current trends and innovating on them.

Until the early 1990s, cholos typically wore their hair short—just a few inches long—and usually slicked back with Tres Flores (Three Flowers) pomade and sometimes a thin hairnet to keep it in place:

We all had hair, you know? Slick straight back, you know? We wore the Three Flowers, you know, every day. Not too many people shaved their head back then. (SC Clanton 14 Street, forties)

---

14. A *fixie* is a fixed-gear bicycle popular in urban areas.

While the shaved head has become the standard for contemporary *Sureño*-affiliated gang members, prior to the early 1990s cholos shaved their heads only in the summer because of the heat:

> The shaved head had been around, but they were not as known. Back then we used to shave our head in the summertime, but it wasn't because we were banging. It wasn't to, you know, you were banging and this and that. It was just to have our heads shaved for the summer, you know? Now people just bang . . . with their head shaved. They bang, so now they think if you shave your head, you're active. Even a lot of older guys, they got their head shaved, man. (ES White Fence 13, fifties)

Cultural innovation is so circumscribed in *Sureño* gang culture that, for some older gang members who were in prison when the transition from slicked-back hair to shaved heads was made in the early 1990s, it presented somewhat of a conundrum as to what to make of it and whether to follow the trend:

> Q: Back when you were a kid what were the popular hairstyles with your friends?
> A: Yeah, people would just slick their hair back. People would wear hairnets, keep the Three Flowers in their hair. The difference now is everyone is bald; everyone shaves their head. When I was in prison, people told me—'cause I was having people send me some grooming supplies—and I would be like, "Send me some grease for my hair!" And my nephew would be like, "No one wears that shit in their hair out here. Everyone is bald now. That's played out!" I said, "I dunno. I can't see myself doing it." Then one day I got tired of going through all of that and I just cut it, and I never went back. And then eventually when I wanted to go back, [my hair] wouldn't grow back, so I'm stuck. [*Laughs*] I'm like "OK, all right."
> Q: When was it when you first shaved your head? Was there a time when you were in the system that you noticed that everyone coming in had their head shaved?
> A: Yeah, you could see the trend. I know I started doing it in 1997, and the trend had started maybe four years before then. People would have their hair much shorter. And now it's not even short; it's bald. They want it bald so you can see the tattoos on their head if they have them. It's really changed dramatically. (ES Varrio Nueva Estrada 13, fifties)

A popular account of the transition is that *Sureño*-affiliated gang members in the prison system started shaving their heads to pay homage to one of the most respected members of the Mexican Mafia, Joe "Cocoliso" Morgan, who wore his head shaved bald and died of liver cancer in prison on November 9, 1993:

> I heard a story that when Joe Morgan died, everybody, his crew, shaved their head out of respect for Joe, and then that just caught on. Yeah, it spread from there. (SC Clanton 14 Street, forties)

There can be no doubt that the timing of the new trend coincides with Morgan's passing. Furthermore, this cultural innovation lacked the kind of negative response that cultural innovations typically evoke among *Sureño*-affiliated gang members. If the trend was initiated to pay homage to Morgan, that would certainly explain the lack of resistance to the new style.

Hairstyle is also an important aspect of cultural identity for Crip- and Blood-affiliated gang members:

> Yeah, 'cause back in the day, braids, like cornrows, braids was pretty much our identity, like living that life being black. (ES 43 Gangster Crips, thirties)

In contrast to cholos, Crips and Bloods in Los Angeles have adopted just about every different hairstyle that has been popular in African American communities across the nation with each passing era. As the trends change from generation to generation and new hairstyles come into common use, they do not necessarily replace older hairstyles but, rather, add to the depth of variety in the repertoire of available hairstyles from which Crip- and Blood-affiliated gang members can choose to express their own individual aesthetic. The Afros of the Civil Rights Movement era gave way to the long, straight "dead hair" pimp style of the Super Fly era in the 1970s. These styles were followed in the 1980s by Jehri curls, French braids, and cornrows, and in the 1990s by dreadlocks, flat tops, waves, tapers, and fades, with and without designs. Mohawks and more are popular in the new millennium. As innovation in aesthetic expression is venerated in the black community, it is not uncommon to see Crip- and Blood-affiliated gang members exhibit current or vintage hairstyles, as each individual uses hair as another medium with which to weave a distinctive presentation of self. As one respondent said:

> Like, blacks, they get, like, braids and cornrows and, uh, French braids or haircuts with designs and, uh, mohawks or something. His-

panics is just more like simple like a bowl cut or fade or something bald. Bald heads really. (Pasadena Denver Lane Bloods, twenties)

Even more than clothing, hairstyles are distinct between *Sureño*-affiliated and Crip- and Blood-affiliated gang members, almost to the point that hairstyle in and of itself can indicate whether an individual identifies as a *Sureño*-affiliated or Crip- or Blood-affiliated gang member. Certain hairstyles unequivocally place one into one identity category or another. A bald-headed Chicano is typically perceived as displaying an active *Sureño*-affiliated gang identity, whereas certain hairstyles popular in the African American community, such as cornrows in the 1990s, can be interpreted as displaying an active Crip- or Blood-affiliated identity. The association of certain hairstyles with distinct racialized gang identities is widely agreed on by gang members, regardless of their affiliation:

Q: Do you think hairstyles are a big difference between Mexican gang members and black gang members?
A: Well, yeah, that's a big difference, hairstyle.
Q: What were the popular hairstyles for your friends when you were growing up?
A: Well, you know, we had, like, braids, ponytail, two ponytail, you know; French braid to the back, however, to the, down to the side. And really, like, [for] Hispanics, it's pretty much majority shave they heads bald, yeah. (Hawthorne 118 Gangster Crips, twenties)

Nonetheless, there is some degree of cultural diffusion between *Sureño*-affiliated and Crip- and Blood-affiliated gang members with regard to hairstyles. For example, some Crip- and Blood-affiliated gang members are shaving their heads, though in many cases they are doing so out of necessity as older generations are aging into hair loss:

Well, for me, I'm going bald, so that's why I choose to shave my head. [*Laughs*] Nowadays you find a lot more black people, the majority of whom have the cornrows and the braids and all that, but every now and again you find, like, some blacks that have bald shaved heads, but the majority of them have, like braids and cornrows and shit like that. (ES 43 Gangster Crips, thirties)

Cultural diffusion also goes the other way, as some *Sureño*-affiliated gang members have their hair cut with a fade or a taper or grow their hair out long and pull it back in a ponytail. Thus, there is often tension between the presentation of self that is expected of gang members and the pressure to follow popular trends:

> Yeah, well, see, like, like in our sense, like, Mexicans always had their hair shaved. You know, we always were like bushy hair or braids, or Afros, or curls, or stuff like that. And nowadays I see Hispanics wearing ponytails, you know, 'cause blacks, you know, we used to have ponytails like that, so now I see Hispanics not shaving their heads anymore too much, and they're wearing their hair, like, bushy, in curls, or in a ponytail, or something like that, and more or less blacks are shaving their heads and keeping their hair designed and stuff like that. So it's, like, the fads. The fads that's coming along with the Hispanic and black community now are more mixed, because it's, like, in this day and age you have the younger generations that semi hang out together. (Compton Mob Piru, thirties)

Like the adoption of urban streetwear clothing styles, the adoption of African American hairstyles by *Sureño*-affiliated gang members has become more common with younger generations and is a source of considerable angst for some elder *Sureños*. While fades have become more acceptable, any other deviation from the traditional *Sureño* hairstyles of shaved heads and slicked-back hair is often met with considerable alarm, even when it comes to gang members' children, as one respondent noted:

> A: Well, you know, how they put, like, drawings and stripes and shit in their haircut. Where with us, if we see a Mexican with that shit on their head, we'll be like, "What the fuck? What you trying to be black for and shit?" For us, it's you got a little bit of hair or you go bald you know.
> Q: Is it still common for them to have like braids and cornrows and all that?
> A: What, black people? Yeah, they still have it. I never liked that. I got mad one time. They did braids on my little girl. I was like, "Naw, what the fuck, aye? She ain't black." You know? "Hell no! Take them shits out!" (SS Florencia 13, twenties)

Vernacular

Linguistic and communicative differences are a major aspect of cultural division between *Sureño*-affiliated and Crip- and Blood-affiliated gang members. Aside from the obvious difference that many *Sureño*-affiliated gang members are bilingual and freely alternate between Spanish and English, *Sureño*-

affiliated and Crip- and Blood-affiliated gang members use distinctly different English dialects in their everyday vernacular. Crip- and Blood-affiliated gang members use a version of what linguists call African American Vernacular English, or Black English, as their primary vernacular.[15] *Sureño*-affiliated gang members typically use a vernacular specific to the American Southwest that linguists call *Caló*, or Chicano English.[16] As linguist Nancy Mendoza-Denton suggests, language is much more than the spoken word.[17] Thus, it isn't just the words that they use that divide racialized gang identities but the totality of how *Sureño*-affiliated and Crip- and Blood-affiliated gang members represent themselves and relate to one another within their own, insular communities. In Crip and Blood culture, one is expected to be gregarious and linguistically expressive, whereas in *Sureño* culture, individuals are expected to be restrained and modestly unassuming in their communication.

As a result of these differences in cultural expectations, each interprets the other's communicative strategy as offensive by their standards of expression, mirroring the findings of research on conflict between the Korean and African American communities.[18] As the sociologist Edward Chang puts it, "Cultural misunderstanding between the two groups plays an important role in fueling and sometimes escalating the confrontations."[19] Crip- and Blood-affiliated gang members are seen as boorish and uncouth by *Sureño*-affiliated gang members, who complain that African Americans "talk too loud" and are too ostentatious:

A: Yeah, it's just very loud, and, you know, almost like shameless style to me. That's how I would perceive it. Like, that's how I perceived it when I was young, you know? I don't, you know— I just feel like they speak their mind, you know? They ain't shy. You know what I'm sayin'? But, you know, they're so outspoken. I mean, that's how I see 'em. They're just very outspoken, you know? They don't, they don't have no reservations.

Q: Did that used to bother you when you were young?

A: It did bother me, when like, "Shut the fuck up, man!" Like, I would just think they would be saying too much, you know, as opposed to how I was raised. Like, you have to be reserved. You have to be a mystery. You have to be a bit cryptic. You can't get yourself away like that, 'cause then you're done, you know? So I

---

15. L. Green 2002; McWhorter 1998, 2017; Smitherman 1977, 1994, 2000.

16. Galindo and Gonzales 1999; Mendoza-Denton 2008; Ortega 1991; Polkinhorn et al. (1983) 2005.

17. Mendoza-Denton 2008.

18. Chang 1999; Lee 1999; Park 1999; Stewart 1989.

19. Chang 1999, 49.

guess I was more guarded, you know, walking around. (ES El Sereno 13, thirties)

Crip- and Blood-affiliated gang members, by contrast, interpret the quiet avoidance of verbal exchange that *Sureño*-affiliated gang members favor as unfriendly and discourteous, often asserting themselves when they feel snubbed with, "I'm talking to you!"

When *Sureño*-affiliated gang members who are not intimately acquainted speak to one another, social convention dictates that they do so without betraying emotion. Discretion is favored, and it is considered uncouth and impolite to speak loud enough for others to eavesdrop on one's conversation. Above all, *Sureño*-affiliated gang members tend to be reticent to let anyone know their business who is not a part of it:

> A: Oh well, the differences in it, in my opinion, is that, uh, I guess blacks tend to use a little more aggressive tones when they speak, depending on the situation. It could differ from the situation, you know what I mean? Umm, opposed to when a homie spoke to somebody, he tried to make it more personal, a little more quiet, so it's not so loud and stuff. Let's handle our business in this manner.
>
> Q: You think black fools talk loud in general?
>
> A: Right off the bat! So it's right off the bat, if the guy thinks he's threatened or something, he's gonna be as loud as he can so he can get enough attention and more people are focused in his business. (ES Little Valley 13, thirties)

There are also significant differences in the use of slang in everyday vernacular by *Sureño*-affiliated and Crip- and Blood-affiliated gang members. *Caló* slang is a combination of English with a little Spanish mixed in, in a modified Mexican Spanish tone and accent and with specific slang terms commonly employed. Some of these slang terms are shared with the Spanish vernacular that many Mexican nationals speak in the Los Angeles area, such as the common affirmations *simon, firme,* and *oralé* and the common greeting *Qué onda?* (What's up?). Words such as *ese, homes, fool,* and *vato* are commonly used to refer to individuals. While calling someone a *fool* might be taken as an insult in Standard English, in *Caló* it is commonly used as a term of endearment. The word *dispensa* is often used for "excuse me" when someone accidentally bumps into someone else or when someone needs to pass by someone who is in their way, or it is used as a short form of apology when one has given offense unintentionally. The word *trucha* (watch out) is commonly employed by *Sureño*-affiliated gang members as a warning when looking out for one another. Police are referred to by the slang term *jura*, common in both *Caló* and Mexican Spanish vernacular:

> 'Cause the blacks, they say the N-word and everything, you know? We'll say *fool*, or we'll say *ese* or *homie* or something, you know? (ES White Fence 13, twenties)

The African American Vernacular English used by Crip- and Blood-affiliated gang members is pronounced with a southern drawl inherited from the generations of African American refugees from the Jim Crow South who came to Los Angeles seeking a better life. As is ubiquitous in black communities throughout the English-speaking world, the most common term of endearment for Crip- and Blood-affiliated gang members is undoubtedly *nigga*.[20] Linguists have long recognized that this is not the same word, with the same meaning and connotation, as the racial epithet from which it was derived; rather, it is employed as a term of endearment.[21] Despite being derived from an unmistakable racial epithet, this term of endearment is ubiquitous as the use of African American Vernacular English has become a de facto lingua franca in youth cultures throughout the English-speaking world, Los Angeles being no exception. Numerous Crip- and Blood-affiliated gang members I interviewed reported that they do not take offense when the word is used, even by someone who is not black, if it is used as a term of endearment in the appropriate communicative context:

> We say, like, "Yo!" or "Ey yo!" or "Hey my nigga!" But now you even got Hispanics sayin' it. But back then they wasn't allowed to say that. Black people'd be like, it was like they being racist. But now anyone can say that. (East Coast Crips, twenties)

In addition to that controversial term, Crip- and Blood-affiliated gang members employ terms of endearment in their common vernacular that identify them specifically as either a Crip or a Blood. Crips call one another *Crip*, *cuz*, or *loco*, whereas Bloods simply call one another *Blood*:

> Like, when we greet each other. . . . Like, "What's happenin', home-boy?" Or "What's happenin', cuz?" Or "What's happenin', Blood?" Or "What's crackin', cuz?" Or "What's good?" That's more of a black

---

20. Where the word *nigga* is used as a term of endearment rather than a racial epithet, I do not elide it.

21. McWhorter 2017, 162–165; Smitherman 1977, 62; Smitherman 1994; Smitherman 2000, 210–212.

approach. Where with Mexicans, it's like, "Aye what's up, fool?" You know? (ES 43 Gangster Crips, thirties)

Verbal exchange among Crip- and Blood-affiliated gang members can be very animated from the perspective of someone who is a *Caló*- or even a Standard English-speaker. Discussants in a conversation often jockey for position, elevating their volume and expressiveness as needed to control the tone, tempo, and direction of the dialogue. Discussants employ clever phrases and figures of speech as the parties test the extent of one another's verbal prowess. The jockeying that goes on between parties to a conversation not only determines the lead in the exchange; it also, to some extent, determines their social status in that specific context.

With linguistic and communicative differences playing a significant role in defining the boundaries between *Sureño*-affiliated and Crip- and Blood-affiliated gang members, crossing the boundaries of these distinct linguistic communities is often confounding and disconcerting on all sides. *Sureño*-affiliated gang members often have a negative reaction to other *Sureño*-affiliated gang members' adopting aspects of African American Vernacular English. The use of *nigga* as a term of endearment by *Sureño*-affiliated gang members can be particularly incendiary, not only with African Americans, but also with other *Sureño*-affiliated gang members:

A: If you pay attention to the youngsters now, especially coming from the West Side and South Central, they use that word a lot, the word *nigga*.

Q: Not all of 'em!

A: A lot of 'em, homes. The youngsters. And right here when some of them are addressing me, I put a stop to that real quick: "Don't you dare call me that! I'll break your fuckin' teeth, homes!" (ES White Fence 13, fifties)

That there is a degree of cultural diffusion in the vernacular employed by *Sureño*-affiliated and Crip- and Blood-affiliated gang members ought not surprise any student of linguistics. Whether as a result of the proliferation of hip hop culture or simply because it is more efficient than Standard English, African American Vernacular English has become somewhat of a lingua franca for youth cultures throughout the English-speaking world, and *Sureño*-affiliated gang members in Los Angeles are no exception.[22] This cultural diffusion of African American Vernacular English is most prominent

---

22. McWhorter 1998.

in younger cohorts of *Sureño*-affiliated gang members, particularly those who live in demographically mixed neighborhoods and grew up with African Americans, though it is by no means ubiquitous among them. While it is not uncommon, it is often perceived as an aberration that must be kept in check to some degree around those who are offended by its use. Older, more traditional *Sureños*, for whom boundary maintenance is highly valued, will often harshly regulate the linguistic boundaries between *Sureño* and Crip and Blood racialized gang identities. Rather than feeling offended when *Sureño*-affiliated gang members employ African American Vernacular English in their presence—even the use of *nigga* as a term of endearment—Crip- and Blood-affiliated gang members can recognize when speakers do not intend offense, particularly if they are well acquainted. However, if they are not personally acquainted, such usage can be interpreted as a provocation to conflict.

Music

Preference in music is another area of cultural division between *Sureño*-affiliated and Crip- and Blood-affiliated gang members. There is a great deal more overlap in music preference than there is in other cultural practices, such as clothing, hairstyles, and vernacular expression. However, even where preference in genres overlaps, there is often distinction in preference for particular artists. The direction of cultural diffusion in music is, and always has been, from black to brown. *Sureño*-affiliated gang members have borrowed some of their most common musical genres, from oldies to rap music, from African American artists, while Crip- and Blood-affiliated gang members have adopted no musical genres from Chicanos.

Prior to the 1980s, the principal musical genre to which gang members—both African American and Chicano—listened is subsumed under the label "oldies." Before rap music became popular, *Sureño*-affiliated gang members also listened to Mexican genres such as *ranchera* music and *corridos*, while Crip- and Blood-affiliated gang members also listened to jazz, soul, and rhythm and blues (R&B). The popularity of oldies was also due to the state of technology and the entertainment industry at that time: there was, of course, no internet, no Napster, no Spotify, no MTV, no YouTube. There were only vinyl records and eight-track cassettes, and music was disseminated primarily by radio broadcast:

Q: The next area is music, what kinda music did you grow up listening to?
A: Oldies, Smokey Robinson, uh, Diana Ross and the Supremes, Mary Wells, you know? The Temptations. . . . All the Motown

music that we could hear. I mean, Midnighters, you know, uh, the Moments, you know?

Q: Was that what was playing on the radio when you were growing up, too?

A: Yeah, it was when Huggie Boy used to be around still.[23] Art Laboe, he's still around.[24] But Huggie Boy, yeah: "Hi, this is the Huggie Boy show," you know? You used to call in, do dedications, your name would come out, you could even say your neighborhood back then: "I'm so-and-so from barrio so-and-so, I wanna dedicate to my *ruca* and woopty-woop, 'You cheated, you lied, you're no good!'"[25] [*Laughs*] (ES White Fence 13, fifties)

The division of preference for certain artists and groups between African American and Chicano gang members was perceived on both sides of the color line, as even Crip- and Blood-affiliated gang members associated certain oldies with a Mexican or cholo audience, even though the performers were by and large African Americans:

The Mexican gangs, they always listened to oldies, but even then there was a kind of set of oldies. They listened to a lot of doo-wop type, and the term isn't really heard lately, but you'll hear it from a older person that say, "Oh, those are Mexican oldies. Those are Mexican oldies." (WS Rolling 20s Neighborhood Bloods, forties)

Even those oldies that *Sureño*-affiliated gang members did listen to were largely produced by black performers, an almost comical irony that is not lost on some of those who grew up listening to them:

Alotta people were on the oldies shit and shit like that, but oldies is pretty much blacks singing, so still. [*Laughs*] You might hate a motherfucker, but you listening to a black dude sing! [*Laughs*] (NELA Toonerville 13, forties)

The first generations of Crip- and Blood-affiliated gang members in the 1970s also listened to the burgeoning funk genre, with the P-Funk subgenre

---

23. Richard "Dick" James Hugg (1928–2006) was a popular radio disc jockey in the Los Angeles region who went by the nickname Huggie Boy.

24. Art Laboe (b. 1925) is a recently retired disc jockey in the Los Angeles region known for a popular oldies radio show.

25. *Ruca* is a Mexican vernacular Spanish term for (female) sweetheart.

gaining particular traction as the popularity of the self-proclaimed Godfather of Funk George Clinton and his bands Parliament and Funkadelic electrified black Los Angeles. This eccentric music complimented the eccentric aesthetic styles of the 1970s as a generation made its pledge to the funk nation, with loud clothes and loud parties lighting up South Los Angeles until the early morning hours each weekend.

In the barrios of East Los Angeles, the emerging genres of punk rock and heavy metal gained traction in the late 1970s and early 1980s as a generation of cholos grew their hair out and went from gangbanger to headbanger. Local Southern California bands with a national audience, such as Slayer, became icons for a generation of headbanging gangbangers, as did local bands with a more regional following, such as Suicidal Tendencies:

Yeah, I mean growing up, I grew up on the punk rock and hardcore and metal, you know? That's what I grew up on. Mexican kids my age, that's what we grew up on. I grew up before the hip hop era. Before there was hip hop, it was metal and punk rock, you know? The hip hop era came in in, like, the late '80s. I mean, I know it was around since the '70s, but no one knew about it—at least, not us. I didn't discover hip hop till, like, '85, '86. (ES State Street 13, forties)

The hip hop subculture, with its break dancing, graffiti art, and rap music, exploded in the ghettos and barrios of Los Angeles in the mid-1980s, nearly eclipsing all other musical genres as the archetypal anthem of gang members on both sides of the color line:

A: Hip hop came around about the same time crack hit South Central, you know, and that changed everything, you know? All these, you know, it was good music back then though, you know? It was different. It was something that you could move to, you know?

Q: And that became the party music?

A: Yeah. Yeah, you know, hip hop, and it took a while to get out here, like, really strong. We had a, we— I remember going to a lot of house parties, I was young—fifteen, sixteen—and it was mostly, like, that '80s freestyle, you know? Debbie Deb, Lisa Lisa, you know? Shit like that. (SC Clanton 14 Street, forties)

As the hip hop culture enveloped the city, the African American gang community in Los Angeles innovated on it and the subgenre of gangster rap emerged, which became virtually ubiquitous in the late 1980s and early 1990s. Gangster rap not only became the primary musical genre for Crip- and Blood-affiliated gang members; it was preferred by many *Sureño*-affiliated gang members, as well. Violent narratives in music were something to which all gang members could relate:

> I think music is— If you can relate to it— And both gangs like violent music, you know what I'm saying? So I don't think that's— We don't listen to no mariachi band or nothing like that, you know? But they listen to our music. (WS Rolling 30s Harlem Crips, twenties)

As with other sources of cultural diffusion, many of the older generation react negatively to the popularity of rap music among younger cohorts of *Sureño*-affiliated gang members. They were raised before the inception of rap music and in many cases were incarcerated during the time period in the 1980s when rap music became popular in Los Angeles. From the perspective of these *veteranos*, listening to rap was just another case of youngsters blurring the lines between racialized gang identities by betraying an affinity for black culture. Their rejection of rap music was as vehement then as it is now:

> A: I cannot stand rap. I'm just doo-wop, rhythm and blues, oldies, that's it. You know what I mean? A rap CD, I'll throw it like a Frisbee. Youngsters got it all fucked up.
> Q: Wannabe rappers and all this shit. [*Laughs*]
> A: Yeah, what the fuck is that? I don't understand it. Be your own self, be your own people! How are you gonna give a black money and support their industry and their record and their CD? How you gonna do that? How come you don't buy Spanish music and support your own people? You understand me? Does that make sense to you? (ES Clover Street 13, fifties)

Other *veteranos* were simply befuddled by the younger cohort's affinity for gangster rap's ballads of drug dealing, degrading women, and gratuitous violence:

> Now the youngsters, they listen to hip hop. They listen to rap. As long as they're cussing and talking crazy, they listen to it, all ethnicities. (ES Varrio Nueva Estrada 13, fifties)

As with preferences for oldies, there are differences in preference between *Sureño*-affiliated and Crip- and Blood-affiliated gang members for various artists, groups, and subgenres within the wider hip hop genre as a whole. Cholos have innovated on gangster rap to produce their own sub-genre commonly called Chicano rap or cholo rap. Some *Sureño*-affiliated gang members make a sharp distinction that the rap they listen to is cholo rap and not rap music made by African American artists:

Q: What are the differences? What kind of music do you guys listen to versus what they [African Americans] listen to?

A: Because, well, the blacks' music, they only write about— It's the same thing, you know? Money, I got this, I got that, and in reality they don't got shit, you know? And, well, the music I listen to is, like, about the mission they fools be doing and how they be getting the money, like, you know, like delivering drugs and trucks and everything across the border and everything, you know? It's things I could prolly relate to, you know, in a way.

Q: Is that mostly like Chicano rap?

A: Yeah, it's like, maybe like, have you ever heard of Brownside? Yeah, like Brownside or some fool named Conejo from Harpys, you know?[26] And like that sorta music, too, you know? Things I could relate to.

Q: So it's rap but a different kind of rap than what black fools listen to?

A: Yeah. (ES White Fence 13, teens)

Crip- and Blood-affiliated gang members are also often cognizant of this distinction. They, too, see the hip hop genre as a product of the black community, but they recognize that cholos have carved out their own subgenre within the larger hip hop genre and that each of these musical subgenres correlate with distinct racialized gang identities:

A: Yeah, it's because, like, it's a identity thing. Like Hispanics, they listen to rap music. But what they listen to, the way they talk and things like that, they pick up alotta their identities and the way that they speak and the music they listen to from us, because those are the neighborhoods that they grew up in. So the things they were exposed to early in they childhood is, like, rap music, old-school R&B, like, alotta the black culture. It's just they have a way of taking some of that and then kinda making it of their own, putting a lil' spin on it.

Q: Like Kid Frost, right? [*Laughs*]

A: Kid Frost and stuff like that, 'cause you have Mellow Man Ace, he's rapping but he put in, like, a Mexican. They got their own

---

26. Harpys is a *Sureño*-affiliated gang in the West Adams district of Los Angeles.

language and their own thing that their people understand. (ES 43 Gangster Crips, thirties)

Despite these differences, there is certainly a large body of mainstream "radio rap" that appeals universally to *Sureño*-affiliated and Crip- and Blood-affiliated gang members. Anyone who's spent time hanging out in the ghettos and barrios of Los Angeles over the years will have heard *Sureño*-affiliated and Crip- and Blood-affiliated gang members alike bumping popular hip hop radio stations such as Power 106, 92.3 The Beat, and KDAY 93.5.[27] The depth of this cultural diffusion was apparent in the wake of the highly publicized murder of the Los Angeles rapper Nipsey Hu$$le by a member of his own gang, the Rolling 60s Neighborhood Crips, in 2019. Nipsey's untimely death resulted in intense public mourning that was not limited by racialized gang boundaries.

Car Culture

While Chicana scholar Denise Sandoval (2014) suggests that lowrider culture can serve as a bridge between African American and Chicano communities, preference in motor vehicles can also be a point of cultural division between *Sureño*-affiliated and Crip- and Blood-affiliated gang members.[28] The vehicle one drives and the way one chooses to customize and embellish a vehicle is a distinct expression of racialized gang identity for *Sureño*-affiliated and Crip- and Blood-affiliated gang members. The archetypal style preferred by *Sureño*-affiliated gang members is the "bomb," a distinctive body style, with smooth curves and a slanted back end, commonly produced by American automobile manufacturers in the 1940s and 1950s. Car club culture dates to at least the World War II era in the barrios of Los Angeles as generations of Chicanos grew up with full-size American sedans as the vehicle of choice. Scholars of lowrider culture have generally acknowledged that it originated in barrio communities, and while many African American gang members grew up with peers and elders who drove lowriders in the 1960s and '70s, they, too, generally acknowledge that Chicanos were the originators of lowrider culture in Los Angeles:[29]

---

27. *Bumping* is slang for playing music (loudly).

28. A lowrider is "a car that is customized primarily to be low to the ground, usually containing a hydraulic set-up, with a fantastic candy paint job, chrome features, and customized upholstery": Sandoval 2014, 196.

29. Bright 1995; Mendoza 2000; Penland 2003; Plascencia 1983; Sandoval 2003, 2014; Stone 1990.

I think . . . the Mexican tradition was even older: the '56 Chevy, even the '55 or '46. There were some cars that they would be driving that you wouldn't see black people driving. The slant backs, the bombs, that was more cholo than it was a black thing. (WS Rolling 20s Neighborhood Bloods, fifties)

In the African American community, the preference was for American coupes, particularly the Cadillac. Owning a Cadillac was once the ultimate status symbol in the African American community in South Los Angeles, an ostentatious display that one had made it, against the odds. In the 1960s, new models of American sedans with distinctive body styles became popular. The Chevy Impala was the most popular vehicle from that era in the Chicano lowrider community and remains so today. Impala models from the early to mid-1960s with pinstripes, lowered on thirteen-inch wheels, with wide whitewalls on the tires, became the ultimate status symbol in the barrios of Los Angeles. In the 1970s and 1980s, African Americans also gravitated toward the lowrider aesthetic. As a result, lowriders, particularly Impalas, were a conspicuous accessory of the gangster aesthetic in the 1980s and 1990s on both sides of the color line. However, virtually any American sedan from the 1950s to the 1980s can be made into a suitable lowrider for the aesthetically minded gang member:

A: Back then you would catch more *eses* in older cars, '50s somethings—'58s, '57s, bombs, per se. You'd catch blacks more in Chevys and Cadillacs, you know, of preference, but more Chevys: the '60s—'61s, '62s, '63s, '64s.

Q: Do you think lowrider culture came more from the black community? Like the Impalas and all that kinda thing?

A: Nah, I think it was something that derived from probably blacks in Compton dealing with the *eses* in Compton, because back out there they were more closely knitted together, you know? They went to school together. They did everything together, mostly. The blacks and Hispanics in Compton, they were best of friends, 'cause my wife even lived in Compton. So, but, yeah, I think the lowrider epidemic derived from the Hispanic culture, you know. (WS Rolling 30s Harlem Crips, forties)

In the 1990s, Crip and Blood gang members began gravitating toward a new cultural trend innovated in black communities around the nation and popularized by the rap industry: putting oversize wheels on cars. This is often accomplished by matching oversize wheels with undersize thin tires and, in some cases, jacking up the height of the vehicle or otherwise modify-

Figure 3.4. Low and slow: *Sureño*-style Impala lowrider. (Courtesy of Estevan Oriol.)

ing it to accommodate even bigger wheels. In the African American community, oversize wheels are typically paired with candy-color paint jobs to achieve the most flamboyant aesthetic possible:

> Major difference. The blacks they, for some reason they love bright colors on their cars. They like humongous rims, the size of the rims on their cars, on a small car, and, yeah. . . . You know what? Might take that back 'cause some homies, Hispanics, in South Central, they like that style, too. It's kinda like a South Central thing, too, huge rims on their cars and their trucks. (ES Longos 13, twenties)

As with other aspects of the rap culture borrowed from the black community, some *Sureño*-affiliated gang members, particularly those from mixed areas, have adopted the preference for big wheels on vehicles from their African American counterparts. This cultural diffusion has been met with the same resistance from *veteranos* as one sees in clothing and music, as older cohorts vigorously enforce the boundaries between *Sureño* and Crip and Blood racialized gang identities:

> Over the years, you know, they started to change it up, and they started to get the cars with the big rims. You know, I think that's a black thing. But now you see a lot of Mexicans or Latinos, or whatever you want to call them, like a lot of *raza* driving these fuckin'

Figure 3.5. Crippin' in Compton: Baby-blue Camaro on twenty-four-inch wheels. (Photograph by the author.)

cars with these huge-ass rims, you know.[30] And I don't give a fuck, but that's a n—er thing. Real lowriders got the small wheels, like thirteen-inch spokes. Know what I mean? (ES State Street 13, forties)

Thus, in the case of car culture, cultural diffusion is a two-way street, with African American and Chicano gang members borrowing vehicle styles from one another over generations, but each putting their own spin on it (pun intended). However, despite a high degree of cultural diffusion in taste for motor vehicles, there remains a pervasive chasm between what is considered a "black" vehicle and a "Mexican" vehicle among gang members in Los Angeles.

Side by Side and a World Apart

I don't know. I can just say that they and we are totally different. Just totally different.
—Inglewood Neighborhood Piru, teens

Racialized gang identities are best understood as regimes of cultural practice and performance, style and behavior, the boundaries of which are often

---

30. *Raza* is a Spanish word that literally means race and is often employed in vernacular to racialize Latinos as a homogeneous racial category.

vigorously policed to preserve the salience of opposing racialized gang identities. As this chapter demonstrates, cultural indicators are often perceived on both sides of the color line as being the cultural property of one racialized identity category or the other. Some facets of cultural identity are universally acknowledged as distinct, such as clothing, hairstyles, and language, all of which were perceived as fundamentally distinct by almost all respondents across all races, regions, and gang affiliations. In contrast, other facets of cultural identity are perceived by most, but not all, respondents as fundamentally different. For example, sixty-one of ninety-seven respondents felt that preference in music was different, and sixty-eight of ninety-seven respondents felt that preference in vehicles was different.

There are also significant differences in where the boundaries of cultural identity fall among different regions of Los Angeles. Generally, for gang members in East Los Angeles, there is less acceptable cultural overlap, whereas in South Los Angeles and the West Side, there is a wider range of acceptable cultural overlap between *Sureño*-affiliated and Crip- and Blood-affiliated gang members. It seems intuitive that where African American and Latino populations overlap demographically, there will be more cultural diffusion between them. That is not to say that there is no boundary or that the boundary is not enforced by gang members in areas that are demographically heterogeneous, but the boundaries proscribing cultural diffusion are more porous in demographically mixed South Los Angeles than in homogeneous East Los Angeles, where there are very few African American residents. Such regional differences are indicative of the cultural diffusion that exposes the fluidity and permeability of racialized identities. Cultural diffusion requires social proximity, and where such proximity is lacking, the identity regime is more rigidly defined and vigorously policed.

4

IDENTITY POLICE

Racial Bias and Racial Boundaries

I n this chapter I examine the extent of explicit racial bias among and between *Sureño*-affiliated and Crip- and Blood-affiliated gang members, as
well as the various forms these biases take on alternate sides of the color
line.[1] The biases I document reflect not merely the naked bigotry of individual gang members but, moreover, the ethnonationalist worldview that
they have inherited, conceptually dividing their communities into opposing
identity camps. The candid expressions of racial bias presented in this chapter demonstrate the divisive progeny of the ethnonationalist worldview that
underlies these biases. Antonia Darder and Rodolfo Torres offer an apt description of this dynamic:

> Founded on this image is what we term the "zero-sum picture" of
> "race relations." Racialized groups in Los Angeles are considered to
> be deeply at odds with one another, their members "naturally sepa-
> rate" and antagonistic toward one another. Benefits to the one are
> perceived as costs to the other.[2]

In expressing racial bias across a range of indicators, gang members are not
merely reflecting the biases of their communities but are actively policing

---

1. I use the term *bias* rather than *racism* because the race concept was invented as a system
of white supremacy. Therefore, I feel that the racialized antagonisms between nonwhite populations are better described as bias rather than racism.

2. Darder and Torres 2004, 56–57.

and reinforcing identity boundaries and the salience of the racial categories in which they imagine themselves. Thus, they act as the agents of their own oppression, focusing on perceived competition with one another rather than their shared material deprivation relative to the ruling classes, thereby sacrificing class-consciousness and solidarity in favor of ethnonationalist identity and division.

While research on racial bias has traditionally been focused around a black/white binary, there has been a burgeoning literature on inter-minority racial bias in recent years, including black/Korean bias and black/Latino bias.[3] This literature has found interracial bias pervasive on both sides of the color line in regions as varied as Texas, North Carolina, and California, as well as in national-level data.[4] This chapter replicates some of the more common racial bias tests in the existing literature, such as willingness to engage in interracial relationships and perceptions of employment competition, with the addition of indicators of racial bias that have not been as thoroughly examined by prior research, such as perceptions of competition for housing and collaboration in the black-market economy. These measures are used to gauge the extent of interracial bias between *Sureño*-affiliated and Crip- and Blood-affiliated gang members in Los Angeles whom I interviewed, whose perceptions largely reinforce the findings of previous research in other regions across the United States.

The first measure of bias concerns the willingness of respondents to engage in amorous relationships across racial lines, a topic that has featured prominently in previous research.[5] The extent of perceived opposition to interracial relationships from family, peers, and the community at large on gang members' willingness to engage in interracial relationships is a useful measure of social distance between *Sureño*-affiliated and Crip- and Blood-affiliated gang members in Los Angeles.

The second measure of bias used is perceptions of employment competition. Perceptions of employment competition are at the core of much of the

---

3. On black/Korean bias, see Chang 1999; Chang and Diaz-Veizades 1999; Choi 1999; Lee 1999; Park 1999. On black/Latino bias, see Barreto et al. 2014; Bean et al. 2011; Cuevas 2014; Frasure-Yokley and Greene 2014; Freer and Lopez 2011; Hutchison 2007; G. Johnson 2014; Jones-Correa 2011; Leiva 2014; Marrow 2009; Martinez 2016; Martinez and Rios 2011; McClain et al. 2006; McClain et al. 2011; McDermott 2011; Mindiola et al. 2002; Morin et al. 2011; Pastor 2014; Quinones 2014; Rodriguez and Mindiola 2011; Sánchez-Jankowski 2016; Sandoval 2014; Sawyer 2011; Vaca 2004; Vigil 2011; Zamora 2011.

4. Jones-Correa 2011; Marrow 2009; McClain et al. 2006; McDermott 2011; Mindiola et al. 2002; Morin et al. 2011; Rodriguez and Mindiola 2011; Telles and Ortiz 2008.

5. Grebler et al. 1970; Telles and Ortiz 2008.

existing research on black/Latino relations.[6] While scholars have provided evidence that suggests these perceptions are empirically unsupported, perceptions of such competition are prevalent and are therefore relevant in gauging the level of bias between *Sureño*-affiliated and Crip- and Blood-affiliated gang members in Los Angeles.[7]

The third measure of bias this chapter introduces—the extent of perceptions of housing competition and willingness to cohabitate in an interracial household or community—has been examined by few prior publications.[8] This is also a significant indicator of social distance between *Sureño*-affiliated and Crip- and Blood-affiliated gang members, as the willingness to cohabitate demonstrates the extent of boundaries of interracial interaction that individuals impose on themselves.

Finally, the chapter examines biases against interracial socializing and collaboration in the underground economy, an area of potential bias that has not been considered in the existing academic literature. The extent to which gang members are willing to socialize and collaborate in the underground economy are important indicators of interracial relations that can complicate the assumption of interracial bias that gang members express regarding less subterranean relationships across racial lines.

Taken together, this chapter demonstrates the extent of racial bias engendered by the cult of identity on both sides of the color line and explores how such biases reinforce the salience of racialized gang identities.

Relationship Bias

The willingness to engage in amorous relationships is a useful measure of social distance and interracial bias that has been explored by prior research. Sociologists Edward Telles and Vilma Ortiz found evidence of relationship bias among Mexican Americans in their landmark longitudinal study continued from Leo Grebler, Joan Moore, and Ralph Guzman's research on Mexican Americans in Los Angeles and San Antonio.[9] Respondents reported extremely limited contact with African Americans compared with whites and Latinos, with a supermajority of original respondents expressing an aversion to intermarriage with African Americans. Although this aversion among the modern subject population was reduced to about half of respon-

---

6. Barreto et al. 2014; Bean et al. 2011; Frasure-Yokely and Greene 2014; Hutchison 2007; Jones-Correa 2011; Marrow 2009; McClain et al. 2006; McDermott 2011; Morin et al. 2011; Pastor 2014; Rodriguez and Mindiola 2011; Sawyer 2011; Vaca 2004.
7. Bean et al. 2011; Pastor 2014.
8. Mindiola et al. 2002.
9. Grebler et al. 1970; Telles and Ortiz 2008.

dents, not one respondent from the first or the second study reported being married to an African American spouse. It is worth noting that a professed aversion to intermarriage with African Americans was especially pronounced among Mexican American respondents from Los Angeles.

I found similar evidence that relationship bias is primarily a one-way street, as antiblackness expressed by an unwillingness to engage in interracial relationships with African Americans was expressed by a majority of *Sureño*-affiliated respondents, while few Crip- and Blood-affiliated respondents expressed unwillingness to engage in amorous relationships with Latinas. Respondents were asked whether they were willing to date or just have sex across racial lines. This is an important distinction, as casual sexual relations are much easier to conceal from parents, peers, and community, whereas interracial relationships beyond sex alone expose those who would engage in such relationships to the social reprobation of parents, peers, and the wider community. Respondents were also asked whether they were opposed to family members' engaging in interracial relationships. The antiblackness of *Sureño*-affiliated respondents was most pronounced on this issue, as nearly two-thirds of *Sureño*-affiliated gang members were opposed to family members' dating African Americans, whereas only one Blood-affiliated gang member expressed opposition to family members' dating Latinas/os.

As Table 4.1 demonstrates, there was a significant difference between *Sureño*-affiliated and Crip- and Blood-affiliated gang members' willingness to engage in interracial relationships. As might be expected, there was also a significant difference between the number of *Sureño*-affiliated respondents who were willing to date African American women and those who were willing to have casual sex absent any substantive relationship. Slightly more than half of *Sureño*-affiliated respondents were unwilling to engage in interracial sex with African American partners, while almost three-quarters were unwilling to engage in interracial relationships that involved more than mere sex. This disparity suggests that, while a number of *Sureño*-affiliated respondents professed opposition to dating African Americans or were opposed to members of their family doing so, a larger number were in fact themselves not opposed to having casual sex with African American women with no substantive relationship attached, as long as such trysts could be concealed from parents, peers, and other community members. In contrast, only five of the thirty Crip- and Blood-affiliated respondents were unwilling to date Latinas, while only one of those reported opposition to family members dating Latinas/os.

Respondents were also questioned about their perceptions of the extent of bias held by their parents, peers, and community. The question of whether their perceptions reflect the true level of such bias among parents, gang peers, and family cannot be known from this research. However, respon-

TABLE 4.1. BIAS AGAINST INTERRACIAL RELATIONSHIPS				
	Sureño		Crip and Blood	
	N	%	N	%
Not willing to have sex	37/67	55	5/30	17
Not willing to date	48/67	72	5/30	17
Opposed to family dating	43/67	64	2/30	7
Note: Rounded to nearest percent.				

TABLE 4.2. PARENTAL, PEER, AND COMMUNITY OPPOSITION TO INTERRACIAL RELATIONSHIPS				
	Sureño		Crip and Blood	
	N	%	N	%
Parents oppose	45/66	68	6/29	21
Gang peers oppose	51/67	76	2/30	7
Community opposes	60/66	91	13/29	45
Note: Rounded to nearest percent.				

dents' perceptions of such bias are telling in and of themselves when considering the potential effect those perceptions have on respondents' own bias.

As Table 4.2 demonstrates, these results show a stark disparity between *Sureño*-affiliated and Crip- and Blood-affiliated gang members' perceptions of their families, friends, and communities, suggesting widespread anti-blackness in the Chicano community compared with less pronounced bias against Latinas/os in the black community. However, there are intriguing distinctions in respondents' perceptions of bias between these different groups. Slightly more than two-thirds of *Sureño*-affiliated respondents reported that their parents were biased against relationships with African Americans, while nine out of ten *Sureño*-affiliated respondents reported that their community at large was opposed to interracial relationships between African Americans and Latinas/os.

Perceptions of bias among gang peers was intermediate but demonstrated strong opposition to interracial relationships, with about three-quarters of respondents reporting that their gang peers were opposed to members of their gang engaging in interracial relationships with African Americans. This is an especially strong finding when compared with Crip- and Blood-affiliated respondents, of whom only one Crip gang member reporting that his gang peers were critical of his penchant for interracial relationships with Latinas. Roughly one-fifth of Crip- and Blood-affiliated respondents reported that their parents were opposed to their dating Latinas, while almost half reported the perception that the black community in general is opposed to interracial dating between African Americans and Latinas/os. This is rough-ly double the rate of parental bias Tatcho Mindiola, Yolanda Flores Nie-mann, and Nestor Rodriguez found in their Houston sample from the mid-1990s; however, the figures for community bias are commensurate with the rate of interracial relationship bias found in their subject cohort.[10] Support-ing my argument from Chapter 3, respondents' perspectives suggest that divergent cultural expectations rather than naked bigotry alone are at the root of these biases. Social taboos against interracial relationships are also at play, as the interview quotes that follow reveal the extent to which respon-dents are apprehensive about the response that engaging in an interracial relationship would invite from disapproving parents, peers, and their com-munity at large.

While some *Sureño*-affiliated respondents recount their carceral experi-ence as being the cause of their feelings of bias toward African Americans, they simultaneously admit that they held those biases before they were in-carcerated. This suggests that the bias was inherited from family, peer, and community networks before they went to prison:

Q: Have you ever dated a black girl or had sex with a black girl?
A: Nope. I'm highly prejudiced. Hell no.
Q: Why the opposition to that? Where do you think that comes from?
A: It comes from numerous things. I just don't like them. And then going to the joint, in the institution, that just sealed it up, you know? I felt like that before I got locked up. My whole life I felt like that. (ES Clover Street 13, fifties)

Some *Sureño*-affiliated respondents had engaged in interracial relation-ships with African Americans in the past but would not consider getting involved in a serious relationship with a black woman again. One respon-dent provided an example of this sentiment while also portraying percep-tions of cultural difference as a significant factor:

Q: Have you ever dated a black girl?
A: Yes, definitely. Actually, my first girlfriend was a black girl.
Q: Lost your virginity to a black girl?
A: [*Laughs*] Yes I did; yes I did.
Q: Would you ever consider marrying a black girl?
A: I never really thought about it. My thing has always been that I prefer Latin and white women. I don't know why. Their [blacks'] culture's a lil' more different. (WS Rockwood Street 13, forties)

---

10. Mindiola et al. 2002

In contrast to *Sureño*-affiliated respondents' reticence to date across racial lines, all but one of the Crip- and Blood-affiliated respondents interviewed had no such compunctions. In fact, a number of Crip- and Blood-affiliated respondents *preferred* dating Latinas to African American women. The little apprehension Crip- and Blood-affiliated respondents expressed about dating Latinas was that such relationships could cause problems with *Sureño*-affiliated gangs or the woman's family, who might be opposed to her dating a black man:

> I actually— I dated a Mexican girl, and she took me to meet her family, but, you know, some of them liked me, but the brothers, no! (Hawthorne 118 Gangster Crips, twenties)

These apprehensions are not entirely unfounded, as a number of *Sureño*-affiliated gangs, particularly those in homogeneously Chicano neighborhoods, have a policy of directly confronting any African American they see in their neighborhood:

> There was this lil' girl, her name was Melina. She wasn't all that. She was kinda fat and ugly, but she was still Mexican. And one time the homies called up and said, "Aye, there's a *mayate* over here!"[11] So we went over and [said], "What you doing here, homes?"
> "I'm here to pick up my old lady."
> "Who's your old lady?"
> And she came out [and said], "That's my boyfriend!" So homeboys told dude to get out of the car, and she started, like, "Aye, that's my old man! That's my old man!" So we pretty much told her this is the last time he comes here. We got his keys, threw them (in the bushes). We told him, "By the time you find your keys in ten, fifteen minutes, and we come back and you're still here, you're not gonna have a car. Don't ever come down here again, homes!" (ES White Fence 13, fifties)

As with the other indicators of interracial relationship bias, there was a stark contrast between *Sureño*-affiliated and Crip- and Blood-affiliated gang members in their reported opposition to family members, particularly female family members, engaging in interracial relationships. Not surprisingly given the sentiments expressed here, some *Sureño*-affiliated respondents were particularly emphatic in their antagonism toward family engaging in interracial relationships with African Americans:

---

11. *Mayate* is a racial epithet in Mexican Spanish slang roughly equivalent to the N-word. The etymology is explained in Chapter 6.

Q: Would you be opposed to a family member dating a black person? Like, if your sisters had ever wanted to be with a black dude?

A: Pssshh . . . yup! [*Shakes head in disdain*]

Q: Has it ever happened? Have you ever had a family member who dated a black?

A: No. *Helll nooo!*

Q: What would you say if it did happen?

A: Shit, I can't tell no one who to love, but if you wanna love 'em, stay with 'em. Fuck 'em!

Q: Would you say something, though, or would you keep it to yourself?

A: No, I would say something. Believe that.

Q: How about your lil' cousins and nephews and shit?

A: I would say something.

Q: Do they know how you feel about that?

A: They know very well how I feel about that! (ES White Fence 13, fifties)

However, as old taboos fade, some Latinas rebel against their families' anti-blackness and date black men in spite of what their siblings and parents think. This can be a source of considerable angst for those who are adamantly opposed to such interracial relationships:

Q: Would you be opposed to your family members, like if your sister wanted to date a black dude when you were growing up?

A: She is dating a fucking black guy right now!

Q: I can tell it bothers you a little bit. [*Laughs*]

A: Fuck, yeah!

Q: Have you said anything to her about that?

A: Yeah

Q: What'd you say?

A: All kinds of shit. But I— You know, at the end of the day I love my sister regardless, you know what I mean? She's all I got left. My other brother's in prison; my other brother's dead; and, you know, so I gotta give her, you know— My principles don't apply to her, you know what I mean? (NELA Frogtown 13, thirties)

While some *Sureño*-affiliated respondents were adamantly opposed to their sisters dating African Americans, others begrudgingly accept that their sisters might want to do so, but even in their acquiescence an implicit stereotype of black men as abusive partners is apparent. Some respondents professed opposition to family members' dating African Americans but were willing to engage in interracial amorous relationships themselves. One respondent found a degree of comical irony in this obvious hypocrisy, as we both had a laugh when I challenged him on the issue:

Q: Would you be opposed to your family members' dating or marrying a black person?
A: Yes. Yes, I would. Definitely yeah. Yes.
Q: Why so? It's OK for you but not for them? [Laughs]
A: [Laughs] Oh, man . . .
Q: Have any of your sisters ever dated a black guy?
A: No. No! Oh God, no! Omigod, dude—this is fuckin' deep, dude! [Laughs] This is fuckin' deep shit, dude, but I gotta be straight. Just say it [like it is]. (WS White Fence 13, forties)

A number of *Sureño*-affiliated respondents attributed their antiblackness to parental and familial influence. One respondent even mentioned how, literally from his deathbed, his father had chided his brother for engaging in an interracial relationship with a black woman when his brother came to pay his last respects:

Q: Were your parents opposed to you guys dating blacks?
A: Well, you know what? My dad, bro—he was dying when my brother was with that [black] girl. He had just had a stroke, and he told my brother—this is what my brother told me when I was in prison, bro—that he was "better off marrying a Mexican prostitute!" [Laughs] That was my dad. Yeah. That was my dad's point of view, bro. That was his philosophy. He didn't give a fuck. (SS Kansas Street 13, thirties)

Another recounted that when he was a child, his parents wouldn't even let him watch television shows featuring African American characters:

I was raised to be racist. My father was very racist because of what he learned from being in prison. My uncles were racist from what they learned in prison. And so they handed it down to me. I was not allowed to watch *The Cosby Show* when I was a little kid. That's how racist my dad was. I couldn't watch *The Cosby Show*! (ES El Sereno 13, forties)

In some cases, these community and familial biases are reinforced by negative experiences *Sureño*-affiliated gang members' parents have had with African Americans. Most provocative among these experiences is that some

Crip- and Blood-affiliated gang members prey on Latina/o immigrants by robbing them, seeing them as an easy target for a quick "lick" (robbery) because they tend to keep their money in cash and are less likely to go to police because of their immigration status. These experiences have had lasting effects on families who have personally experienced this predation at the hands of African American gang members:

> A: [My mother] used to tell my sister . . . "Don't ever bring a black dude over." She had her reasons, dude. She had her reasons.
> Q: What do you think her motivation was?
> A: Being robbed, maybe, by them back then, you know? I witnessed it too when they robbed my mom, so, yeah, we were younger, so . . .
> Q: In your neighborhood?
> A: No. In LA. Right here in downtown. We used to come out here a lot to do shopping, and her purse got snatched a couple times, so I would hate them, too, [because of that]. (ES Stoners 13, forties)

This has become a particular point of contention for *Sureño*-affiliated gang members in recent years. With the proliferation of smart phones and surveillance technology, these robberies and assaults are often caught on film and disseminated widely on social media, fueling further racial animosity. When videos of these incidents appear on Instagram and Facebook, *Sureño*-affiliated gang members invariably identify with the victims on the basis of identity and react with extreme prejudice. These incidents are incredibly incendiary, particularly when they go viral on social media, which has occurred more than a few times in recent years. In one recent incident, a pair of youngsters from the Hoover Criminals (formerly Crips) were caught on video assaulting a street vendor who was selling them *aguas frescas* (juice). In an attempt to assuage the racial animosity the incident created after the video went viral, other Hoover gang members forced each youngster to fight another member whose fighting prowess far outmatched their own. The video of them getting "checked" was likewise posted online to assure *Sureño*-affiliated gangs that the perpetrators had been appropriately disciplined for the incident.

While far from a majority, at least some Crip- and Blood-affiliated respondents reported that their parents were also biased against interracial relationships. It is not uncommon for African American parents to discourage their children, either directly or indirectly, from engaging in a serious relationship with a non-black spouse. However, some African American parents want their kids to engage in interracial relationships for the novelty of grandchildren with mixed phenotypic features.

Q: Would you be opposed to your family members dating Latinos?

A: No, 'cause my mother always says, "I want me a mixed baby, can you get me a mixed grandchild?" [Laughs]

Q: So it's a good thing?

A: Yeah, yeah it's something she's looking forward to, she said, "I'm tired of all you nappy-headed kids running around here." (Pasadena Denver Lane Bloods, twenties)

More *Sureño*-affiliated and Crip- and Blood-affiliated gang members reported community bias against interracial relationships than parental or peer bias against such relationships. While community bias against interracial relationships between African Americans and Latinas/os is particularly pronounced in the Chicano community, it is also present in the African American community as well, to a lesser extent. A *Sureño*-affiliated respondent from the Rampart area recounts how harsh the social reprobation against such relationships often are.

Q: Were there other people in the neighborhood, just like regular *raza* that were like that (biased against African Americans)?

A: There were some, well there's racism, there's racism in the hood, like I would hear people all the time like, "Fuckin' stupid n—ers!" Talking shit you know, but, yeah, that's always been noticeable . . . like, "Damn! What is she doing with that n—er?" (WS La Mirada Locos 13, thirties)

Some *Sureño*-affiliated respondents who had dated African American women in the past reported having problems with African American men who were jealous that they were with an African American woman:

I used to walk down the beach with my wife, and she was mixed, but she looked like she wasn't. Her hair was straight, and her name was Maria, so she had some Hispanic. . . . She was pretty and thick, and a lot of black guys used to look at me and look at her like, "What is she doing with that Mexican?" (WS Venice 13, forties)

Roughly half of Crip- and Blood-affiliated respondents reported perceived community bias against engaging in interracial relationships with Latinas, suggesting that interracial bias against Latinos is also somewhat prevalent in the African American community. However, black bias against Latinos is often a bit more subtle in its expression. Rather than making garish remarks or confronting people involved in interracial relationships with outright insults and racial epithets, members of the African American community who oppose interracial relationships more often express their disapproval by giving judgmental looks and making snide but subtle comments either directly to the subject of their disapproval or to others in the vicinity. This is a dynamic I have witnessed on numerous occasions and on which a respondent remarked:

> Q: Do the [black] residents in the community feel that blacks should only be with blacks and give you a hard time [for dating Latinas]?
>
> A: It's like, yeah, you feel me? They don't give me a hard time with it when they see it. They just be like— You can tell, like, yeah. That look, yeah. (PJ Watts Crips, twenties)

While only one Crip- or Blood-affiliated respondent reported that his peers were outright opposed to African Americans dating Latinas/os, most reported that their homeboys either don't care or are interested in dating Latinas themselves. There is also an apparent gender dichotomy in the occurrence of this bias, as many of the Crip- and Blood-affiliated respondents reported that few if any of their male peers had anything against interracial dating, whereas their female peers were often jealous of such relationships:

> Q: How about . . . your homeboys from your neighborhood? Are any of them like that, you know? Or [do] they only date black girls and that type of thing?
>
> A: Yeah, I know a few guys like that. That just, well now, in this day and age they see that, you know, Hispanic women are dating black men and more white women are dating black men, so some of the guys that I hang out with now when we go out, they're like, "Aww, man, she's cute." You know, because they probably seen me with a Hispanic women before, so it's like, "Aww, man, I gotta get me a Hispanic woman then." I know I've seen it before when I've dated a Hispanic woman or a white woman and I take them around my old neighborhood and some of my old homegirls or just females that I had flings with or whatever be looking up at 'em, like turning their nose up. Like going, "What the hell is he doing with her?" It's mostly from the girls, not the guys—you know what I mean? The girls be like, "Oh, he left me for her." and this and that, you know, so it's like, it's kinda different.
>
> Q: Shit! You gonna fuckin' get a Mexican girl beat up. [*Laughs*]
>
> A: Yeah, or I'll be sitting there trying to fight the [black] girl to stop it! [*Laughs*] (Compton Mob Piru, thirties)

Whereas perceived peer bias against interracial dating was rare among Crip- and Blood-affiliated respondents, it was reported by an overwhelming majority of *Sureño*-affiliated respondents. In some cases, this boundary policing can be extreme, exposing the offender to harsh social repudiation and even a punitive beating or, in some cases, outright excommunication from the gang:

Q: How about your homeboys from your neighborhood? How do they feel about dating black girls?

A: Naw. My homies won't do that. They'll just be like, "I'll hit it if I'm drunk." They always bring that up, but naw. . . .

Q: They won't bring a black girl around and be like, "Aye, this is my old lady over here. Say, what's up"?

A: [*Laughs*] Helll nooo! We'll jump them out, you know.[12] (SS Florencia 13, twenties)

In some cases, the status of the offender could deflect the negative ramifications of violating that taboo. Older, more respected gang members in some cases are beyond reproach, whereas younger, lower-status gang members face vigorous opposition if they engage in interracial relationships:

Q: Are your homeboys also from your neighborhood, you think, generally opposed to— Like if a homeboy wanted to date a black girl, homies would have a problem with that? Like, people would say something to him?

A: If a homeboy, like a ordinary homeboy— It's not allowed pretty much. If you're a homeboy with status and you've earned the right to pretty much do what you want, then that's how it is, you know what I mean?

Q: What about if a youngster tried to do that? How would they get regulated?

A: Nowadays, homes, the color lines are being broken every day, homes. It's not too big of a deal nowadays. I know that if one of the lil' homeboys decides to, he won't be able to bring her around the neighborhood. That's a fact. He could go and do whatever where she is. He cannot bring her around our neighborhood, no. (ES White Fence 13, fifties)

However, in other neighborhoods, peer bias against interracial relationships amounts to little more than playful banter and racist jokes about

---

12. *Jump out* means to kick a member out of the gang, literally.

"playing in the mud" and "jungle fever," with minimal loss of status for the offender:

> Q: Did anyone from your neighborhood ever give you a hard time about being with a black girl?
>
> A: Naw— Well, you get jokes and shit, this and that, but nothing that, like, no one straight turned on me or cut me off or anything like that. (NELA Toonerville 13, forties)

Employment and Housing Competition

Much of the existing research on black-Latino relations focuses on perceptions of employment competition between African Americans and Latinos.[13] Starting with Chicago School sociologist Herbert Blumer, sociologists have long theorized employment competition as a proximate cause of what sociologist Edna Bonacich has termed "ethnic antagonism."[14] Blumer's classic *group threat* framework suggested that established labor populations possess "a feeling of proprietary claim" to privileged labor-market access that compels them to perceive incipient labor populations as a threat to their hegemony.[15] British sociologist Michael Banton suggested that as competition among racial groups intensifies, so does the salience of their racial/ethnic identities, a hypothesis that found support in subsequent research.[16]

Sociologist Laurence Bobo of Harvard University suggested that perceptions of competition can be founded on actual material threat that incipient labor populations pose to the "real resources and accepted practices" of established ones.[17] However, sociologist Manuel Pastor of the University of Southern California argues that such concerns are largely unfounded in the Los Angeles context.[18] While Pastor points to evidence that Latinos earn less in wages than African Americans, as Bonacich has suggested, this may actually be a source of resentment among African Americans who feel that Latino immigrants undercut wages, a sentiment that was expressed by Crip- and Blood-affiliated respondents.[19]

---

13. Barreto et al. 2014; Bean et al. 2011; Frasure-Yokely and Greene 2014; Hutchison 2007; Jones-Correa 2011; Marrow 2009; McClain et al. 2006; McDermott 2011; Morin et al. 2011; Pastor 2014; Rodriguez and Mindiola 2011; Sawyer 2011; Vaca 2004.
14. Blumer 1958; Bonacich 1972.
15. Blumer 1958, 4.
16. Banton 1983; Quillian 1995, 1996.
17. Bobo 1983, 1197.
18. Pastor 2014.
19. Bonacich 1972.

TABLE 4.3. PERCEPTIONS OF COMPETITION FOR EMPLOYMENT AND HOUSING				
	Sureño		Crip and Blood	
	N	%	N	%
Employment competition exists	45/60	75	21/29	72
Housing competition exists	44/60	73	21/29	72
Note: Rounded to nearest percent.				

Examining the role of desegregation on racial animosity, sociologist Susan Olzak suggested that the influx of ethnic interlopers into previously segregated communities predicated hostility between dominant white and subordinate black labor populations, culminating in some cases in race riots and interracial violence.[20] Subsequent research on the Los Angeles Riots of 1992 and interracial violence in New York found support for the *defended neighborhood* perspective, as a team of Yale sociologists christened it.[21] While defended neighborhood perspectives have largely focused on conflict and violence between white and black populations in the United States, recent work by sociologist Martín Sánchez-Jankowski of the University of California, Berkeley, found a similar dynamic at play between established African American populations and immigrant Latino populations in Los Angeles and Oakland.[22]

Racial resentment rooted in perceptions of labor-market competition has been shown to be present in both African American and Latino communities in different parts of the country. Therefore, it is an obvious measure to use in evaluating the levels of bias between *Sureño*-affiliated and Crip- and Blood-affiliated gang members in Los Angeles.[23] To that I add perceptions of housing competition, a measure that has seen little attention from scholars of interracial relations.[24] Unlike bias against interracial relationships, which was mostly a one-way street, perceptions of employment and housing competition were rampant among *Sureño*-affiliated and Crip- and Blood-affiliated respondents alike at comparable levels (Table 4.3). In contrast to that against interracial relationships, the rate of bias expressed by *Sureño*-affiliated and Crip- and Blood-affiliated respondents on these

20. Olzak 1992; Olzak and Shanahan 1996; Olzak et al. 1996.
21. Bergesen and Herman 1998; Green et al. 1998; Pinderhughes 1997.
22. Sánchez-Jankowski 2016.
23. Frasure-Yokely and Greene 2014; Jones-Correa 2011; McDermott 2011; Morin et al. 2011; Rodriguez and Mindiola 2011.
24. Mindiola et al. 2002.

TABLE 4.4. BIAS RELATED TO EMPLOYMENT AND HOUSING				
	Sureño		Crip and Blood	
	N	%	N	%
Oppose working with	16/66	24	0/30	0
Interracial workplace conflict	19/63	30	8/29	23
Latinos harder workers	51/65	78	12/29	41
Oppose living with	49/66	74	7/29	24
Note: Rounded to nearest percent.				

measures almost perfectly mirrored one another, with roughly three-quarters of both groups reporting concerns regarding competition between African Americans and Latinos for employment and housing. "You will not replace us!" could easily describe the racial anxieties between black and brown communities over perceived threats of competition from one another, just as it is used by tiki torch–wielding white nationalist sycophants to voice their racial anxieties.

All but four *Sureño*-affiliated respondents and one Crip-affiliated respondent had been employed in an interracial workplace environment. However, while occupational bias is far less pronounced than relationship bias, as discussed in this section, it would be fair to say the data on occupational bias are also quite polarized (Table 4.4), with almost one-third of *Sureño*-affiliated respondents reporting that they were opposed to working with African Americans while not a single Crip- or Blood-affiliated respondent reported being opposed to working with Latinos. Similar proportions of *Sureño*-affiliated (30 percent) and Crip- and Blood-affiliated (27 percent) respondents reported having had a conflict with a coworker from the opposing identity group. It's worth noting that for the *Sureño*-affiliated respondents who opposed working with African Americans, no relationship was found between opposition to working with African Americans and having had a conflict with an African American coworker, suggesting, again, that these are social biases that are not provoked by specific negative experiences. Negative experiences reinforce rather than trigger racial biases, which are a reflection of the racial worldview gang members have absorbed from ethnopolitical entrepreneurs.

Among the most common stereotypes examined in previous research is the extent of the perception that black workers are lazy and that Latinos are harder workers.[25] This perception was prevalent among the *Sureño*-affiliated respondents, but surprisingly, it also was not uncommon among Crip- and Blood-affiliated respondents, as well. More than three-quarters of the *Sureño*-affiliated respondents reported the perception that Latinos are harder workers than African Americans, along with more than 40 percent of Crip- and Blood-affiliated respondents. The remainder of respondents reported the perception that laziness is an individual rather than a group trait or that both groups are lazy workers. No respondent reported the perception that African Americans are harder workers than Latinos.

The results for measures of housing bias are an even more striking reflection of the extent of antiblackness among *Sureño*-affiliated gang members, as Table 4.4 shows, with almost three out of four *Sureño*-affiliated respondents reporting opposition to living with an African American roommate or living in a predominantly African American community and fewer than one out of four Crip- and Blood-affiliated respondents reporting opposition to living with a Latino roommate or in a predominantly Latino community. However, as the qualitative data show, *Sureño*-affiliated and Crip- and Blood-affiliated gang members held these reservations for very different reasons.

Sureño-affiliated respondents who perceived employment competition with African Americans often felt that African Americans had an unfair advantage in that they lacked honor and thus were shameless in their willingness to gain favor with employers, as a *Sureño*-affiliated respondent complained:

Q: Have you ever felt you had to compete with blacks for work that causes resentment?

A: Yeah, because a lot of times they're good at sucking up real good, homes, and I think us, we have a little more pride, so we have to sometimes prove ourselves more, but more, like, through our work ethic. They don't have a problem with—you know what I mean?—licking the boss's boots. (SS Kansas Street 13, thirties)

A number of *Sureño*-affiliated respondents reported negative personal experiences with African American coworkers, which served only to reinforce the stereotypes they have of African Americans. These experiences are also often coupled with resentment over coworkers' referencing the history of slavery and repression African Americans have suffered in the United States, which many *Sureño*-affiliated respondents see as firmly in the past and not connected in any way to the plight of contemporary African American populations:

---

25. Marrow 2009; McClain et al. 2006.

Q: Do you think blacks are hard workers?

A: Whoa, man. . . . You know what? Honestly, from what I know and over the years working, from what I've seen, I say this not to disrespect the race, but a lot of them are lazy. They don't like to work. They're fucking lazy. And, you know, what with the Mexican culture, we're hard workers, you know. We're here, and we struggle. We know what it's like not to have money, so, you know, all the Mexicans I know like to work, and we save our money. But a lot of these black fools I've worked with, they like to just kick back. They like to take it easy, or they always bring the race card in and bring up fuckin' slavery. But you know what? Slavery's been gone for, like, five hundred years, so get over it. They always complain about being slaves and shit. You know what? They like to complain a lot. It's like, do your fucking job and work. We're here to work, so work. From my experience, they're lazy. I would always take a Mexican or Latino over a black any day to do a job because they actually bust their ass. (ES State Street 13, forties)

Even for those *Sureño*-affiliated respondents who do acknowledge the effects of structural racism and intergenerational disaccumulation in American society, African Americans are seen as excessively characterized by a sort of pathology of the perpetual victim.[26]

For those who begrudgingly accept working with African Americans, their acceptance is contingent on maintaining rigid cultural, social, and physical boundaries between themselves and African American coworkers. Willingness to work with African Americans does not necessarily denote an absence of antiblackness:

Q: Are you opposed to working somewhere where you have to work with blacks?

A: I prefer not to, but if I have to, I will, you know what I mean? Just you stay on your side of the tracks, and I stay on mine. I ain't gonna eat lunch with you. Don't ask me for shit. I got nothing to say to you. (ES Clover Street 13, fifties)

While not a single Crip- or Blood-affiliated respondent reported opposition to working with Latinos, most reported perceptions of employment competition with Latinos, at exactly the same rate as *Sureño*-affiliated re-

26. Brown et al. 2003.

spondents. However, these biases were rooted in very different perceptions and experiences from those of *Sureño*-affiliated respondents. Crip- and Blood-affiliated respondents overwhelmingly felt that Latinos had a distinct advantage in the workplace because of the stereotype that Latinos are harder workers than African Americans:

> Mexicans do have the reputation of working hard, so like if somebody want to hire somebody, they'll probably hire the Mexican before the black guy. (WS Rolling 60s Neighborhood Crips, teens)

Another common perception is that Latinos undercut African American employment opportunities because Latinos are willing to work for less pay than African Americans, not just taking jobs, therefore, but also suppressing wages for everyone:

> They have a big advantage because a lot of these companies know that Mexicans will work for whatever just to put food on the table. It's just like us, if we go apply, it's, "Oh, y'all making $5 a hour," we gone be like, "Oh, hell naw! We could make that on the block." Like so, yeah, I think Mexicans got a better chance of getting what we ain't got. (WS Rolling 30s Harlem Crips, twenties)

There is also a perception that Latinos will work beyond what should reasonably be expected by employers, such as working unpaid overtime. Crip- and Blood-affiliated respondents think it is not only unfair to curry favoritism, but it also undermines labor relations by leaving employers with unreasonable expectations that employees will do extra work off the clock:

> A: What tends to happen is a lot of the Mexican workers are— What I don't like about working with them is that they overcompensate, and 'course an employer would like to get as much as they can out of an employee, so if work starts at seven, what bothers me is that they're there at five-thirty and they're working.
> Q: To make everybody else look bad?
> A: Right, or make themselves look good. Either way. And it's not fair because even though I'm not penalized directly for that, starting at seven— But, of course, if you're the boss, and you getting production out of these guys, keep 'em even later, get off at three-thirty, they're still there at four, four-thirty. Circumstances may need for that. If there's— [If] you gotta clean up something, something went wrong, but just because, you know, quit time is quit

time, pick it up tomorrow, you know, not just because you want brownie points. (WS Rolling 20s Neighborhood Bloods, forties)

The perception that employers favor hiring Latinos even if they're less qualified because they acquiesce to exploitation was pervasive among Crip- and Blood-affiliated respondents. One point of particular contention is the perception that Latinos make up the vast majority of the workforce in fast-food franchises, where African American residents commonly dine but are rarely employed. This is an almost daily reminder to African Americans that their business is welcome, but their labor is not:

> Go to any fast-food restaurant in these South Central communities and look at the employees. You'll find 85 to 90 percent Latino. Go to a drive through restaurant. The person doesn't speak very good English or gets the order wrong or doesn't understand what you're saying, and it's like, "Man, but we can't have nobody black working up in there, right?" So it does create problems, and I hear it a lot. (WS Rolling 20s Neighborhood Bloods, fifties)

While prior research suggests that one bias Mexican immigrants hold is that African Americans are lazy workers, numerous Crip- and Blood-affiliated respondents shared this perception, along with the concern that many African Americans maintain a disposition that is not conducive to a workplace environment.[27] A number of respondents felt that, to stay competitive with Latinos in the labor market, they have to make a conscious effort to maintain a positive mental attitude:

> Q: Do you think, in general, that Mexicans are harder workers than blacks? Or do you think that's a misconception?
> A: I think it's 'cause they're more willing to work than a lot of blacks, you know? Some people just want a easy ride, you know? If it's not gonna be too easy— That's why I swallowed my pride. So you know what? Shit, if they can do it, I can do it! Let's put a dollar in my pocket. But the predicament I'm in right now, I have no choice. How can I say I want $12 an hour and I'm on parole and probation? So it's like— I mean, some people just don't . . .
> Q: You're more realistic about it.
> A: Yeah.
> Q: Where you think some people still have that pride that holds them back?

---

27. Marrow 2009.

A: That pride is kicking a nigga's ass![28] (Pasadena Denver Lane Bloods, twenties)

One particularly candid respondent even stated outright that he was a lazy worker compared with his Latino coworkers and that he would rather hustle if legitimate employment opportunities are not satisfactory:

Q: In general, do you think blacks or Mexicans are better workers? Do you think there's a difference?

A: I, honestly— I'm'a be honest with you 'cause I don't lie about stuff like that, 'cause such as myself, I'm a lazy worker and I see Mexicans work hard. I see them from the U-Haul places, you know, and . . .

Q: Standing on the corner and all that?

A: Yeah, and they work for whatever, just to put something on they kids' table. Just like us, . . . We have different intentions, like, "Oh, I can't get no job. I'm finna go to the block and hustle," you know? And Mexicans, I feel they harder workers than us. (WS Rolling 30s Harlem Crips, twenties)

Whether Latinos are harder workers than African Americans is an issue this research cannot resolve, and I would be highly suspect of any methodology that purports to confirm the stereotype. However, it is clear that the perception that African Americans are lazy and Latinos are hard workers is indeed prevalent among *Sureño*-affiliated and Crip- and Blood-affiliated gang members across the board.

While perceptions of housing competition are about even with perceptions of employment competition, bias against cohabitation is much more pronounced than bias against working in an interracial environment. More than three times as many *Sureño*-affiliated respondents were opposed to cohabitation as were opposed to working with African Americans, and while no Crip- or Blood-affiliated respondents were opposed to working with Latinos, roughly a quarter were opposed to living with or among Latinos. The willingness to cohabitate across racial lines is an important measure of bias for two reasons. First, willingness to interact in public spaces is one level of tolerance, but willingness to share private space is an even more suggestive indicator. The willingness to open up the most private spaces in one's life—one's own living space—gets to the core of how comfortable re-

---

28. Where the word *nigga* is used as a term of endearment rather than a racial epithet, I do not elide it.

spondents are with interracial interaction. Second, bias against sharing private spaces is further evidence of the kind of perceptions of cultural division discussed in Chapter 3.

For many *Sureño*-affiliated respondents who grew up in homogeneously Latino neighborhoods, even the thought of living in areas with African American neighbors is abhorrent:

> Q: Would you ever live with a black roommate or live in a black neighborhood?
> A: I wouldn't live with a black roommate. No. Fuck no! I mean, what do you mean? No, no, no!
> Q: Would you ever consider living in a black neighborhood?
> A: I mean, personally I wouldn't want— I wouldn't want to. But, you know, sometimes—you know what I mean?—I . . .
> Q: Worst comes to worst?
> A: Yeah. Worst comes to worst. You might have to. But, I mean, I'll be damned, I'm'a look everywhere before I do that, you know what I'm saying? [*Laughs*] (NELA Frog Town 13, thirties)

Those who grew up in demographically mixed areas often draw a line at sharing private living space with African Americans:

> Q: Would you ever consider rooming with a black guy?
> A: Oh, hell no!
> Q: Why's that?
> A: Because they're dirty. [*Laughs*] I mean, I seen Mexicans who are dirty, too, but I been to a lot of black houses, and they're fuckin' dirty! They'll, like, take their shit off and throw it wherever. Me, I'll come home from work and take my shit off and fold it and put it in the hamper. But if it's dirty these fools, [they'll] just throw it on the floor and go about their business and leave it right there, you know? I can't have that. I'm a clean freak. That shit gets on my nerves. (SC 38 Street, twenties)

The perceptions that African Americans are too loud and have poor hygiene were pervasive among *Sureño*-affiliated respondents. To a significant degree, these perceptions are due to divergent cultural expectations, as a respondent suggested:

> Q: Are there any other, like, cultural differences that you can think of between Crips and Bloods and South Siders, or just blacks and *raza* in general?

A: Really, the way they do things was the way— Their hygiene wasn't there. The way they talk, too loud, it bothers me. They could be near each other, you know, not even a couple inches apart, and they'll be talking loud, you know what I mean? Like if they're deaf. (ES White Fence 13, fifties)

A number of *Sureño*-affiliated respondents associated their perceptions with experiences they had with African Americans while incarcerated, where they were forced to share living space to some extent:

A: I mean, I'm here to keep it real. With my experience being locked up in the system with them, the majority of them have bad hygiene, you know? They smell. They don't like to shower. I don't know what it is with them. Them dudes are just dirty. It causes a lot of tension in jail 'cause of their fuckin' hygiene, you know? Shit will kick off just because of them being fuckin' dirty, you know. It's bad. It's like, "Take a fuckin' shower!" There's something about them. They just don't like to shower for some reason.
Q: Do you think they're too loud? Does that ever offend you?
A: Yeah. Fuck yeah, dog. They're always loud. Everywhere I go and I see black people, they're always loud. Like even if I'm just walking down the street and they're talking on their phone, they're talking so loud it's like they want everyone to know their business. If I'm on the phone in the streets, I'm keeping that shit personal, you know? I don't want you to hear my conversation. I could be on the fuckin' train, the bus, the sidewalk, and they be on the phone, and they're so loud they're just like putting their business out there. I think it's just a black thing. No matter where they're at—at a club, in the street, wherever—they just like being loud. (ES State Street 13, forties)

Apprehension among Crip- and Blood-affiliated respondents about cohabitating with Latinos was also common, although for very different reasons and informed by very different experiences than for *Sureño*-affiliated respondents. There is a fair amount of apprehension in the African American community in Los Angeles about living in areas that are homogeneously Latino. This trepidation is even more acute for gang members, who have to worry not only about being black in the barrio but also about being a Crip or Blood in a community that is exclusively the territory of *Sureño*-affiliated gangs. More often than not, these misgivings are not merely paranoia but, rather, the result of negative personal experiences Crip- and Blood-affiliated respondents have had in homogeneously Latino communities or of secondhand reports of such experiences from peers or family who have had them:

Q: Would you ever move into a Latino neighborhood? Would you feel comfortable?

A: Really, like, I never even thought about that. Yeah, I will 'cause I lived in Montebello for a couple of months. So, yeah, I was staying with this Latino family. Yeah, it was cool, but they was, like, racist, though, 'cause Montebello, East LA, all that, they, like, more racist.

Q: You experienced racism over there? What kind of things happened?

A: Yeah, man. I was on the bus. Motherfuckers jumping on the bus staring at me, gang members. I got a gun put in my face before. Like, "Fool, you know where you at?" I'm like, "Yeah, I know where I'm at, man." They like, "You not supposed to be over here."

Q: Where you lived at that kind of thing would never happen?

A: Never. We would never do that to no Hispanic.

Q: Have you ever lived in any other community where you felt like Hispanics were biased against you?

A: Nope. That's it. That's the only place. Everybody know about that place over there.

Q: Do you feel like that's just Latino gang members acting that way or members of the community are biased, as well?

A: Yeah, that's what it was. It was them and, yeah, . . . and, like, parents, and, yeah, like, they're not used to seeing a black person. So when they see one, they like, "What the hell are you doing over here?" Yeah. That type of thing. (PJ Watts Crips, twenties)

Such racial intolerance was also reported by some Crip and Blood respondents in the West Century and Crenshaw areas on the west side of South Los Angeles, where the few majority–African American neighborhoods in the city remain, particularly areas controlled by the Rolling 90s Neighborhood Crips, Rolling 40s Neighborhood Crips, and Black P Stones Bloods. These communities and their gangs take pride in maintaining black demographic hegemony over these areas and are quick to confront any attempt by *Sureño*-affiliated gangs to encroach on their territory, as one respondent told me:

A: We don't let no bald heads in our hood. Not even gardeners, you know? Like, not even gardeners.

Q: You think there's competition for housing between blacks and Mexicans? Like, especially like, you know a lot of Mexicans moving into areas that used to be predominantly black, you think there, that causes conflict, resentment, and stuff?

A: Yeah. You let them move in, and you don't get ahead, you know? They're coming and they're coming, like, I don't know, think power in numbers, you know? And that's how they— I don't know.

Q: Like, you mentioned you guys and all that. You don't let them come to your neighborhood?

A: No, not even gardeners. We nip it in the bud fast. (WS Rolling 90s Neighborhood Crips, twenties)

Lamentably, this type of "ethnic cleansing" is not unheard of in regions of Los Angeles County that are homogeneously black or Latino. There is indeed a great deal of resentment in the African American community generally, and among Crip- and Blood-affiliated gang members particularly, over the demographic transition much of South Los Angeles has experienced since the 1980s, as Latino immigrants have moved in where African American families have moved out. These resentments often underlie the racialized gang conflicts described in the following chapter.

With almost three-quarters reporting perceptions of housing competition with Latinos, Crip- and Blood-affiliated gang members' perspectives reveal that resentment of Latino demographic encroachment is prevalent throughout the African American community in Los Angeles and is a primary source of racialized animosity toward Latinos. This resentment and animosity reflect the group threat and defended neighborhood frameworks discussed earlier, which suggest that such encroachment by outside groups can often be a source of racial animus and hostility.[29] The perceptions reported by Crip- and Blood-affiliated respondents in this study overwhelmingly support these perspectives. Latino immigrants' encroaching on African American neighborhoods also creates practical problems, as immigrants often live with extended families in a single residential space, increasing the population density of the whole neighborhood. This leads to other problems, such as limited street parking, language barriers, and loud parties playing unfamiliar music.

While African American residents suffer Latino demographic encroachment in historically homogeneously African American neighborhoods in South Los Angeles, their plight is perceived as even more unfair because of the widespread perception that African Americans are not welcome in many homogeneously Latino areas of East Los Angeles:

---

29. On group threat frameworks, see Blumer 1958; Quillian 1995, 1996. On defended neighborhood frameworks, see Bergesen and Herman 1998; Green et al. 1998.

Q: Do you think that there's also competition over housing that causes conflict and resentment?

A: Yes. They get resentful, and then individuals end up getting hurt, and there is loss of life over that issue. Up in the Watts area alone has probably risen to close to 80 percent Latino, but the 20 percent African American are part of the PTA at school, are part of the Watts Gang Taskforce, and they continue to run the projects. When you talk about the Jordan Downs Housing Project, ... even though the majority of residents are Mexican or El Salvadorean or whatever, the black gang [Grape Street Watts Crips] still continues to dominate that project. I think that's a issue. But also, like, Ramona Gardens, where my mother grew up, there are, like, two percent African Americans, and they are uncomfortable. In that project, they like, "Man, we can't even go nowhere because they trippin'!" They don't like us 'cause we're black, so that's it. (WS Rolling 20s Neighborhood Bloods, fifties)

The cruel irony of the sentiments expressing racialized hostility over perceived employment competition by respondents is that both *Sureño*-affiliated and Crip- and Blood-affiliated gang members represent, at best, the most marginal segment of the labor population: Marx's classic surplus labor population, absorbed into the labor market when useful to capital, and just as easily discarded when they are not.

Hanging and Hustling

Not unlike rules governing interracial relationships, there were significant differences between *Sureño*-affiliated and Crip- and Blood-affiliated gang members in the level of bias they reported against socializing and collaborating in the underground economy across racial lines. As can be seen in Tables 4.5 and 4.6, Crip and Blood respondents generally reported much more tolerance for interacting with *Sureño*-affiliated gang members than *Sureño*-affiliated respondents did for interacting with Crip- and Blood-affiliated gang members. When asked whether they felt it was acceptable in their neighborhood to interact socially or to hustle with Crips and Bloods, a majority of *Sureño*-affiliated respondents reported that it would not be acceptable to do so. In contrast, Crip- and Blood-affiliated respondents overwhelmingly reported that it would be perfectly acceptable to hang out and hustle with *Sureño*-affiliated gang members in their community, with only four out of twenty-nine respondents responding in the negative.

While working in an interracial environment was viewed as acceptable by gang members across the spectrum, *Sureño*-affiliated respondents from

TABLE 4.5. TOLERANCE FOR INTERRACIAL SOCIALIZING

	Sureño		Crip and Blood	
	N	%	N	%
OK to socialize	29/66	44	25/29	86
Not OK to socialize	37/66	56	4/29	14

Note: Rounded to nearest percent.

TABLE 4.6. TOLERANCE FOR INTERRACIAL UNDERGROUND ECONOMY COLLABORATION

	Sureño		Crip and Blood	
	N	%	N	%
OK to hustle	30/66	45	26/29	90
Not OK to hustle	36/66	55	3/29	10

Note: Rounded to nearest percent.

East Los Angeles—particularly members of older barrio gangs not centered in housing projects—expressed the most intense misgivings about interacting with African Americans outside a workplace environment. For one *veterano* from East Side White Fence 13, enforcing taboos on social and underground economy interaction between *Sureño*-affiliated gang members and African Americans is just as important out of prison as it is in prison. He had no tolerance of any such contact across racial lines. Maintaining such boundaries is particularly important for *veteranos* because they see doing so as a continuance of the racially exclusive biases with which they were raised. As legal scholar Ian Haney-Lopez suggested, antiblackness is, in their view, a fundamental component of a Chicano identity.[30] From their perspective, the observation of these biases by each successive generation has enabled the gang to successfully reproduce itself generation after generation and should be perpetually maintained to preserve the bond between the gang, its community, and a Chicano identity. Such biases are passed down from generation to generation, both within the gang and in overlapping family units of multiple intergenerational gang families, that form the historical core of the gang and root it firmly in the barrio community in which it exists:

Q: So what are the rules for interacting with blacks in the streets?
A: My neighborhood, it's not allowed, period. Other neighborhoods—especially, like, in South Central—it's allowed. The West Side, it's allowed.

---

30. Haney-Lopez 2003, 211–212.

Q: Do you think that's because your neighborhood is more traditional and sticks to the old rules?

A: Well, my neighborhood is an old neighborhood. Our neighborhood has lasted so long because of the structure we have, homes. So the rules, we don't break. The rules, we keep. And we're deeply rooted. There's already been generations upon generations of family members in the barrio. (ES White Fence 13, fifties)

Many *Sureño*-affiliated respondents expressed a lack of trust in African Americans, whom they saw as lacking the integrity required to engage reliably in black-market transactions. African Americans are perceived as impulsive, shameless, and unpredictable. As a result of these perceptions, many *Sureño*-affiliated gang members avoid engaging in distribution-level black-market transactions with African Americans, particularly Crip- or Blood-affiliated gang members:

Q: How about hustling with them? Is that acceptable?

A: Slanging dope to them? You know, I wouldn't. I wouldn't trust the motherfucker.

Q: No getting from them?

A: Fuck that. No major deals or nothing like that. I always stay away from it, you know, because they're unpredictable, you know what I mean? They're grimy. (ES Evergreen Locos 13, thirties)

This reticence among *Sureño*-affiliated gang members on the homogeneously Latino East Side might be attributable to a lack of familiarity with African Americans. However, similar sentiments were expressed by *Sureño*-affiliated respondents from the West Side, where *Sureño*-affiliated and Crip- and Blood-affiliated gangs often share overlapping territories. While there is a little more wiggle room on the West Side, especially where money is concerned, the conceptual division remains:

Q: So let's talk about under what circumstances it would be acceptable to hang out with blacks on the street. Would it be all right to hang out with blacks on the street?

A: You know, there's sometimes— There's drug deals that happen.

Q: So it's all right to hustle with them?

A: If it's just a money thing, then that's all right.

Q: So you wouldn't invite them to a barbecue in the neighborhood, huh?

A: [*Laughs*] Hell no! "Chicken and watermelon anyone?" [*Laughs*] Fuck no! (WS White Fence 13, forties)

In demographically heterogeneous areas, there is also more acceptance among *Sureño*-affiliated gangs when it comes to socializing and hustling with Crip and Blood gang members on the streets, and with African Americans more generally. Some *Sureño*-affiliated respondents drew the line at engaging in large-scale narcotic transactions, whereas small drug sales to individual African American users were considered an acceptable source of income:

Q: Under what circumstances do you think it's all right for blacks and South Siders to interact on the street? Is it cool to work together?

A: I mean, if you have to, you know? You gotta pay your bills, you know? That's— That's, like, a total different subject.

Q: You think it's acceptable to hustle together, to serve black fools, as users or to serve them weight?[31]

A: I would draw the line. I would draw the line on— Well, you know what? I mean, I would draw the line on serving them a lot of weight, but if it's just a crackhead coming to buy, you know, twenty or thirty [dollars], as long as you're a smart drug dealer and you're not doing it from your home, you know? Slang it to them, you know? Make your money. (SC Clanton 14 Street, forties)

Regardless of whether *Sureño*-affiliated or Crip- and Blood-affiliated gang members have more or less integrity, it is undeniable that Crip- and Blood-affiliated gang members, and the African American community in general, are much more amenable to interracial interaction with *Sureño*-affiliated gang members and Latinos in general than *Sureño*-affiliated gang members are to interacting with African Americans. When observing Crip- and Blood-affiliated gang members interact with *Sureño*-affiliated gang members with whom they are not personally acquainted, there is certainly a visible degree of circumspection, a pang of anxiety over the possibility of conflict, but once the ice has been broken and each party is satisfied that the intentions of the other are not confrontational, Crip- and Blood-affiliated gang members generally do not look negatively on interacting with *Sureño*-affiliated gang members. Thus, there is no general taboo in the African American community against interacting with or being seen interacting with *Sureño*-affiliated gang members, or with Latinos in general, as one respondent noted:

Q: In the streets, under what circumstances is it unacceptable to interact with cholos?

A: For me, there's no circumstances.

---

31. *Weight* is a slang term for distribution-level quantity of narcotics.

Q: So there's no barriers at all? Hustling is cool?

A: No barriers at all. Yes. All that. It's all good. (Watts Bounty Hunter Bloods, twenties)

Both Crip- and Blood-affiliated gang members, and the African American community in general, are generally rather accepting of Latinos with whom they are on good terms, without any of the kind of social stigma that can tar *Sureño*-affiliated gang members who dare to violate taboos against socializing with African Americans. With social mores that emphasize the autonomy of individuals, Crip- and Blood-affiliated gang members who choose to socialize or hustle across racial lines do not suffer any sort of social reprobation, either from their gang peers or from the larger black community:

Q: Not counting prison politics, on the street [under] what circumstances is it acceptable to interact with Mexican gang members? Like, is it OK to work with them?

A: Yup.

Q: Is it OK to hang out with them otherwise? Like, do your homeboys ever kick it with the Harpys?

A: As far as the black, there is no boundary. Whatever an individual chooses, he chooses. There are no consequences in the black community for having Latino friends or dating Latinos or whatever.

Q: How about hustling with them?

A: There's no consequence for that, either. (WS Rolling 20s Neighborhood Bloods, fifties)

The only real limit to interacting with *Sureño*-affiliated gang members from the perspective of most Crip- and Blood-affiliated gang members is whether there is an ongoing conflict between them. If there is not, then interaction across racial lines is considered perfectly acceptable, though it may still warrant caution until the intentions of the unfamiliar party are satisfactorily determined to be nonthreatening:

Q: On the streets, what are, like, the boundaries as far as hanging out with Mexicans? Assuming they're not from Florence, of course . . .

A: Man, it kinda all depends on where they from. Like, if I seen somebody from up inside of here and he was from South Los, you know I'll be cool with him.[32]

---

32. South Los 13 is a *Sureño*-affiliated gang that has amicable relations with East Coast Crips in the Carson/South Bay area of Los Angeles County.

Figure 4.1. Graffiti by South Central 18 Street Lagos and 83 Hoover Criminals proclaiming, in no uncertain terms, that the area where this photograph was taken—at 82nd Street and South Vermont Avenue—is their shared territory. (Photograph by the author.)

Q: So it just kinda depends on where they from? If they ain't a enemy, then it's all good?
A: Yeah, but you still gotta, like, watch them too though. (East Coast Crips, thirties)

In many cases, open alliances and friendships are made among *Sureño*-affiliated and Crip- and Blood-affiliated gangs across racial lines by virtue of shared conflicts with rival *Sureño*-affiliated or Crip- or Blood-affiliated gangs. Nothing makes friends like having enemies in common. For example, there is a loose alliance between the *Sureño*-affiliated West Side 18 Street gang and African American gangs such as the Rolling 30s Harlem Crips, Rolling 60s Neighborhood Crips, East Coast Crips, and Hoover Criminals (formerly Crips), as Figure 4.1 shows. These alliances are due to common rivals, as 18 Street has had a long-running conflict since the early 1990s with the Black P Stones Bloods and their allies, the West Side Rolling 20s Neighborhood Bloods in the West Adams/Crenshaw area, both of which are traditional enemies of Crip-affiliated gangs 18 Street is friendly with:

Q: What about hanging out with Mexican gang members? Is that acceptable in your hood? Like, is there any Mexican gangs you guys get along with?

A: Yeah, like 18s, we cool with 18 Street just 'cause . . . they got everybody— Like, they have everybody mostly is they enemy, and
plus all Blood gangs, they beef with Blood, so they cool with us
mostly because we beef with, like, all the same gangs. (WS Rolling 60s Neighborhood Crips, teens)

Even Florencia 13, which has a reputation for bitter racialized conflict
(discussed in Chapter 5), associates with African American gangs with
whom they share territory and with whom they share common rivals, such
as the Five Deuce Pueblo Bishop Bloods. The Pueblo del Rio Housing Project
located on the east side of South Los Angeles (east of the 110 freeway around
53rd Street off South Alameda Street) is the traditional territory of the Pueblo Bishops, an African American gang that predates the inception of Crip
and Blood identities in Los Angeles. With Florencia and the Pueblos sharing
a common enemy in the East Coast Crips, a de facto agreement to cohabitate
has developed between them, which has an active clique in the projects
called the 54th Street Locos. They cooperate in drug retail and distribution
and socialize, interact, and coexist with one another amicably, contrary to
what moral panic-provoking media sources suggest:[33]

Q: With other blacks, is it cool in your neighborhood to hang out
with them—like, you said, with Bloods or whatever? Do homies
trip on that?
A: My neighborhood got a projects and they share the projects with
the black people, the Bloods, the Five Deuce Pueblos.
Q: Oh, you guys are in the Pueblo Projects also?
A: Yeah, so pretty much they know it as a Pueblo Projects, but it's us
there, too, you know? They get along, because pretty much their
hood and our hood; we beef with pretty much all the same hoods,
you know? So if we see one or they see one going into the hood,
then we'll let them know, you know?
Q: Do you guys hustle with them, too?
A: Yeah. Yeah. Well, sometimes the homies don't have shit. They'll
go hit those fools up, like, "What you fools working with?" (SS
Florencia 13, twenties)

The ability and willingness to cooperate in the narcotics trade is the oil
that lubricates the wheels of interracial relations between *Sureño*-affiliated
and Crip- and Blood-affiliated gangs, particularly in demographically mixed
areas where cooperation among gang members in the narcotics trade is a

---

33. See *Gangland* 2010.

virtual necessity if conflict is to be avoided—at the distribution level, at least, if not at the retail level. However, conversely, the inability to cooperate in the narcotics trade can be the catalyst for a protracted racialized gang war, as Chapter 5 demonstrates.

For Crip- and Blood-affiliated gang members, working with *Sureño*-affiliated gang members is unavoidable if one is employed in the narcotics trade. Crip- and Blood-affiliated gang members often have to go through *Sureño*-affiliated gang members to get the narcotics they require to supply their retail operations, because narco-traffickers use *Sureño*-affiliated rather than Crip- and Blood-affiliated gang members in Los Angeles for distribution. This is a reality that Crip- and Blood-affiliated gang members employed in the narcotics trade have to accept. In fact, a good connection in a *Sureño*-affiliated gang who is willing to provide them, consistently and reliably, with the quantities of narcotics they need to supply their retail market is an invaluable ally and cherished partner, indeed. In communities where opportunities for employment in the regular economy are scarce, collaborating in the narcotics trade is in everyone's interest, on all sides:

Q: Are there any boundaries for interacting with people from Mexican gangs?

A: No. No: most everybody does 'cause, you know, Mexicans get the dope now. Back in the days, the blacks used to get the dope, but we started jacking and robbing Colombians and people who coming from Mexico, so they started letting the Mexicans, young Mexicans, gangbangers, get it. So you dealing with them if you wanna get weed or cocaine.

Q: Nobody thinks anything of that?

A: Naw, no. Nobody think nothing 'bout it when you getting some money. [*Laughs*] (Blood Stone Villains Bloods, forties)

These kinds of relationships, rooted in the narcotics trade and a shared history of growing up together in demographically mixed communities, often result in very close friendships between *Sureño*-affiliated and Crip- and Blood-affiliated gang members. In some communities, *Sureño*-affiliated and Crip- and Blood-affiliated gangs share not only territory, rivals, and narcotic retail and distribution operations but also their very lives, coming of age together facing the same struggles and triumphs despite the racialized divisions that surround them. These lifelong friendships can be so close, as the Blood Stone Villains respondent quoted previously notes, that they endure each other's conflicts, as well, even where their rivals accuse them of being "race traitors" because of their willingness to maintain relationships with one another across racial lines:

A: I bought a house in Torrance. They went and wrote "Fuck N—ers" on the wall.

Q: What? Because you moved in the house?

A: Yeah, Tortilla Flats [an unincorporated area just east of Torrance]. . . .

Q: Did they ever do anything beyond that?

A: They was hot about it. Well, yeah, it was a big ol' thing. The news came out there and everything. What was ironic about it, they were saying "Fuck N—ers," but how this all started was over some Mexicans. I took some young Mexican homeboys that stay on my block [in South Los Angeles], 'cause the block I grew up on had a Mexican gang, too, and they claim the same street I claimed: 56th Street. But I'm their big homeboy because when their part of the hood started, they didn't have no homeboys my age. I was the oldest. They kinda learned . . . how to fight from me. So when they became [the] Playboys [gang], . . . I got them to help me move my girl over there, and, while they were standing around, some of the dudes from Tortilla Flats— You know how Mexicans do. They bold, like, "Where you from, homie?" They told them where they from, but they had a strap [firearm].

Q: So they got into it themselves?

A: Yeah, so when they did that, they was like, "Why he over there with these black dudes?" So naturally, instead they couldn't get with them. . . .

Q: So they got at you instead? [*Laughs*]

A: Yeah! [*Laughs*] Alotta people don't even know that story. They just know, "Oh, you black. There's Mexicans over there tripping on him." But it's ironic.

Q: Because it was actually between them, not you?

A: Yeah. But being they was young dudes, and they older dudes now—it's crazy because they in and out of the penitentiary, and still, even though they Mexicans, they some gangbanging-ass Mexicans with tattoos and all that—they still don't like Tortilla Flats 'cause about what happened with me, you know, and they *Sureños* and everything. (Blood Stone Villains Bloods, forties)

Unfortunately, childhood friendships can grow frayed when gang members assume racialized gang identities in their teens. When interracial gang feuds erupt between the gangs to which childhood friends belong, those friendships become much more difficult to maintain, particularly when people on both sides start getting killed. As one respondent reported:

No, it wasn't really weird 'cause where we grew up in Watts, it was a lot of blacks and Hispanics all right there together. Before we started beefing— When I was a kid back then, we all got along. Then everybody started beefing and breaking off, but our older brothers and sisters had babies together. It's crazy. (East Coast Crips, twenties)

Even where personal trust and friendship are maintained, a certain social distance must be enforced, if for no other reason than that one's gang peers will almost certainly attack a rival gang member on sight, even if he is a friend of one of their homeboys. Therefore, even if members of rival *Sureño*-affiliated or Crip- or Blood-affiliated gangs choose to maintain personal relationships with one another regardless of the larger conflict in the wider gang community, they must generally do so outside the conflict area to protect themselves, and one another, from becoming victims of one another's confederates. Friendships and relationships that exist across racial lines that do not cross the lines of partisan gang conflicts, by contrast, might be perfectly acceptable:

Q: You mentioned you had a friend that was black, but he's a Blood, and you told him he couldn't kick it in your neighborhood?

A: Well not because of my beliefs. 'Cause of my homies don't like him. So why am I gonna bring him over when they're just gonna beat him up? It's like bringing a piñata out to a Mexican party. They're gonna fuck that shit up.

Q: So it's more a neighborhood thing that he can't come around?

A: Yeah, it's a neighborhood thing. Not a racial thing.

Q: So if a black fool from a different black neighborhood that you don't have beef with— He'd be good to come and kick it if he wants?

A: Yeah. I mean, I got a lot of friends that are black and come to my neighborhood. But people know them. I mean, they're black, but people don't trip on them, so it's cool.

Q: So the only reason homies would trip on those other fools is 'cause they're from a rival neighborhood?

A: Yeah, because they got beef with the Bloods. (SC 38 Street, twenties)

Where racialized gang conflicts have been especially costly to communities on both sides of the conflict, the ability of individual members to maintain some vestige of previous friendships and relationships with members of the rival gang with whom they grew up can perhaps be interpreted as fulfilling an unconscious need to preserve their sanity by recognizing the humanity in people they once knew. Finally coming to terms with the pain and devastation that they have suffered as a result of the conflict can bring moments of circumspection to even the most hardened gangsters on both sides of the color line:

> Q: What happened to that friendship when you got older? Did you stay friends?
>
> A: We had to become enemies because he joined my rival gang. He joined— He became an East Coast Crip. So now I'm from Florence, so that doesn't go, but I ran into him twice already in the last four or five years, and we said— We talked a little bit: "Aye wassup?" 'Cause we've known since we were kids, so his mind was like, "Sorry it had to be this way." We chopped it up a little bit.[34] "Wassup, man? How you doing? How's your mom? Oh, all right man, you should be careful. You know you told me to be careful. I tell you to be careful." You know, whatever happens happens. It's going on, but we try not . . . to let that affect my relationship and his—I mean, whatever we had since we was teenage kids. So we know each other since we was kids, so I felt the amount of weight, like, 'cause I know he's with the business and I'm from Florence, like, you know? It is hard for me to accept it, but the other way around, you know, we were childhood friends so— But he's black, so it's, like, OK. . . .
>
> Q: So you guys aren't gonna bang on each other?
>
> A: So we're not gonna bang 'cause I know where he's from, and I'm from Florencia.
>
> Q: He gave you a pass?
>
> A: Yes, he gave me a pass, and I gave him a pass a couple of times, so that kind of works both ways, you know? Likewise. (SS Florencia 13, thirties)

Indeed, such relationships across lines of racialized gang conflict can potentially save one's life—for instance, when one finds oneself facing the barrel of a gun with a childhood friend on the other end. In Chapters 3 and 4, I examined the biases and boundaries that enforce the salience of racialized gang identities. In Chapter 5, I turn my attention to how these divisions play out in the streets of Los Angeles, providing case analyses of specific racialized conflicts between *Sureño*-affiliated and Crip- and Blood-affiliated gangs in different regions of Los Angeles County.

---

34. *Chop it up* is slang for engaging in a conversation.

5

RACE WAR?

Case Studies in Racialized Gang Conflict

I n the prior chapters, I examined and critiqued the historical foundations of racialized gang identities, the cultural divisions that emerged as a result of that history, and the identity boundaries and racial biases that define racialized identity boundaries and interracial relations between *Sureño*-affiliated and Crip- and Blood-affiliated gang members. In this chapter, I provide brief case studies of the origins and trajectories of specific racialized gang conflicts in communities throughout Los Angeles County, where they have occurred, to demonstrate the fratricidal progeny of ethnonationalist ideology and identity politics. Rather than simply cataloguing the trajectory of such conflicts in Los Angeles, an endeavor that would require volumes to cover comprehensively, I use selected narratives to explore how racially charged perspectives on all sides—including from third parties, such as law enforcement and the media—perpetuate and exacerbate racialized gang conflict. These conflicts typically originate over nonracial issues arising out of the narcotics market or personal disputes or competition for amorous attention, for example, rather than racial animus for the sake of pure bigotry. However, racialized interpretations of the events as they unfold function to define conflicts in racial terms and thereby perpetuate and exacerbate interracial conflicts when they do occur. As Rogers Brubaker puts it so eloquently:

> Violence becomes "ethnic" (or "racial" or "nationalist") through the meanings attributed to it by perpetrators, victims, politicians, offi-

cials, journalists, researchers, relief workers, and others. Such acts of framing and narrative encoding do not simply *interpret* the violence: they *constitute it as ethnic*.[1]

These specific narratives are followed by an examination of the rules of engagement that operate among and between *Sureño*-affiliated and Crip- and Blood-affiliated gangs in different community contexts and how members of rival gangs navigate these formal rules and informal mores in selecting targets to engage during the course of racialized gang conflicts.

Some might mistakenly assume that interracial gang violence erupts as a result of racial animus between gangs—that hate *initiates* conflict. The reality reported by gang members is far more complex. It indicates that racial mistrust and anxiety over access to resources and space in the face of changing demographics are very much on gang members' minds, providing a foundation of racialized hostility that informs the trajectory of interracial conflicts, even though these conflicts most often flare up around isolated issues as a proximate cause. Racial animosity emerges from conflict *because* conflicts are defined as racial. Racialized conflict doesn't result from racial animosity. The multitude of micro-analyses that follow demonstrate that, even as scholars have emphasized the prevalence of intraracial gang violence, interracial gang conflict is indeed endemic in Los Angeles County, as a majority of respondents reported that their gangs had been or are currently embroiled in interracial gang conflicts.[2] Of the fifty *Sureño*-affiliated gangs sampled, twenty-six reported that they had been involved in interracial conflicts, including eight of the eighteen gangs sampled from homogeneously Latino East Los Angeles. Likewise, nineteen out of the twenty-four Crip- and Blood-affiliated gangs sampled reported having been involved in interracial gang conflicts. Sectarian violence between *Sureño*-affiliated and Crip- and Blood-affiliated gangs therefore is far from uncommon and, in many cases, has been carrying on continuously for decades.

Many of these conflicts trace back to the 1980s and 1990s, when Latino immigration, primarily from Mexico and Central America, triggered demographic transitions in South Los Angeles to which Crip- and Blood-affiliated gangs responded by provoking conflicts with *Sureño*-affiliated gangs in defense of their racial hegemony in historically African American majority communities. In other cases, *Sureño*-affiliated gangs have attacked Crip- and Blood-affiliated gang members to defend their racial hegemony in historically Chicano-majority communities in East Los Angeles. The classical group threat and defended neighborhood perspectives conceptualize

---

1. Brubaker 2004, 16, author's emphasis.
2. On interracial and intraracial gang violence, see Hipp et al. 2007, 2009.

interracial conflict across a racial binary with whites in the dominant position.[3] However, in the narratives that follow, marginalized communities of color trade the roles of established and interloper population in different contexts, depending on the historical demographic profile of different regions of Los Angeles. And, as sociologist Laurence Bobo has suggested, concerns that interlopers threaten the hegemony of established populations are not always unfounded.[4] In the narratives of specific racialized gang conflicts presented in this chapter, it should be apparent that the racialized divisions discussed in previous chapters don't initiate interracial conflict. Rather, they provide a framework that informs how parties to interracial conflicts respond to events as racialized interpretations fuel the trajectory of the conflicts. Racialized divisions and racialized interpretations on all sides are the accelerant that turns a spark into an inferno.

Long Beach

The community with the longest-running racialized conflicts in Los Angeles County is undoubtedly Long Beach, a demographically diverse harbor community in South Los Angeles County of stratified middle- and upper-middle-class communities on one side and working-class marginalized communities of color on the other. Conflict between *Sureño-* and Crip-affiliated gangs has plagued the city since the 1980s. The three largest *Sureño*-affiliated gangs in Long Beach, the East Side Longos, the West Side Longos, and the North Side Longos, have been engaged in a decades-long conflict with the two largest African American gangs in the city, the Insane Crips and the Rolling 20s Crips, of which the popular rap artist Snoop Doggy Dogg is a member. While these gangs have also engaged in intraracial conflicts among themselves, the conflicts that cross racial lines have resulted in a racially charged atmosphere in which racialized violence has flared up intermittently for more than three decades. The history of racialized conflict in Long Beach between *Sureño-* and Crip-affiliated communities is paramount in the perspective of gang members in Long Beach:

Q: Has your neighborhood ever gone at it with black neighborhoods?

A: That's who we go at with: all blacks. Ninety percent of my enemies in my neighborhood are blacks, and Samoans and Asians.

---

3. Banton 1983; Bergesen and Herman 1998; Blumer 1958; Bonacich 1972; D. Green et al. 1998; Olzak 1992; Olzak and Shanahan 1996; Olzak et al. 1996; Pinderhughes 1997; Quillian 1995, 1996.

4. Bobo 1983.

Q: What neighborhoods do you go at it with?

A: We go at it with 20s, [Rolling] 20 Crip, Insane Crip, Tiny Rascal Gang, Asian Boyz [Crips], Sex Money Murder [Crips], West Coast Crips, Sons of Samoa [Crips], West Side SOS [Crips], North Side Mac Mafia [Crips]. Ninety percent are black or Samoan.

Q: How did beef start with these black and Samoan gangs?

A: Well, this was back before my day. So I figure— I don't know, honestly. I couldn't say. I couldn't call it. It's been going on for generations, but I'm thinking just because of shootings, you know? That's what I'm guessing. Back in the days with my neighborhood—back in, I'll say, what? The '80s? We ain't beefing so much with black neighborhoods back in the days. It wasn't no beef like that. It just blew out of proportion. (ES Longos 13, twenties)

It is also worth noting that in Long Beach, Samoan- and Asian-majority gangs generally take on Crip gang identities, along with the corresponding cultural identities of African American gang members.[5] They are therefore associated with African American identities from the perspective of *Sureño*-affiliated gang members.

Gang enforcement officers in the Long Beach Police Department also share the view that interracial conflicts predominate in Long Beach. While intraracial gang conflicts do exist, as well, they are eclipsed by the interracial conflicts between the larger *Sureño*- and Crip-affiliated gangs in the city:

Q: What specific interracial conflicts between black and Latino gangs are you aware of in your jurisdiction? What are the different gang rivalries?

A: As far as the gang rivalries, it's almost a standing order: blacks versus Hispanics, and vice versa. If they see one in their territory, they will shoot it out on the spot. (Long Beach Police Department gang intelligence officer)

Race thinking is also reflected in a recent pact among *Sureño*-affiliated gangs—the East Side Longos, West Side Longos, and North Side Longos—who put aside their differences to form a united coalition:

Q: What's the major Latino gangs?

A: Our biggest Hispanic gang is East Side Longo, followed by West

---

5. Annie Le, a postdoctoral scholar at Stanford University, is working on a manuscript on Asian gangs in Los Angeles County that I am eagerly anticipating, but, unfortunately, it was not published as of this writing.

Side, and North Side Longo. Currently they are all getting along. They have a pact or a truce now, which hasn't always been the case. (Long Beach Police Department gang intelligence officer)

While the various *Sureño*-affiliated Longo gangs have agreed to a truce and formed a coalition, the various Crip gangs in Long Beach fractured decades ago and have suffered ongoing conflicts among themselves in addition to their common rivalry with *Sureño*-affiliated gangs. This fracture is only recently beginning to heal:

Q: What are some of the names of the black gangs?
A: As far as the black gangs go, Insane and Rolling 20 Crips are the biggest. . . .
Q: Do they have a confederation?
A: No, they are bitter enemies. Because . . . well, most of the youngsters don't know, but they use to be one gang back in the day, back in the '80s. One group wanted to be dope dealers and one wanted to be professional gangsters, and they split off that way, and they've been warring ever since. The Rolling 20s were in it for the money and Insanes were out for the violence. None of the kids out here now know that history. (Long Beach Police Department gang intelligence officer)

Unfortunately, the specific catalyst that initiated the conflict between Crip- and *Sureño*-affiliated gangs in Long Beach was also not known to any of the gang members I interviewed. Perhaps it has been lost to history, taken to the grave with those who lost their lives during these decades-long racialized conflicts. However, some respondents believed that the conflict started over a narcotics transaction gone wrong. Given that the conflict started during the crack era, when tons of cocaine were being imported into South Los Angeles to fund an illegal war in Nicaragua, it is not unwarranted to speculate that the narcotics market played a role in the commencement of hostilities.[6] While no gang member I interviewed, formally or informally, could recall a specific incident that served as a catalyst for the conflicts that exist today, one respondent suggested that the narcotics trade could have played a role:

Q: Do you know how those beefs started with the black gangs? Have they always had beef with your neighborhood?
A: Hmmm, when it started off, when both gangs started off no, they didn't have beef. It all started over girls, like always. Girls and dope.

---

6. G. Webb 1998.

Q: People fighting over girls or burning each other over drug deals?
A: That's how all these neighborhood beefs happened. (ES Longos 13, twenties)

However, whether narcotics played a role or not is impossible to corroborate because I got a different answer from almost every gang member I interviewed, even those who were close friends and "crimees" (crime partners):

Q: Do you know what started the beef with them in the streets?
A: I heard, uh, we were just talking about this the other day. Created a little documentary, but— I think it was, uh— What was it? I have no idea, to be honest, streetwise, I have no idea.
Q: Was it over dope or . . .
A: I think it was over them killing a Hispanic, and it just went on.
Q: It just went off from there?
A: Something to do with a black killing [a] Hispanic. (ES Longos 13, twenties)

Regardless of what the catalyst was that provoked the initiation of hostilities between *Sureño-* and Crip-affiliated gangs in Long Beach, the war between Crips and Longos carries on to the present day, as gang identities and gang conflicts are perceived by both the African American and Chicano communities as synonymous with racialized divisions. Like all racialized gang conflict in Los Angeles, this perception is rooted in the racial nationalist identities African American and Chicano gang members have inherited, which lead them to think of themselves as inherently exclusive, insular, oppositional communities. It is no accident that these racialized conflicts first emerged in Long Beach during a period of significant demographic transition that followed the collapse of the Civil Rights Movement.

West Side

Narcotics transactions gone wrong are explicitly recognized as the catalyst for ongoing racialized gang conflicts between *Sureño*-affiliated and Crip- and Blood-affiliated gangs on the West Side. However, it is apparent that there are underlying racial animosities that inform the trajectory of these conflicts. A particularly noteworthy example is the long-running conflict between West Side 18 Street and the Black P Stones Bloods (BPS) and their allies, the Rolling 20s Neighborhood Bloods, which resulted in the murder of my childhood friend Eddie in 1996, as described in the Introduction. The origin of the conflict lies in a dispute over a popular narcotics retail location, a particular apartment building on the edge of Baldwin Village, otherwise known as "The Jungles." This dense complex of low-income low-rise apartment buildings just west of the historically African American Crenshaw Boulevard corridor has been dominated by BPS since they migrated to the community from Chicago in the early 1970s. Throughout the 1970s and 1980s, all three gangs—18 Street, BPS, and Rolling 20s—shared an overlapping territory, regularly interacting and functioning together both socially and in the narcotics trade. During that time, 18 Street gang members were deeply outnumbered by BPS and Rolling 20s members, as the Baldwin Village/West Adams area where they coexisted had long been an African American community.

However, as the demographic balance shifted with increased Latino immigration in the 1980s, 18 Street expanded its membership base as older cliques, such as the Smiley Drive Gangsters, grew and newer 18 Street cliques, such as Rancho Parque, Rimpau Locos, and Alsace Locos, were established. This demographic shift set the stage for the bitter conflict that emerged across racial lines in the early 1990s:

Q: Was there when you were growing up— Was there, like, racial tension in the high schools? Like, you know, how in the '90s there was all that tension at Dorsey, with Mexicans and blacks and stuff? Was there anything like that when you were growing up?

A: Nah, 'cause I went through there, I would have been class of '85, so, there were no issues at all.

Q: When do you think that tension started up?

A: Maybe mid-'90s.

Q: Do you know what the beefs were over?

A: Probably the influx of Hispanics. The influx, and then as . . . Mexicans began to adapt the black culture, that brought about a— That brought about a sort of a clash, if you will. Also, the drug— The drug trade also contributed a lot to it.

Q: Competition?

A: Right, because before, the Hispanic gangs were sort of submissive, and if you were Mexican and you weren't in a gang, you were really submissive to blacks or particular black gangs, and blacks saw them as a nonthreat. Some individuals even were predatorial to Hispanics, yeah.

Q: Robbing them and stuff?

A: Robbing them, kinda like bully tactics.

Q: That was a racial thing? Or you think it was just an easy lick?

A: A combination of the two, combination of the two, I want to be careful when I say racial because, it wasn't that they hated.

It wasn't a hatred thing. It was more or less of a sense of social imbalance.

Q: That they were a different group?

A: They were a different group, and a lot of them are humble because maybe they didn't live here long. They were finding their way, or they didn't want any trouble, and individuals may have taken that as a sign of weakness of some sort.

Q: You think that was, like, around the time that the population shift happened and a lot of Mexicans moved into the area?

A: Yeah, it was gradual.

Q: You think from, like, the mid-'80s to the mid-'90s?

A: It's always increasing from early on.

Q: Even to today?

A: Yeah, it's still increasing. (WS Rolling 20s Neighborhood Bloods, forties)

The influx of Latino immigrants into the area engendered an explosion in the membership of *Sureño*-affiliated gangs such as 18 Street, which many Crips and Bloods interpreted as a threat to their long-standing hegemony in the historically African American community. This is a classic case of the group threat and defended neighborhood perspectives, but with African Americans playing the role of dominant population defending their hegemony against Latino immigrants perceived as interlopers. This perception was not entirely unwarranted as Latino families demographically supplanted African American families in one of the oldest African American communities in Los Angeles. From the perspective of the existing African American community—and particularly Crip- and Blood-affiliated gang members—the influx of Latinos and the growth of *Sureño*-affiliated gangs presented the kind of direct competition for housing, employment, and proceeds acquired in the underground economy discussed in Chapter 4. *Sureño*-affiliated gangs such as 18 Street also encroached on the territories of existing African American gangs, competing for physical space, as well as limited resources. As their growing demographic advantage overwhelmed smaller African American gangs, large gangs saw the writing on the wall and assumed a defensive posture:

Q: How did the beef with the 18 Street start?

A: You know what? That escalated because they had a problem with Gear [Gang Crips]. I don't know if you know the history with that. They shared a neighborhood with the Gear Gang Crips, and they kinda like overpowered them and took over, which didn't sit well with a few [black] people. But pretty much everybody

Figure 5.1. West Side 18 Street Lil Locos: Blood Killer, with arrow indicating claim to territory. (Courtesy of Alex A. Alonso.)

goes, "Oh, that's their problem." But when it started to spill over, it got bigger. It's kinda like the thing of "give a inch, take a mile." So they were allowed to exist there, but then they got to where there was a altercation, and it didn't go— It didn't go away easily. It escalates, and, you know, that's when it just boiled over, and boiled over, and boiled over. (WS Rolling 20s Neighborhood Bloods, forties)

The specific catalyst for the initiation of hostilities was competition over clientele at a specific narcotic retail location: an apartment complex in a particularly high-traffic location on the periphery the Jungles that narcotics users had long frequented. Reportedly, in 1993 a simple argument over a parking spot escalated into competing claims to territory, resulting in the shooting of an 18 Street member in the face, initiating a racialized conflict that continues through the time of this writing:

Q: Has your neighborhood ever gone at it with any Mexican gang?
A: Yeah, we been at war with the 18 Streets since 1993.
Q: How did that start?
A: It started because the 18 Streets were selling dope in the Jungles, and they had an altercation about sales, and the 18s and the Black

P Stones in the Jungles went to war. And there is an affiliation of the Stones that is not in the Jungles that are part of the Rolling 20s hood called the City Stones, and the 18 Streets started attacking the City Stones, and they started accidentally killing Rolling 20s and other Blood gang members to the point where they said they don't give a fuck. If you over there wearing red— The 18 Streets are Blood Killers, so if you over there wearing red, you getting hit. . . .[7]

Q: Do you know what the dispute was with the 18s? Was it about location, or was it someone had burned someone?

A: Well, it was about location. There was an apartment building on Gibraltar [Avenue] and that's where it started. I get two sides of the story: I get the story from the 18 Streets and the story from the Black P Stones. The 18 Streets was saying that the Stones were telling people not to buy from them and taking their customers and things like that, and then they confronted them, and they were arrogant and saying, "This is our neighborhood," and the 18 Streets were just like, "Naw we just want to work together." The Black Stones wouldn't have it, and it led to a fight, and then it went from there. From the Black P Stone side, they saying just the opposite: that the 18 Streets were saying this is their neighborhood and they gonna sell wherever and they don't give a damn, so that's what the Black Stones say about it. Basically, it started over both of them wanting to sell drugs at the same location on Gibraltar where there wasn't a lot of money to be made, so they started fighting over customers. And it led to a fight, and the Black P Stones shot at the 18 Streets and told them to get up outta there, and the 18 Streets came back shooting, and it turned into a war and it's never stopped. (WS Rolling 20s Neighborhood Bloods, fifties)

This particular racialized conflict has cost dozens of lives over the course of its quarter-century duration. As a result of the animosity engendered by such heinous violence and racialized interpretations of events as they have unfolded, the conflict has been perceived and defined consistently in racialized terms by both sides. Racialized animosity is not only expressed in intermittent spates of deadly violence; it is also often spelled out on the walls of the community for all to see, sending moral panic through entire communities on both sides of the color line whenever hostilities ignite. While racial bigotry was not the proximate cause of the conflict, race thinking underpinned the gang members' conceptualization of their interests as oppositional that led to the initiation of the conflict. Race thinking also pro-

---

7. *Blood Killers* means that they are known for targeting Blood-affiliated gang members.

Figure 5.2. West Side Black P Stone City Stone Bloods, 18 Street/Mexican Killa, Fuck Krabz 4 Life. (Courtesy of Alex A. Alonso.)

vides a ready repertoire for the opposing parties to demonize and dehumanize their rivals and creates a seemingly impenetrable invisible wall between the combatants, precluding the possibility of negotiation in good faith.

Compton

The racialized animosity gang members harbor for their rivals is often expressed in starkly racial terms, with the use of racial epithets on all sides. Since I was a teenager I have been familiar with *Sureño*-affiliated gang members' using racial epithets such as the N-word and *mayate* to dehumanize their rivals, and I have heard Crips and Bloods use racially charged terms such as *wetbacks*, *beaners*, or just *Mexicans* for the same purpose. When used in a context of conflict, these words are charged with just as much animosity and hatred as the N-word. One also finds racial epithets spelled out on the walls in the community, with incendiary phrases such as "Fuck N—ers" and "Mexican Killer" scrawled in graffiti for all to see. Such blatantly racial provocations can have a chilling effect, especially on unaffiliated community members and their families, spreading a self-fulfilling moral panic through the entire community on both sides of the color line. It can be terrifying for children especially, whose fears of being targeted on the basis of race alone, even if they have no association with gangs, are not entirely unfounded. Such racially targeted violence is often the result of the extreme animosity that is engendered when gang conflicts erupt across racial lines. Racialized divisions provide a ready repertoire of hateful caricatures to be employed in demonizing rival gang members across racial lines whenever such conflicts erupt. The availability of racial epithets as a rhetorical weapon in an escalating conflict over territorial, economic, or romantic competition, for example, inevitability provides for the possibility that the conflict will become interpreted as racial, thereby further exacerbating the conflict and potentially dooming it to intractability.

Voicing a racial epithet during the course of a violent crime can lead to prosecution on hate crime charges, even if the impetus for the violence has nothing to do with racial bigotry. Once a racial epithet is used, the motive is automatically presumed to be racial bigotry according to both state and federal law. As a Los Angeles Sheriff's Department (LASD) Operation Safe Streets (OSS) detective from the department's Compton Station put it to me in a formal interview, "As far as what constitutes a hate crime, just because a Hispanic gangster shoots at a black gangster doesn't mean it's a hate crime. I can attribute that to a turf war, but the moment they yell out 'n—er' or they start writing on the walls, that becomes a hate crime." Thus, the underlying motive behind an incidence of gang violence is irrelevant to law enforcement, because what constitutes a hate crime in the eyes of the law is the use of a racial epithet, regardless of the underlying motive for the violence. While hate crime enhancements were ostensibly legislated to protect people of color, they are often used to criminalize and demonize gang members who are themselves people of color. However, the "justice" of neoliberal hate crime legislation is hardly color-blind in its application.

There are no cases known either to me or to anyone I spoke with in law enforcement or the Los Angeles County Hate Crimes Commission of a Crip- or Blood-affiliated gang member being charged with a hate crime against a Latino victim, despite the fact that perpetrators and victims are to be found on all sides of racialized gang conflicts. This could be due to an enforcement and reporting bias that casts African Americans as the victims rather than the perpetrators of hate crimes, but it could also be due to the fact that the most common term used by *Sureño*-affiliated gang members to demonize rival African American gang members, the N-word, is a universally recognized racial epithet. By contrast, the most common term used by African American gang members to demonize their *Sureño*-affiliated rivals is simply *Mexican*, which is not interpreted as racial slander by authorities, even though it is often employed that way. Casting *Sureño*-affiliated gang members as solely or even disproportionately responsible for interracial gang violence is neither accurate nor constructive, as the biased enforcement and false narratives that drive such policy operate not only facilitate the

Figure 5.3. Graffiti by Compton Varrio 155 Street crossed out in Compton. (Photograph by the author.)

demonization and criminalization of gang members but also further inflame, rather than assuage, racialized animosity between them.

An incident that occurred in the city of Compton on New Year's Eve of 2013 is a pertinent example. In December 2012, an African American family moved into a predominantly Latino area near the intersection of Central Avenue and Compton Boulevard, which is claimed by Compton Varrio 155 Street (CV 155),[8] one of Compton's larger and more active *Sureño*-affiliated gangs. Perhaps unknown to the new residents, CV 155 had engaged in decades of racialized gang conflict with neighboring African American gangs in Compton. As a result, CV 155 members generally interpret the presence of any male African American youth in their territory as a potential threat to their security, an apprehension that is far from unwarranted. They therefore engage in the practice of confronting any male African American youth they see to determine his gang affiliation, if any. This practice exists to determine whether action is warranted to proactively neutralize a potential threat. Thus, when the new African American family moved into their neighborhood, CV 155 members harbored suspicions that the new neighbors were somehow associated with rival gang members and might provide information to them that would threaten the security of CV 155 members and their families.

---

8. Pronounced "One-Five-Five."

While the three teenage members of the newly arrived family were not gang members, a young woman in the household had a boyfriend who was. When the boyfriend, who was affiliated with a local Crip gang, came to the house on New Year's Eve, the CV 155 members' suspicions were validated.[9] They then did what any active gang member would do: attacked their rival when they saw him in front of the house, beating him around the head and body with a length of steel pipe. When he escaped the initial attack and ran into the house, the CV 155 members returned in greater numbers and allegedly yelled racial epithets at the house with the teenagers inside, brandished a firearm, and threw a bottle through the front window. If not for the use of racial epithets, this simple assault of a rival gang member would not have garnered much attention from the mainstream media or law enforcement. Such assaults occur almost daily in Compton and throughout Los Angeles County. Indeed, there were more than thirty gang-related murders in Compton in 2013 alone, yet none received the level of media attention that this incident did.

The allegation that racial epithets were used during the incident—suggesting a connection between an isolated incident and a larger policy of racially motivated, antiblack ethnic cleansing on the part of *Sureño*-affiliated gangs in Los Angeles County—provided the local media with fuel to feed the flame of racialized antagonism. This is exactly the kind of sensationalist journalism Karen Umemoto critiques in her analysis of the role of the media in intensifying perceptions of gang conflicts as racially motivated.[10] As Umemoto explains, such incendiary reporting influences perceptions of gang conflicts by framing them within a narrative of racial bigotry rather than simple gang rivalry. Such inflammatory narratives color the perceptions the community has of such incidents, inducing moral panic over the concern that racial bigotry is the underlying reason behind such attacks and that any African American resident therefore could be similarly targeted for attack solely on the basis of racial identity. Such incendiary narratives can also act as self-fulfilling prophecies, reinforcing racialized tensions already at play in interracial gang conflicts.

"Attack on Family in Compton Latest Incident in Wave of Anti-Black Violence," a story published in the *Los Angeles Times* on January 25, 2013, clearly pushes the idea propagated by law enforcement that such attacks are part of a wider campaign of racial bigotry and aggression against African Americans by members of *Sureño*-affiliated gangs:

---

9. The young man's gang affiliation was confirmed to me by LASD Compton OSS officers.
10. Umemoto 2006.

The attacks on the family are the latest in a series of violent incidents in which Latino gangs targeted blacks in parts of greater Los Angeles over the last decade. . . . Federal authorities have alleged in several indictments in the last decade that the Mexican Mafia prison gang has ordered street gangs under its control to attack African Americans.[11]

Such marriages between overzealous law enforcement and sensationalist journalism serve to advance a narrative that connects unrelated, isolated incidents of interracial gang violence to a purportedly wider campaign of antiblack ethnic cleansing allegedly orchestrated by the Mexican Mafia. Such incendiary claims are both divorced from reality and devoid of any substantive understanding or analysis as to why such incidents occur on an individual basis. Provocative narratives advance the careers of individual journalists and law enforcement officials at the cost of exacerbating, rather than mitigating, perceptions among parties to a conflict that perpetuate racialized gang violence.

The two principal assailants in this case pled guilty to federal hate crime charges as part of a plea deal to avoid the draconian sentences they would have faced had they gone to trial and lost. However, members of CV 155 I have spoken with informally feel that the hate crime prosecution was unwarranted and excessive because the impetus for the assault was the gang affiliation of the victim and not his racial identity in and of itself. This claim was supported by deputies assigned to OSS, the LASD's gang unit, who conceded during an informal interview that the attack took place not because of the victim's racial identity, but because of his gang affiliation. Such sensationalist reporting and overly zealous prosecutions of *Sureño*-affiliated gang members, without corresponding prosecutions of Crip- and Blood-affiliated gang members who also engage in interracial violence, only serve to inflame racialized animosities rather than mitigate them, constituting these conflicts *as racial* in the process.

In every racialized gang conflict I'm aware of in Los Angeles County, institutional favoritism on the part of law enforcement and the media has consistently been shown toward African American gangs, with *Sureño*-affiliated gangs cast as the unprovoked aggressors in what are actually mutually hostile racialized gang conflicts. Federal law enforcement agencies headed by African Americans, which use their discretionary authority to pursue hate crime cases exclusively against *Sureño*-affiliated gang members, lend credence to the perception that racial favoritism is responsible for the

---

11. Quinones et al. 2013.

grossly disproportionate enforcement of federal hate crime statutes against *Sureño*-affiliated gang members in Los Angeles. At the time the indictments were brought, the U.S. President, the Attorney General, and the Special Agent in charge of the Federal Bureau of Investigation's Los Angeles field office were all African American.

The appearance of such bias only inflames racial animosity that *Sureño*-affiliated gang members feel toward their Crip- and Blood-affiliated rivals, providing yet another source of antagonism that exacerbates rather than abates racialized gang violence. The influence exercised in such biased reporting and enforcement thus becomes a self-fulfilling prophecy, as racial motives are ascribed to gang conflicts, which, in turn, leads gang members to interpret conflicts as revolving around racial identities rather than gang identities, thereby exacerbating racialized conflicts rather than mitigating them. Racialized interpretations of events as they unfold are the accelerant that fuels the fire of racialized animosity between *Sureño*-affiliated and Crip- and Blood-affiliated gang members in Los Angeles.

East Los Angeles

Another case of interpretive provocation on the part of the media and law enforcement occurred in 2014 in the aftermath of the firebombing of four apartments in the Ramona Gardens public housing project, in the Boyle Heights section of East Los Angeles. On the evening of Mother's Day of that year, three African American couples and one mixed-race couple had windows broken and Molotov cocktails thrown at their units, causing minor damage to a window and a handful of exterior walls. With three of the four units attacked occupied by African Americans in a housing project that had long been the territory of a local *Sureño*-affiliated gang, Big Hazard, and a prior precedent of allegedly racially motivated firebombings that occurred in the early 1990s, law enforcement and the local media set about promulgating a narrative that ascribed racial bigotry as the sole motive for the attacks and conjectured a nefarious conspiracy blaming the Mexican Mafia in the immediate aftermath of the incident. However, as is always the case, the specific circumstances that led to these attacks are considerably more nuanced than a simplistic narrative of racial bigotry suggests.

Beginning in the first decade of the twenty-first century, the Housing Authority of the City of Los Angeles (HACLA) began a concentrated effort to remove Hazard gang members and their families from the housing project they had traditionally occupied for generations. Families that harbored Hazard gang members (e.g., let their children sleep in their apartments) were evicted from the projects, and families from outside the community were brought in to replace them. In some cases, African American residents from other housing projects were transferred to Ramona Gardens, replacing Chicano residents who had long called the complex home. Some of the new residents were hostile to Hazard-affiliated families and have worked openly with local law enforcement, calling the police whenever they see Hazard gang members on the premises and having regular meetings with local law enforcement in the gymnasium on the grounds of the housing project, as one respondent told me:

> A: I dunno. Those projects are so weird right now, I even seen a *jura* [cop] bring a birthday cake to this lady's pad, you know? Like, what is this all about? These cops come around, like, in their lil' unit, and they start coming around and, like, knocking on doors and talking to the ladies, you know? Getting information. Like, on Saturday mornings, we have a spot called "*La Rachon.*" Like, a lot of people come . . . and start selling like food and clothes and electronics and stuff, and the cops will just come and start talking to the ladies. Pretty much just like passing info and stuff.
>
> Q: Like, they're talking to homies' moms?
>
> A: Yeah, but naw—to the other ones that don't even got family from the hood. They prolly moved in, like, five, ten years ago. The newbies, you know? Yeah, and they wanna, like, get rid of us. And, man, once a month they have a meeting in the gym. The *juras* come, and they tell them everything. Plus the cameras. (ES Big Hazard, forties)

Furthermore, while HACLA has made a concentrated effort to evict Hazard gang members and their families, some of the new African American residents brought into Ramona Gardens by the authority included active gang members from other housing projects, such as the Bounty Hunter Bloods from the Nickerson Gardens Housing Project in Watts. Amid the mass eviction of longtime Chicano residents and the influx of new residents from outside the community, HACLA installed security cameras throughout Ramona Gardens and increased the law enforcement presence. Housing police began regular foot patrols in the projects, focusing their attention primarily on harassing and intimidating Hazard gang members and their families into withdrawing from the public space. Gang members who had been evicted or who were named in a local gang injunction were regularly arrested for trespassing or being in violation of the injunction when they attempted to visit friends or family who still lived in Ramona Gardens. One Hazard gang member I interviewed had been to jail five times in as many years for being in violation of the injunction:

Q: Are you named in the injunction?

A: Yeah, since, like, '07. There's this one *jura* that just would keep harassing me. I used to come out of my pad just to take out the trash, and he would get me. Like, "Come over here!" I'm like, "What? I'm just taking out the trash." "You ain't supposed to be here!" "What? I live here. I'm not with the homies. What the fuck?" "It don't matter. The gang injunction—you're not supposed to be here." So that's what he took me in for, gang injunction. He took me in twice, by myself. Don't even have to be with nobody. He just take me in by myself, 'cause I couldn't be in the neighborhood, but I lived in the neighborhood! I fought those cases, but I lost them both. I did, like, two months, then, like, forty-five-to-sixty days. For nothing, though.

Q: How many times you get hit with that?

A: Five times. Five times!

Q: Damn. You got five convictions for gang injunction violation? Wow, that's crazy.

A: Yeah, and I ain't even did nothing. Five times, fool. *Serio!* (ES Big Hazard, twenties)

Such aggressive and racially selective enforcement engenders perceptions of institutional bias and feelings of resentment among Hazard gang members and their families: they are being expelled from their own community while known gang members from an African American community on the other side of Los Angeles County have moved in to replace them. The perception of group threat among Hazard gang members therefore is well founded, as Hazard gang members and their families have been physically supplanted by African American families at Ramona Gardens as a result of HACLA policy. When HACLA first started moving African American residents from outside the community into Ramona Gardens, Hazard gang members engaged in a campaign of harassment in an effort to intimidate residents from outside the community into leaving. However, when law enforcement attempted to connect gang members in prison who had grown up in Ramona Gardens to the harassment campaign against African American residents, the *veteranos* implored the youngsters to leave African American residents alone as long as they were respectful and did not engage in gang activity in the projects:

A: You know, before in the projects there was never no black people. But there's alotta black people right there now. Even on Thursdays the homeboys go right there in the hood and play basketball. They play against, like, blacks. Homies don't trip no more. It ain't nothing no more.

Q: That just changed in, like, the last five years, though, right? The housing authority decided to move blacks into the projects on the East Side?

A: Yeah, prolly in like '09 it started.

Q: That's actually kinda more fucked up for you, right? 'Cause alotta people like you that lost their pad, black people moved in, huh?

A: Yup, at first. But then, like, they were just bringing them in like too many. And then the homies were, like, pssshh. And then they put the cameras up. They got cameras all over now, so—

Q: You think at first the fools from your neighborhood were tripping, though?

A: Yeah, 'cause I was part of it, you know? We were robbing these fools, fucking up their cars. They didn't get the message, you know? Like, get the fuck up outta here.

Q: Did any move out 'cause of that?

A: Yeah, most of them. But they just kept coming in, though.

Q: So they'd move new ones in?

A: Yup. Yeah. And then, plus, like, a couple older homies got busted for hate crime, you know? Older homeboys who had nothing to do with it, you know? We said: "You know what? Forget it." They had nothing to do with it, though. . . .

Q: Any of those black families that are moving in— Are there any black fools from neighborhoods, too?

A: Yeah, there's even a fool from Bounty Hunters right there right now.

Q: Are they trying to, like, set up shop right there?

A: Naw. They just, like, keep to themself. (ES Big Hazard, twenties)

That détente lasted until 2014, when gang-affiliated African American residents flagrantly disrespected Hazard members and their families on Mother's Day. Members of the Bounty Hunters, some of whom live in Ramona Gardens, were socializing in a parking lot on the evening of Mother's Day, and a young woman in their group exposed herself while performing the popular dance known as "twerking." This offended the families of Hazard gang members. When Hazard gang members objected to the display and asked that the Bounty Hunters tone it down or take it inside, the Bounty Hunters told them to go fuck themselves and claimed their gang affiliation, throwing up (displaying with a hand sign) a "BH" and yelling out "Bounty Hunters!" This bravado was a blatant provocation that violated the precarious peace that had existed between the gangs. The firebombings occurred that evening.

Indeed, HACLA's campaign to evict Hazard gang members and their families from Ramona Gardens while allowing Bounty Hunter members from Watts to move in and socialize freely in public spaces that Hazard gang members are forbidden from by injunction creates tremendous racialized resentment by betraying the impression that HACLA intends to provoke racialized conflict between the two gangs. It seems a rather unlikely coincidence that the Bounty Hunters (BH), the African American gang that was moved into Ramona Gardens, uses the exact same acronym as Big Hazard (BH), the Latino gang already living in the project. Whether that is by intent or mere coincidence, that fact certainly lends itself to the speculation that HACLA intentionally provoked racialized conflict at Ramona Gardens to justify the removal of Big Hazard–affiliated families from the community, which the city ultimately intends to convert into faculty and student housing for the adjacent County-University of Southern California Medical Center.

To further fan the flames of racial hostility, Los Angeles Police Department (LAPD) officers allegedly went to Nickerson Gardens after the Mother's Day firebombings and told residents there that the attack had likely been ordered by the Mexican Mafia. This encouraged Bounty Hunter gang members to interpret the attack as part of wider conflict between *Sureño*-affiliated and Crip- and Blood-affiliated gang members in prison and throughout Los Angeles. However, it is incumbent on me to acknowledge that, at a community meeting held on July 9, 2014, at Bethel AME Church by the Southern California Ceasefire Committee, LAPD Chief Charlie Beck denied that officers had made these statements. The original allegation that they had done so had come from a representative of the Bounty Hunter Bloods living in Nickerson Gardens at an earlier meeting of the Southern California Ceasefire Committee, and two officers from the LAPD South Bureau Criminal Gang/Homicide Division who were present did not contradict it. Of course, it is certainly possible that someone from the LAPD did make those statements to Nickerson Gardens residents in the emotionally heated aftermath of the Ramona Gardens firebombings and did not want to own up to it in the presence of Chief Beck. It is also certainly possible that Chief Beck honestly was unaware that such an incendiary statement had been made.

Thanks in large part to the dedication of gang interventionists working for the Mayor's Gang Reduction and Youth Development (GRYD) program in Ramona Gardens and Nickerson Gardens, and the Southern California Ceasefire Committee in South Los Angeles, cooler heads prevailed, and the narrative suggesting a larger racial conflict was ultimately rejected, narrowly averting further violence. These facts came out during a gang intervention meeting held by the Southern California Ceasefire Committee on the Wednesday after the firebombings at which intervention workers from both Ramona Gardens and Nickerson Gardens explained, and acknowledged, that the conflict had resulted from the confrontation earlier on Mother's Day. However, despite the fact that one of its reporters was in the room during the meeting, the *Los Angeles Times* ran an incendiary story a few days later promoting a narrative of racialized conflict rooted in racial bigotry:

> Once controlled by a Latino gang, the Boyle Heights housing project had seen crime drop dramatically. Moreover, black families were beginning to move back into the rows of garden apartments—more than 20 years after the firebombing of two black families prompted most African Americans to flee.
>
> Then on Monday night, someone threw flaming Molotov cocktails at four apartments in Ramona Gardens. It had all the hallmarks of the racial attack from the area's darker years.
>
> Three of the four apartments targeted just after midnight were occupied by black families. The other housed a Latino family. No one was injured in the attack. Police have no suspects and have been careful to say the motive remains unclear.
>
> But several law enforcement sources familiar with the investigation said officials believe the attack was racially motivated.[12]

Who these unnamed "law enforcement sources" are remains unclear, but the story the *Times* chose to run is devoid of any mention of the confrontation between Big Hazard and Bounty Hunter gang members that was the motive for the firebombings and, of course, makes no attempt to understand any role law enforcement or HACLA may have played in framing and exacerbating the circumstances surrounding the incident. Anyone who depends on the *Los Angeles Times* for their news would be left with the impression that racist Latino gangs engaged in a campaign of ethnic cleansing against innocent African American residents who did nothing to provoke such racial bigotry. While this provocative narrative sells newspapers, it fails to faithfully reflect what actually occurred and exacerbates rather than mitigates the possibility of retaliatory violence.

The truth was also no defense for the Hazard gang members accused of involvement in the firebombings. Eight Hazard members were charged by federal prosecutors under federal hate crime statutes. All of them ultimately pled guilty to avoid spending the rest of their lives in prison. Their sentences ranged from five to fifteen years in federal prison for the incident, in which no one was even injured.

---

12. Becerra and Winton 2014.

South Los Angeles

Such media-induced moral panics have also surrounded one of the more prominent racialized gang conflicts in South Los Angeles: the twenty-year conflict between Florencia 13 and East Coast Crips. The roots of this conflict are also a great deal more nuanced than a narrative of racial bigotry alone suggests. The proximate origin of the conflict lies in a narcotics transaction gone wrong. Unknown to many, particularly in the media, a cooperative relationship existed between Florencia and East Coast in the distribution and retail of narcotics before the conflict began:

> Q: Before all that beef happened, did you guys get along with them?
> A: Yeah, everything was really cool. I mean, it was more like they had the money; we had the drugs. They had all the money; we had all the drugs, so it's gonna benefit both of us. It'll make alotta money. We gonna make alotta money, and they gonna get alotta drugs. That's how it was, and we call this— Everybody called this "the pipeline." (SS Florencia 13, thirties)

I was told slightly different versions of the story by respondents on both sides of the conflict, but the basic circumstances are undisputed. In 1999, a member of the East Coast Crips absconded with a load of cocaine that was allegedly worth more than $1 million. Based on an estimated wholesale value of $10,000–$15,000 per kilogram of cocaine, the amount stolen could have been in the range of one hundred kilos. Whatever the exact amount, though, members on both sides of the conflict universally acknowledge that this narcotics transaction gone wrong was the original catalyst for the conflict:

> Q: How did the beef with the Florences start?
> A: Man, drugs. Some of my homeboys had robbed them for, like, over a hundred keys [kilos]. The 69 East Coast [Crip]s. This was in, like, '98, '99. It was just on from there. Like, you said about dealing with them, my homeboys had robbed them. I mean, they took a truckload of drugs from them.
> Q: Did they rob them, or were they just dealing together and they burned them for the shipment?
> A: They was dealing together. Yeah, and it's been on ever since. They put a green light on us, and it's been going on since then.[13] (East Coast Crips, thirties)

---

13. A green light means that gang members are encouraged to attack the subject at any opportunity.

This fundamental violation of the trust that had existed between the two gangs shattered the relationship. Members from both sides who had grown up together and had close personal relationships reached out in an attempt to negotiate terms and avoid a full-blown gang war. But the inability or unwillingness of East Coast members to produce the perpetrator(s) of the theft led to a breakdown in their mutually beneficial relationship. A bitter racialized gang conflict erupted between the two gangs that carried on for two decades:

A: I sit down; I talk to some of the OG homeboys, and they told me, "Sorry, man. I'm from East Coast." I go, "I know where you from. I'm from Florence." So he told me like this: "You know what? Look, the people that did it, they're gone, man. They left us with the problem." So the guy that did the thing, both of them, they got all the money. They split. So who stayed with the problem?

Q: They left it to everybody else?

A: Yeah, so all— So the rest of them, they didn't want nothing, but . . . .

Q: But what was done was done, right?

A: What was done was done. The *raza*'s gonna be like, "Fuck that. We gonna do what we gotta do," you feel me? So just because— Because two individuals . . . left, and now they're, like— Now they're mad at the two individuals, like, "You guys took off with all the money, and then you guys left us with all these . . . problems."

Q: Those two fools, they just vanished?

A: They're gone. They're gone. They don't even— They don't even know where they're at. I mean, even they're looking for them.

Q: Probably moved out of state.

A: Yeah, come on. You got all the money; I'm gone. I mean, so, they're like, "Man, how can you fix it?" Well, you can't. "Well you bring the guys over here," I'm like, "Bring them." Even if you do, they can't . . . find them. We can't find them. Nobody can. So we're just stuck with the problems. (SS Florencia 13, thirties)

Despite the fact that the proximate cause of the conflict—a robbery—had nothing to do with racial identities, once hostilities were initiated, the conflict increasingly took on racial undertones as gang members and their communities on both sides interpreted acts of violence as expressions not just of gang rivalry but also of racialized hostility. As a result, gang members themselves began to express the conflict in explicitly racialized terms, not just by writing racial threats and epithets on walls, but also by targeting civilians in the African American and Chicano communities within the

Figure 5.4. South Side Florencia 13: ECK (for East Coast Killer), 18K (for 18 Killer). (Photograph by the author.)

conflict zone, whether intentionally or with reckless disregard for differentiating between bona fide gang members and unaffiliated civilians.

In response to the violence, a multiagency task force headed by the FBI executed a concentrated gang-suppression campaign that led to the conviction of around one hundred Florencia members on state and federal charges, six of whom were given life sentences in federal prison.[14] The vast majority of the remaining members who were arrested in the sweep were convicted of minor crimes and served less than one year in jail. The *Los Angeles Times* quoted the judge in the Florencia case as having stated in open court, during the sentencing of one defendant to life in prison, that he had "preyed on victims because they were black and for no other reason."[15] Of course, gang members on both sides of the conflict were guilty of targeting civilians, but law enforcement focused the hate crimes investigation exclusively on Florencia members, apparently based on the assumption that African Americans can only be the victims, and not the perpetrators, of racially motivated violence.

This perception is further fueled by sensationalist accounts of the conflict in popular cable-television docudramas such as the History Channel's popular *Gangland* series, which cast Florencia as a rabidly racist gang bent on killing African Americans at every opportunity, regardless of whether

14. Quinones 2010.
15. Ibid.

they were affiliated with the East Coast Crips.[16] Perhaps the most absurd moral panic proliferated by *Gangland* was that Florencia gang members had put a "green light" on any African American wearing a white T-shirt. Once such a rumor starts, it can take off throughout the community. I've heard this unsubstantiated rumor repeated regularly among members of the African American community in South Los Angeles. Even one of the Florencia members I interviewed was disturbed that his own family, after watching the *Gangland* episode, was convinced that he and his homeboys were unrepentant racists:

Q: Do you think that your parents know what's going on with East Coast?

A: Well, my parents, they think what's going on is just racist, because my mom saw that *Gangland* thing, too, so my mom thinks we're just racist. [*Laughs*] You know? My mom thinks we're racist and shit, and my brother-in-law doesn't want to come over to my house and shit, 'cause he thinks I'm racist against him, too. [*Laughs*] He seen that thing, too. Pretty much everyone did. [*Laughs*] You know? So now everybody thinks we're racist. We're not. It's not like that.

Q: It's a neighborhood thing, right? 'Cause if you were racist, why would you be getting along with the Pueblos, right?

A: Yeah pretty much in *Gangland* they shoulda said that part, too, right? They left that part out, right? They thinking that we beef with all Crips, and they say we're all CK [Crip Killer]. I mean, we are CK, but it's pretty much we're all on them [East Coast Crips], you know? That's it.

Q: How about, like, when people write on the wall, like "N—er Killer" and "Mexican Killer," right? You think that's just, like, flossing [hyperbole]? They're not really gonna shoot every black or Mexican person they see, right?

A: Yeah, that's ridiculous. (SS Florencia 13, twenties)

He was equally incredulous about the rumor that Florencia gang members would shoot African Americans for simply wearing white T-shirts. In fact, although he had heard hints about it, he was largely unaware of the rumor until I mentioned it in a formal interview:

A: You know what? Alotta people will say that because of the *Gangland* documentary. . . . It was so stupid, because it made it seem

---

16. *Gangland* 2010.

like we're racists, you know? Like, fuck, we just want black people for no reason. We don't even know what it's for. But it's not like that. Why we gonna want to hurt someone that's not even involved with it and shit, you know?

Q: What about that lil' *chisme* [rumor] that your neighborhood put out a green light that any black person wearing a white T-shirt in South Central would be shot on sight?

A: Naw. Well, all right. That's where he got it from then. . . . So one day I was walking, and some black guy told me, "Didn't you hear about it? If a black person wears a white T-shirt, you gonna kill us!" and I'm like, "For reals?" And I dunno—he just kept on walking and shit, but he made it seem like everybody that's wearing a white T-shirt around here is gonna die and shit. So I'm like, "What the fuck? I'm wearing a white T-shirt, too, and shit!" [*Laughs*] So what the fuck, aye? But in my hood, we never heard of that, you know? I think that was just a rumor, you know, because I don't think, like, just the Cheese Toasts [a disrespectful nickname for the East Coast Crips] wear white shirts and shit, you know? Everybody does. (SS Florencia 13, twenties)

Such media-fueled rumors do little to reduce feelings of racial animus that inevitably surface as a result of racialized gang conflicts. Instead, they serve to provoke moral panic, causing unaffiliated residents to feel a greater degree of fear and insecurity than is warranted by actual events. While unaffiliated civilians have been killed and wounded on both sides of racialized gang conflicts, this violence is most often the result of mistaken identity, wherein gang members mistakenly target civilians because they are unable to differentiate between them and active gang rivals.

As the remainder of this chapter illustrates, during the course of racialized gang conflicts gang members typically target rival gang members exclusively. When innocent people become victims of interracial gang violence, it is almost always due to a case of poor marksmanship, mistaken identity, or mistakenly attributed gang affiliation. Indeed, it makes little sense for gang members to intentionally target innocent residents who are not affiliated with gangs, because innocent residents do not present any substantive threat to the personal security of gang members and their families. Unfortunately, this obvious point is lost on law enforcement officials, politicians, journalists, and certain colleagues of mine in the academy, who would rather propagate a narrative of racially motivated violence and feed the sort of moral panics that can only make these conflicts worse, thereby constituting them *as racial conflicts*.

Figure 5.5. 76 Neighborhood 76 East Coast Crips: hand signs translate as "fuck Florencia"; FK (for Florencia Killer). (Courtesy of Alex A. Alonso.)

Rules of Engagement

While gang members typically target rival gang members exclusively when engaging in gang feuds, there is always potential, when conflicts cross racial lines between *Sureño*-affiliated and Crip- and Blood-affiliated gangs, for the violence to be perceived as racially motivated and for unaffiliated civilians to be targeted. When one considers the intricacies of how gang members go about targeting their rivals, it becomes apparent how cases of mistaken affiliation occur that lead to the unintended targeting of non-gang-affiliated residents. Such incidents can occur as a result of mistaken identity or affiliation and then act as a catalyst for retaliatory attacks that involve the intentional targeting of unaffiliated residents on a racial basis. However, it is equally important to emphasize that in many cases they do not. Rather, gang members respond to the targeting of unaffiliated civilians in their community by targeting active gang rivals specifically, as the rules of engagement dictate.

The rules of engagement that operate to limit the acceptable range of targets to be engaged in a gang conflict operate on both a formal and an informal level, within and among *Sureño*-affiliated and Crip- and Blood-affiliated gangs. For *Sureño*-affiliated gang members, a formal set of *reglas* [rules] dictate the protocols that must be followed when engaging in gang conflicts. These protocols apply universally to conflicts with other *Sureño*-affiliated gangs and conflicts with Crip- and Blood-affiliated gangs. Violations of the *reglas* expose members of the gang both in prison and on the streets to the threat of being victimized by other *Sureño*-affiliated gang members as punishment.

One of these rules proscribes the practice of drive-by shootings by *Sureño*-affiliated gang members. To limit the number of innocent victims hit by gunfire, the *reglas* forbid drive-by shootings by *Sureño*-affiliated gang members. As a result, the modus operandi of *Sureño*-affiliated gang members is to approach their target(s) on foot and shoot from as close range as possible. This ensures they are hitting the intended target and not innocent bystanders. If they do fire from a vehicle, they will typically bring it to a complete stop and open a door so they can put a foot on the ground and then fire the weapon, which does not violate the rule against drive-by shootings. Certainly, firing a weapon from a moving vehicle is not conducive to accurate marksmanship, so forbidding *Sureño*-affiliated gang members from engaging in drive-by shootings inevitably reduces the number of innocent victims accidentally hit by gunfire as a result of gang conflicts.

The *reglas* also forbid *Sureño*-affiliated gang members from engaging rival gang members if they are with their families, particularly if children or elders are present, to reduce the possibility of hitting innocent family members or children unintentionally and minimizing emotional trauma inflicted on family members, particularly children and the elderly. *Sureño*-affiliated gang members are also forbidden from shooting into occupied structures, such as family homes, for the same reason. All of these *reglas* implemented in order to reduce the collateral damage gang violence has on unaffiliated family, children, and residents in the community. While law enforcement and media narratives habitually demonize *Sureño*-affiliated gang members, the enforcement of these formal rules of engagement since their implementation in 1993 has undeniably saved countless lives by reducing the number of innocent victims hit by stray bullets in gang shootings, as one respondent noted:

> Like us, we can't do drive-bys. If you were my enemy and I seen you at your front porch, I can't get off and fucking blast at you, 'cause if I miss you and I hit a little kid, then that's my ass or my neighborhood's ass. Black fools, they don't give a fuck. You could be with your mom, your grandma, your son—they gonna get off . . . and blast you. Yeah, 'cause they can't get green-lighted. They can't. We could, though. Yeah, 'cause they could blast you from the car—boom—hit all kinds of people and nothing will happen to them or their hood if they do it, but if we do it, then that's our ass. So we know better. We

have, like, rules and regulations to follow out here. (ES Indiana
Dukes 13, twenties)

With no overarching structure to enforce formal rules of conduct,
Crip- and Blood-affiliated gang members are not structurally compelled to
observe such formal limitations. Crip- and Blood-affiliated gang members
have no repercussions to fear in terms of gang politics and therefore can
engage rivals in the presence of their family or children, shoot randomly
into rivals' residences, and engage in drive-by shootings without suffering
consequences beyond those presented by the incident itself. Crip- and
Blood-affiliated gang members are even known to shoot rivals and family
members at funerals. Such wanton disregard for innocent victims is almost
unheard of among *Sureño*-affiliated gangs.

The absence of organizational structure that allows these types of attacks
by Crip- and Blood-affiliated gang members provides another reason for
Sureño-affiliated gang members to interpret violence perpetrated across racial lines in the worst possible light. The willingness of Crip- and Blood-
affiliated gang members to engage in drive-by shootings, to target rivals in
front of their families, and to shoot recklessly into the residences of rivals
without regard for innocent family members, children, and neighbors is
perceived by *Sureño*-affiliated gang members as a severe violation, not
just of their rules of engagement, but also of their Catholicized cultural
frame, which deeply values the family and the innocent. When such shootings do occur at the hands of rival African American gang members,
they are thus interpreted as unambiguous evidence of the depravity of their
Crip- or Blood-affiliated rivals. Thus, a structural difference between
Sureño-affiliated and Crip- and Blood-affiliated gangs becomes interpreted
as a cultural difference between racialized gang identities—an interpretation that is at the core of the ethnonationalist ideology that informs their
perceptions, as illustrated by one respondent:

A: Like you know, if you're on the street with your lady, with your
mom, with your little girl, we're not even gonna look at you.
We're just gonna keep on going, man, you know? I mean, it's a
waste of time. I mean, you're with your mom, you know? We're
not gonna disrespect you like that. And them [Crip- and Blood-
affiliated gang members], you know, they don't care; they don't
give a fuck, you know? They put a gun in front of your face and
you're with your kid, or they just pass by and they doing a drive-
by. They start shooting anybody, you know? Most of the blacks
right now, like, they don't get along with Mexican gangs. They
don't get along with the Mexicans, you know, then they go and

try to do a little *jale* [job; here, a shooting], and they go look for you at your hood, and they see any Mexican—they gonna kill them, you know? It's like that. Only because you a Mexican and you walking around at the wrong neighborhood, you know?

Q: Do they pull that kind of thing on purpose? Do you think they do it more often than you? That they make sure the person is a gang member and not a little kid?

A: Yeah, you know, we don't get down like that, you know?

Q: Even if they do dirty shit? Are there some homies that want to retaliate and do dirty shit, too?

A: Yeah, 'cause, you know— I mean, the other people, they don't got nothing to do with it. So how you gonna go kill anybody and they don't got nothing to do with that?

Q: Why do you think they do that? Do you think they intentionally target people they know aren't gang members?

A: I mean, it is what it is, my boy. Like, that's how they handle business. Like, they can't handle things, you know? So, like, for them, they go and kill any Mexican and they're cool with that, you know? That's their *estilo* [style]. (SS Florencia 13, twenties)

However, perhaps unsurprisingly, *Sureño*-affiliated gang members weren't the only ones to report the perception that their rivals intentionally target unaffiliated civilians across racial lines. Many Crip- and Blood-affiliated gang members perceive their *Sureño*-affiliated rivals as being more willing to target innocent civilians than they are. Crip- and Blood-affiliated respondents were actually just as likely to report that *Sureño*-affiliated rivals had intentionally targeted innocent African American civilians as *Sureño*-affiliated respondents were to report that their Crip- and/or Blood-affiliated rivals had intentionally targeted innocent Latino residents of their community. Where Crip- and Blood-affiliated respondents did admit intentionally targeting innocent civilians in the Latino community, it was in retaliation for what they perceived as their *Sureño*-affiliated rivals' intentionally targeting African American civilians. With both sides of a racialized gang conflict interpreting events in the worst possible light, violence can quickly spiral out of control, with innocent civilians being inadvertently or intentionally targeted on both sides:

Q: Is it a thing where, like, everyone [is] just trying to get gang members on both sides? Or do innocent people get hit, too?

A: I mean, with them, they don't care. They gonna come through shooting anything, you know, like, man. . . . From the way I see it, that's the way it go down.

Q: Do you think they do it intentionally? Or do you think it's by accident, where they don't know who is and isn't actually a member of East Coast?

A: Intentionally, I think. They finna come through and just shoot up anything black. Anybody they see, it's kinda like vice versa from retaliation. If y'all come through just trying to shoot up anybody, then we finna do the same thing.

Q: Have innocent people on your side got hit?

A: Oh, yeah. I know some innocent people that got shot before.

Q: So if it happens, that's when your homeboys will retaliate in kind?

A: Yup.

Q: Other than that, is it usually only try and get gang members? Or is it open season all the time?

A: Naw. Yeah. It's only get gang members. We want to get the big fish, triple OG. I mean, not even the young one that's, like, fifteen. I'm talking, like, the one that's like thirty-seven.

Q: Trying to get the main shot callers, huh? Don't make a lot of sense to hit someone that ain't gonna hit you, right?

A: Yeah, exactly. (East Coast Crips, thirties)

There are a number of different strategies that gang members employ in targeting their rivals to accurately determine the affiliation of potential targets to be engaged. Easily the most common method is by "hitting up" potential targets—challenging them with the notorious three words, "Where you from?"—to find out whether they claim affiliation with a rival gang. Certainly, during the course of my fieldwork, and in my life growing up in Los Angeles, I have been met with a challenge of "Where you from?" more times than I can possibly recall, yet a minuscule fraction of those occasions have actually resulted in my being shot at. When gang members challenge a potential target with the ominous "Where you from?" the challenge in most cases is a genuine attempt to discern whether the subject is a member of a rival gang and therefore a suitable target to be engaged. If the person is not a member of a rival gang, gang members will typically hold their fire and continue on searching for a suitable target.

This is exactly why the "Florencia white T-shirt" moral panic is so absurd. Florencia gang members—or any gang members, for that matter—have no interest in shooting someone who is not a threat to them, so it makes little sense to suggest that they or anyone else would be targeting innocent unaffiliated residents for merely wearing white T-shirts. Rather, when on a "mission" to do a *jale*, Florencia gang members' common practice is to either hit up a potential target or yell out a "diss" to see what the potential target's reaction to the insult is. For example, the most common diss for East Coast Crips is to refer to them as Cheese Toast, a clever, unflattering play on the gang's name. East Coast members do the same thing, using the diss "Flowers" to insult a potential Florencia member. Such disses are common among and between gang members in Los Angeles. So when a Florencia member is on a mission to find a member of the East Coast Crips to shoot, he will yell "Fuck Cheese Toast!" at African American youths in East Coast Crips' territory and gauge their reaction to the insult. Likewise, an East Coast Crip will yell out "Fuck Flowers!" at cholos to gauge their reaction. If they react defensively, their reaction is interpreted as proof of affiliation, and they are thus legitimate targets to be engaged. If they react indifferently—for example, by responding, "So what? Fuck Cheese Toast!" or "Fuck Flowers!"—the shooter will likely hold his fire:

> Q: So if a black fool's wearing a white T-shirt, your homies aren't gonna necessarily think he's from East Coast?
> A: Naw. Pretty much what all of the homies do is when they see a black person, they always tell them, "Fuck Toast! Fuck Toast!" even if it's not in their hood, just to make sure. I guess our hoods don't like them at all. Even if we're in Orange County and we see a black person, we'll be like, "Fuck Toast!" 'cause, you know, I guess they just don't like them.
> Q: But black fools somewhere else won't know what they're talking about, right?
> A: [Laughs] Yeah. They'll be like, "What he talking 'bout?" [Laughs]
> Q: So you think that's the strategy homies use to see if it's a enemy or not? They'll just tell them, "Fuck Toast," just to see how they react?
> A: Yeah, either "Fuck Toast!" or tattoos. But you can't really see their tattoos 'cause they're so black. [Laughs]
> Q: Do you think that, when they try to bang on your hood, they make sure they're getting gang members only? Or do you think they get a lil' more loose with it?
> A: No, them, they're like that, too. If it's in their neighborhood and they see any Mexican passing by, they diss my hood and shit just to see what they do.
> Q: But if they're not from your hood, they'll just leave them alone?
> A: Naw. You know what? They'll prolly jack [rob] them or something.
> Q: But they're not out, like, trying to shoot Mexicans left and right just to get off, right?
> A: Nah. But they'll bang on every Mexican passing by. And if you look gang-related, they'll be like, "Woopty-woop!" [confrontational]. But they ain't gonna shoot you just for being Mexican. Neither are we. (SS Florencia 13, twenties)

When civilians are targeted, as noted earlier, the incidents almost always start out as cases of poor marksmanship, mistaken identity, or mistakenly attributed gang affiliation. Very few respondents reported that they would be willing to intentionally shoot innocent residents with no gang affiliation on the basis of racial identity alone, but most acknowledged that such mistakes had happened in the course of racialized gang conflicts. In some cases, these incidents are caused by Crip- and Blood-affiliated gang members' propensity to engage in drive-by shootings, which result in unintended victims' being inadvertently hit by stray bullets. *Sureño*-affiliated gang members generally view these incidents with contempt:

Q: When your homies are going at it with black gangs, do you think they try to target only gang members?

A: Yeah.

Q: Or does it ever cross over where they'll hit whatever black fool they see?

A: Naw, it's not like that. They homies, they make sure it's a enemy.

Q: Do you think black fools respect that too?

A: Well, not really. Like, the homies told us that now you can't just go and shoot anybody, like a drive-by, like, back in the days. Now we gotta get off the car and do all the extra—go up to them and ask them.

Q: Make sure he's actually from the neighborhood?

A: Yeah, make sure. Yeah.

Q: Do you think black fools follow the same rules?

A: Well, black fools, they drive-by. Like, every time they go dump on us, it's drive-bys.

Q: So they don't really care who they hit?

A: Yeah.

Q: Have they ever hit anybody that wasn't from your neighborhood?

A: Yeah.

Q: Like someone's brother or sister?

A: Yeah, my homie's little brother. They killed him.

Q: Do you think they did that on purpose, or do you think it was an accident?

A: It was a accident 'cause we were— We're all kicking it, and they drived-by shooting. They shot him in the head.

Q: He's the one that got hit?

A: Yeah.

Q: Have they ever hit anybody that wasn't from the neighborhood just for the fuck of it?

A: Naw, not that I know of.

Q: Do you think that they try and hit somebody that's actually a gang member?

A: Yeah.

Q: But they're just not as thorough as . . .

A: Yeah, they just don't make sure. (WS Drifters 13, teens)

Mistaken affiliation is another common reason unaffiliated civilians get targeted during racialized gang conflicts. As discussed in Chapter 3, *Sureño*-affiliated and Crip- and Blood-affiliated gang cultures are so different from one another that members of rival *Sureño*-affiliated and Crip- and Blood-affiliated gangs often have a genuinely difficult time identifying who is and is not a bona fide gang member by aesthetic appearance alone. Many of the cultural symbols that might denote gang affiliation within each gang culture are not recognized, or are misinterpreted, by members of the opposing gang. Couple that with the proliferation of gang injunctions in Los Angeles—and the corresponding trend among gang members on all sides to dress more casually and not conspicuously display their gang affiliation through clothing styles—and one can start to appreciate how difficult it is for gang members looking for suitable targets in a rival's territory to discern who is and who is not a bona fide gang member.

In the minds of a particularly overzealous or emotionally agitated gang member, anyone and everyone in a rival's territory could be perceived as a rival. Without prior knowledge of who specific rival gang members are by face, such confusion often leads to the shooting of unaffiliated civilians in cases of flat-out mistaken identity. However, it is worth noting that even when that does happen, as in the case recounted by an interviewee, the Blood gang whose neighborhood in which the civilian was killed decided to retaliate by targeting rival gang members rather than intentionally targeting an innocent civilian in the rival's territory:

Q: Has there ever been any innocent people, like, in your community—black people—that got hit that weren't actually gang members?

A: Yeah, actually. Just recently.

Q: That wasn't a gang member but got hit anyways?

A: Yes.

Q: Do you think that was something that they— That the other side did on purpose? Or [do] you think it could have been a case of mistaken identity?

A: Mistaken identity.

Q: You think they just saw someone and 'cause he was black and was the right age and everything, they thought he was a gang member but he wasn't?

A: They think everybody from our hood.

Q: And how did people in your neighborhood take that when an innocent person got hit? Did they feel like they need to go back and hit an innocent person to make even?

A: Yes, well, we didn't feel like we should go get an innocent person. We just felt like that's unacceptable.

Q: You should still retaliate?

A: Yeah, retaliate, but try to get them, not any innocent people.

Q: 'Cause you know how Mexicans say, "Only blacks shoot innocent people." That's bullshit, right?

A: Yes. I wouldn't shoot an innocent person 'cause I think, "I'm'a bang on him and see where he from." But I ain't gonna shoot the burner [firearm] until I see where he from, and then if he tell me some other hood that I beef with, then, yeah, you know?

Q: But if he's just some dude that's fucking coming home from work, just some regular guy?

A: Nah, I ain't gonna do nothing to him. (WS 235th Street Scottsdale Piru, teens)

Unfortunately, such restraint is not universal among Crip- and Blood-affiliated gangs. Some Crip- and Blood-affiliated respondents emphasized that they *would* intentionally target unaffiliated civilians in a rival's community, without compunction, if innocent residents were shot or killed in their community:

Q: Do they— Do you think when that was going on that there was, like, boundaries that certain people wouldn't cross? You know, like shooting up houses or shooting up people's brothers and sisters and shit like that?

A: When they came to our hood and shot a fifteen-year-old boy, we went back to they hood and found a fifteen-year-old boy and shot his ass. When the 18s go to the BPSs and killed that innocent black girl by accident, the BPSs went to the 18 Streets, found a innocent girl, and smoke her. (WS Rolling 90s Neighborhood Crips, twenties)

Such unapologetic willingness to target innocent victims was not reported by any *Sureño*-affiliated respondents, but, of course, such incidents are alleged to have occurred by law enforcement and the local media. Perhaps the most notorious such incident was the murder of fourteen-year-old Cheryl Green by Barrio 204th Street gang member Jonathan Fajardo in the

Harbor Gateway area of South Los Angeles in December 2006. Fajardo was convicted of first degree murder and later murdered by a fellow *Sureño*-affiliated gang member while on death row at San Quentin State Prison in 2018.[17] While law enforcement, local politicians, and the local media propagated a narrative of the murder as a racially motivated hate crime, Green was in fact an unintended victim of a careless shooter seeking revenge for having been beaten up earlier in the day by an African American motorist.[18] In his rage, Fajardo apparently either didn't realize or didn't care that children were playing directly in his line of fire when he began shooting at a group of African American men socializing at the end of a driveway. Nonetheless, the tragic murder became a media spectacle not only because the victim was a child, but also because the murder had occurred as a result of interracial violence. Ironically, Fajardo was himself Afro-Latino.[19]

When incidents occur across racial lines, emotions can run high, and gang members can, and do, cross lines they otherwise might not if the conflict was intraracial. As one insightful respondent pointed out, the level of maturity of individual gang members can determine how they respond to such incidents when they do occur. Mature, seasoned gang members are more likely to respond with calculated violence targeting those specific individuals they hold accountable, while younger gang members may react with emotion and intentionally target innocent civilians in their rivals' community for retaliation. While gang members, law enforcement, and the public may perceive certain gangs as more prone to targeting innocent victims intentionally, it is important to recognize that different individuals interpret and respond to events in different ways, even within a single gang. Furthermore, gang members who do intentionally target innocent victims are often held in contempt by those who do not. That is certainly true for *Sureño*-affiliated gangs, but it is also true for Crip- and Blood-affiliated gangs. I have never seen or heard of anyone "getting props" [being praised] for intentionally targeting civilians. When it does occur, those responsible invariably keep it to themselves:

> Q: As the beef unfolded over the years, of course, people have been hit on both sides. On the Blood side, how do people identify who's an acceptable target? Is it only 18s that are targeted? Is it considered acceptable for someone to go to the 18s' hood and anyone with a bald head they see, just hit them?
>
> A: I think it matters, but it depends on the individual who's doing it. There are individuals who are older, who are sneaky, [and] who

---

17. Lozano 2018.
18. Kim 2010.
19. Quinones 2007.

know how to get who they want. In other words, they know how to dress up like a bum or how to wait around a liquor store and catch the individual they're looking for. However, there are some that are young, and they'll just go out and shoot anything that looks like— So that's how a lot of, like, skateboarders and other people in that community that have that look get shot. But some of the older guys in the community knew how to do what it is they wanted to do. There was also a guy from 18 Street who for about seven years prolly killed fifteen people, between the Jungles [BPS] and the Rolling 20s, and he never shot a innocent child, either. He knew what he was doing, too.

Q: So you think it varies on an individual level, where some people are very focused on only getting gang members and some people are just loose and will hit whoever?

A: Right. I hate to say it, but it's the maturity level. The mature individual who knows who he wants is gonna wait on the opportunity to get the right person, as opposed to someone that is immature and wants to make a name for theyselves or wants to play like he big and bad. [He] will go and shoot something and say it was the toughest guy from 18 Street [when] it really might have been a stand-up father of two or something. (WS Rolling 20s Neighborhood Bloods, fifties)

The long-running conflict between 18 Street, Black P Stones, and Rolling 20s unfortunately has seen numerous incidents in which unaffiliated family and community members have been shot or killed. Without talking to the shooter in each case, however, it's hard to know whether the victims were intentionally targeted or, perhaps more likely, were victims of mistaken identity or suspected affiliation. It is certainly conceivable that, in most of the incidents of which I am aware, the shooters honestly mistook their victims for bona fide gang members. As good an example as any is the murder of my childhood friend Eddie.

Similar murders of young men with no bona fide gang affiliation in the BPS and Rolling 20s community have been committed by 18 Street gang members that were interpreted as provocative violations of the rules of engagement by BPS and Rolling 20s gang members when they occurred:

Q: Do you think people ever get to the point where they intentionally hit innocent people? Or you think if innocent people get hit, it's probably an accidental misidentification?

A: Yeah, I would never say that, because I never heard that or experienced it. I know a lot of people say that. That a young child—a thirteen-year-old in Baldwin Village—got killed, a basketball player who didn't gangbang at all, [that] really raised a lot of eyebrows, because they were saying a 18 Street came and shot him in cold blood. But I knew the youngster, and even though he didn't gangbang, he would play basketball in red shorts all the time, and he was getting tall—he was about five-foot-eight, five-foot-nine, at thirteen years old. So it could very well appear that they thought he was from Black Stone even though he was loved by so many people and it was a tragedy that he was killed. Or in the case of Jamiel Shaw, the young kid who went to LA High—was a football player—and he had a Spider-Man backpack, and it was red. They say the guy who been found guilty of his murder, they say he shot [Shaw] 'cause he was from Rolling 20s, but, of course, he wasn't from Rolling 20s, but he coulda gave that impression by living in the community and adapting to the color of red. That's just a community color, but that does not mean that an individual is a member of a gang.

Q: When things like that happen, do you think there are those who will intentionally go out and hit innocent people to retaliate, just to make a statement? Like, if you hit someone on our side, we gonna hit someone innocent on your side just to make a statement? On either side: Blood or 18 Street?

A: Yeah, with emotions so high, it's possible. I don't personally know of it, but is it possible? Of course it is. I'm gonna agree that it could be possible. I mean, some of these young kids with emotions so high are like, "Shit, I don't care who it is. I'm gonna hit something." (WS Rolling 20s Neighborhood Bloods, fifties)

As with all other aspects of gang violence, victims and perpetrators are found on all sides of the racialized gang conflicts that have plagued the Los Angeles region for decades. Focusing blame and prosecutions on one side or the other—as the local media, opportunistic politicians, and overly zealous law enforcement have done in Los Angeles, continually laying the blame for "racial violence" on *Sureño*-affiliated gang members—is an obfuscation of the complexity of racialized gang violence and an abdication of their obligation to mitigate rather than aggravate such conflicts. Such institutional favoritism only intensifies the animosity gang members feel for one another across racial lines. By defining gang conflicts in racial terms, gang members, law enforcement, the media, and the community do not just *interpret* such sectarian conflict as such, they *constitute it as racial conflict*, which has very real, material repercussions for the trajectory of the conflicts, and their ramifications, for both gang members and their communities.

6

CROSSING BOUNDARIES

Transracial Gang Identity

Despite the depth of division between *Sureño*-affiliated and Crip- and Blood-affiliated gang members in Los Angeles, the race-thinking logic that informs their racialized perceptions has some auspicious cracks in it that expose the porous boundaries of the invisible walls that divide them, culturally and conceptually. One of the most telling is the preponderance of *transracial* gang members, whose ubiquity in *Sureño*-affiliated and Crip- and Blood-affiliated gangs shatters the racial myths of exclusivity and immutability. Transracial gang members are gang members whose personal racial identity, by standards of phenotypic appearance, familial descent, or primordial origin, does not align with the racialized identity of the gang faction of which they are aligned—that is, non-black members of Crip- or Blood-affiliated gangs and non-Latino members of *Sureño*-affiliated gangs. The historical phenomenon of whites assuming a black identity has been generally referred to as "reverse passing."[1] However, in the case of transracial gang members, boundary crossers of this kind can be of virtually any ethnoracial origin. There are not only white Crips and Bloods but, more common, there are Crip- and Blood-affiliated gang members who are of Latino, Asian, and Pacific Islander origin. *Sureño*-affiliated gang members can be of virtually any ethnoracial origin, from Anglo to Armenian, Puerto Rican, Asian, Pacific Islander, Iranian, Jewish, or any combination of these and more, *ad infinitum*. The preponderance of transracial gang members in *Sureño*-affiliated and Crip- and Blood-affiliated gangs throughout Los An-

---

1. Brubaker 2016.

geles demonstrates both the illusion of racialized gang identities and the centrality of cultural praxis in determining the boundaries of racialized gang identities.

Contemporary ethnopolitical entrepreneurs on the neoliberal left have vigorously policed racial boundaries by viciously attacking anyone who dares to cross them. Of course, the most obvious example of this boundary policing is the moral panic that revolved around Nkechi Amare Diallo (formerly Rachel Dolezal) and the very public inquisition that she was subjected to as a result. In many cases, as I discussed in Chapter 2, these attacks were made under the guise of defending transgender identity transformation—in particular, the gender transformation of Caitlyn Jenner (formerly Bruce Jenner). This occurred around the same time that Diallo was being propelled to national pariah status as a result of a scheme by her Christian fundamentalist birth family to cover up the sexual abuse she and her adoptive (black) sister had suffered at the hands of their (white) elder brother. Diallo's birth family succeeded in that the criminal case against their son was dropped as a result of the moral panic around Diallo.

While I am reluctant to further entangle myself in the debacle of discourse surrounding the identitarian moral panic that ignited as a result of Diallo's mere existence, there is an aspect of the debate that remained almost entirely unexamined in the numerous rounds of hostile exchanges between scholars and pundits: the material existence and experience of transracial people and their communities. The debate over Diallo's identity largely revolved around theoretical and conceptual arguments as to whether she "is black" or "is white"; what defines "blackness"; and whether the conceptual coherence of racial categories has any salience for such a determination to have any meaning in the first place. What the debate did not do is consider the prevalence, circumstances, or experiences of actual transracial people and their communities. On one hand, this is an empirical matter. One commentator questioned whether "being transracial is actually a thing."[2] (This was considered the moderate position in the debate.) Another, more partisan pundit proclaimed that "transracial identity is *not* a thing!"[3]

Actually, as an empirical matter, the transracial experience *is* a thing, and it has been a thing for a very long time here in Los Angeles and in the American context more generally.[4] As I discussed in Chapter 2, Ann Morning and Rogers Brubaker remind us that reverse passing is not a new phenomenon in American society and prior to the moral panic surrounding Diallo, never garnered any comparable disapprobation or charges of appro-

---

2. Barbato 2015.
3. Blay 2015, author's emphasis.
4. Brubaker 2016; Liebler and Ortyl 2014; Liebler et al. 2017; Morning 2015.

priation from the putative left. Likewise, transracial gang members have long been an accepted anomaly in both African American and Chicano gangs in California. For example, two Cuatro Flats gang members discussed in barrio anthropologist James Diego Vigil's book *A Rainbow of Gangs* were transracial—one African American; the other of Asian descent.[5]

Despite the race-thinking logic of racialized gang identities, gang members are infinitely more accepting of those who dare to cross racial boundaries and live transracial existences than ethnopolitical entrepreneurs in academia ever will be. Even the principle racialized inmate organizations themselves have long histories of accepting transracial members, even at the highest levels. Perhaps the most renowned among them was the aforementioned Joe "Cocoliso" Morgan, who was one of the most highly respected members of the Mexican Mafia throughout his life, from the 1960s to his passing in 1993. Morgan was entirely of Slavic descent, by way of Yugoslavia, and had no Mexican heritage whatsoever. Nonetheless, he had grown up in the barrios of Boyle Heights in East Los Angeles and was a lifelong member of one of the oldest barrio gangs in that community: La Primera Flats.

The Black Guerrilla Family (BGF) also had a prominent Latino member: Hugo "Yogi" Pinell. He had joined the BGF under the leadership of George L. Jackson, whose exploits have become legendary in California penal history. Pinell was with Jackson when they and other African American and Latino inmates seized control of the Administrative Segregation Unit at San Quentin State Prison in 1971.[6] Pinell was well known throughout the African American prison community, and his murder in 2015 was mourned in African American communities from the Bay Area to Baltimore.[7]

In this chapter, I examine the existence, experience, and perceptions of transracial gang members and their peers in Los Angeles, particularly those who have crossed the boundary between black and brown. This is not only useful in that it is the first case study of a contemporary transracial population in the academic literature; it also demonstrates the conceptual incoherence of racialized gang identities, divisions, and conflicts. In total, forty-one out of sixty-seven *Sureño*-affiliated respondents reported that their gang had at least one black member, whereas only one Blood-affiliated respondent could not think of a Latino member among the thirty Crip- and Blood-affiliated respondents I interviewed. I interviewed one Latino Crip of Mexican descent and three black *Sureño*-affiliated gang members, two from the Boyle Heights section of East Los Angeles and one from the Long Beach area. One of them was fully African American; another was half–African

---

5. Vigil 2002b.
6. Weide 2020.
7. St. John 2015a.

American and half-Mexican; the third was Afro-Latino of mixed Caribbean and Central American ancestry but with a phenotypic appearance indicative of modern Sub-Saharan African origin. This chapter concludes with a consideration of their experiences and perspectives.

What's in a Name?

Along with the existence of transracial gang members, which has been documented for more than a half-century, another indication of the pervasiveness of transracial gang membership in *Sureño*-affiliated and Crip- and Blood-affiliated gangs is the widespread use of terms and monikers in the *Caló* and African American English Vernacular dialects to describe and name gang members in Los Angeles. Chicano culture has long recognized transracial identity and even has words to describe transracial members of the Chicano community, including whites, African Americans, and East Asians. The most common term of endearment ascribed to white and white mixed-race people accepted into the Chicano community is *güero* or, in common *Caló* vernacular spelling, *huero* (diminutive: *güerito* and *huerito*). This word originates in Mexican Spanish vernacular to describe someone of light complexion or someone of European origin who is an accepted member of Mexican society and cultural identity. The late Michael "Trigger" Pebley, from the Toonerville community in the Atwater/Glendale area of Northeastern Los Angeles, is a good example of a *güero*, or white *Sureño*-affiliated gang member (Figure 6.1).[8] The term contrasts with *gabacho* (or *gaba*) and *gringo*, terms that refer to Anglos who are not accepted members of Mexican or Chicano communities and culture and that carry the negative connotation of outsider status. Likewise, the common terms of endearment used to refer to Afro-Latinos or African Americans who identify as Chicano are *negro* and *moreno* (diminutive: *negrito* and *morenito*). These terms contrast with the Mexican Spanish vernacular racial epithet *mayate*, which is roughly equivalent to the N-word in American English. The unflattering etymology of the word traces back to the Nahuatl word *mayātl* (a type of black beetle).[9] Asians are commonly referred to as *chinos* (diminutive: *chinitos*), a neutral term that can be used either endearingly or derogatorily, depending on the context. Whether the object of the term is of Chinese descent or not is immaterial.

Sureño gang culture also has its own particular repertoire of monikers for transracial members. Of course, many of the terms that describe transracial members explained earlier are also used by transracial and mixed-race gang members as monikers. *Huero* is the most common moniker used

8. I delivered the eulogy at Pebley's funeral in 2014.
9. Pensinger 1974.

Figure 6.1. Mr. Trigger RIP, transracial white Toonerville gang member. (Courtesy of Estevan Oriol.)

by *Sureño*-affiliated gang members who are light-complected, of mixed European and Mestizo ancestry, or of entirely European origin. Another common term used to refer to transracial or mixed-race *Sureño*-affiliated gang members with light complexions or of European descent is *Ghost* or, in Spanish, *Spanto*. Also popular is *Casper*, the name of the friendly ghost from the popular post–World War II cartoon. Another common name for *güeros* in *Sureño*-affiliated gangs is simply the word *white* in Spanish: *Blanco*—the moniker of the late Eddie "Sleez" Testa, who was both an LA graffiti legend and a member of WS White Fence 13.

Likewise, *Negro* is a common moniker used by *Sureño*-affiliated gang members who are dark-complected, of mixed Afro-Latino ancestry, or entirely African American. *Moreno* is less common—in my experience, at least—though far from unheard-of. Other common names reserved for *Sureño*-affiliated gang members of modern Sub-Saharan African descent are *Blacky* and *Shadow*. The most common monikers used by *Sureño*-affiliated gang members of East Asian descent are *Chino* and *China Man*, whether or not the individual is of Chinese or other Asian descent. A mixed-race and transracial *Sureño*-affiliated gang member I have worked with in gang intervention uses both of those monikers, and his ancestry is half-Scottish and half-Korean. (He was not interviewed for this study.)

Crip- and Blood-affiliated gangs likewise have a repertoire of nicknames reserved for transracial gang members. Crips and Bloods of at least part-

Figure 6.2. Boo Ya Tribe Carson Piru. (Courtesy of Estevan Oriol.)

Mexican descent most often assume the moniker *Taco* or *Uno*. Another not uncommon practice is to simply add the word *Mexican* to one's given name. For example, a respected member of the Santana Blocc Compton Crips is an individual of Mexican descent who goes by the name Mexican Pete. (He was not interviewed for this study.) White members of Crip- and Blood-affiliated gangs are also not unheard-of, by any means. *Casper* is also a common moniker used by white members of Crip- and Blood-affiliated gangs, which should not be surprising, given the popularity of the cartoon character. Another common name for a white member is *Milk*, for obvious reasons. *Milk* is reportedly the moniker of Cameron Terrell, a blue-eyed, dirty-blond-haired member of the Rolling 90s Neighborhood Crips who grew up in the exclusive seaside community of Rancho Palos Verdes. Terrell was catapulted to media fame when he was charged in a gang-related murder and later acquitted at trial in 2018.[10]

A significant number of Crip and Blood gang members are of East Asian or Pacific Islander descent, particularly in the Long Beach and Harbor Area regions of Los Angeles County. Asian Crips and Bloods also use the monikers *Chino* and *China Man*, as well as *Budda* or *Buddah* for, perhaps, the more rotund homeboy. However, as some Crip- and Blood-affiliated gangs comprise majority-Asian or majority–Pacific Islander members, such as the

10. Santa Cruz 2018.

overwhelmingly Samoan American West Side Pirus in the city of Carson and the primarily Cambodian, Crip-affiliated Asian Boyz in Long Beach, they make proliferous use of monikers that are ubiquitous among African American gang members. Readers familiar with underground hip hop culture will recognize popular artists such as the classic 1990s hip hop group Boo Ya Tribe as affiliated with the Pirus and the contemporary artist Stupid Young as affiliated with the Asian Boyz, all reflecting a transracial Crip or Blood gang identity. Asian and African American Crips and Bloods freely intermix and interact in many regions of Los Angeles County, sharing community, culture, lovers, and, in many cases, enemies.

Transracial Identities, Cultural Categories, and Racialized Gang Membership

As Chapter 3 demonstrated, *Sureño*, Crip, and Blood identities are determined primarily by both cultural praxis and social location. Generally, those who grow up with members of a *Sureño-*, Crip-, or Blood-affiliated gang and adopt the racialized cultural identity associated with that affiliation will be accepted as members of the gang, irrespective of their ethnoracial phenotypic appearance or family heritage. African American youth who grow up in Boyle Heights, an almost universally homogeneous Chicano neighborhood in East Los Angeles, will likely grow up with Chicano peers and adopt their cultural practices, perspectives, and identity—and join predominantly Chicano *Sureño-*affiliated gangs. Likewise, some Latino youth who grow up in Leimert Park, Century, and Crenshaw—predominantly African American neighborhoods on the West Side of South Los Angeles—will likely adopt the cultural practices, perspectives, and identity of their predominantly African American peers and join predominantly African American Crip- or Blood-affiliated gangs in that area. In demographically mixed areas, individuals of any race can go either way.

However, while predominantly African American Crip- and Blood-affiliated gangs are almost universally accepting of non-black members, there is some degree of variation in the rules and practices of *Sureño-*affiliated gangs with regard to accepting African American members. Of the sixty-seven *Sureño-*affiliated respondents interviewed, twenty-six reported that their gangs have no African American members whatsoever. *Sureño-*affiliated gang members from South Los Angeles I interviewed were more likely to report having African American members in their gangs than were *Sureño-*affiliated gang members from racially homogeneous East Los Angeles. *Sureño-*affiliated gangs from mixed regions—mostly in South Los Angeles and the Harbor Area—were generally accepting of African American members as long as they

grew up with Chicano members of the gang and display the cultural repertoire, perspectives, and identity that correspond with a *Sureño* gang identity:

> Q: What do you think is different from black members in your
> neighborhood and other blacks?
>
> A: Well, he's— The color of his skin is black, but really he's Puerto Ri-
> can. But there's— There are blacks, full-blooded African Ameri-
> cans, in my neighborhood. It's just the way; the setting where you
> grew up in and how you grew up at, like, who— How can I put
> this? Let's say if I was to grow up in a black neighborhood with
> nothing but blacks, all my life. Obviously I'm'a act like them. I'm'a
> judge their way of living and the way of being based on the way of
> you growing up. Just like there's whites, but they act like homies.
>
> Q: So you think where you grew up plays a role in how you act?
>
> A: That definitely plays a major role. The way you grew up and the
> people you grew up with. (ES Longos 13, twenties)

Such cross-racial members are perceived and identified as full-fledged
Sureño-affiliated gang members and are sharply differentiated from African
Americans who are members of Crip- or Blood-affiliated gangs and who
maintain an African American cultural identity:

> Q: You mentioned your neighborhood had a couple of guys that
> were half-black, half-Mexican. Did you know of anybody that
> was full black?
>
> A: Yeah. Also my homeboy [name elided] was full black, I believe.
> Never met his parents, though, so— But I think he was real dark.
> But he might've been the only one.
>
> Q: But he didn't act like he was black?
>
> A: No. He spoke better Spanish than me.
>
> Q: Does it make it OK to have homies that are black or half-black in
> the neighborhood if they don't act black?
>
> A: Yeah, pretty much.
>
> Q: Do you think that's the boundary that determines if the guy is cool
> and can kick it or not?
>
> A: It's more— Yeah, you know what I mean? Like I said earlier:
> there's a difference between blacks and n—ers. You know, this
> guy was pretty— He was just black by skin, you know? He was a
> straight-up Chicano. He was straight-up, you know? This dude
> dressed like us, walked like us, talked like us. If he wasn't black
> or it was a dark room, you would swear he was one of us. He had
> the accent, everything, you know? (SC Clanton 14 Street, forties)

This respondent is clearly making a sharp conceptual distinction between an African American who happens to be "black by skin" but displays the appropriate indicators of a Chicano cultural identity and those he describes using the N-word because they maintain an African American cultural identity. While he did not use a racial epithet to differentiate between African Americans who assimilate to Chicano culture and those who don't, another respondent from South Central also made this distinction and connected it to which African Americans could be considered for membership and which could not:

Q: Is there a rule against that? Like, if somebody wanted to— Had a friend that was black and wanted to get in? Think homies would be like, "No way!"
A: Nah.
Q: So it depends on the individual?
A: Yeah, it depends on them. Yeah.
Q: You think it would be more acceptable if it's a black dude that grew up in the neighborhood, and, you know, like we were saying, acts Mexican and talks—
A: I'd rather have somebody in there that [has been] hanging around Mexicans all his life than somebody that just comes in like, "Hey, cuz. I wanna get jumped in, cuz."
Q: Do you think it's all good, like, for, like, you know, a lot of South Side neighborhoods have black fools, but it's cool because they act like South Siders—
A: Like Mexicans, the way they carry themselves. Like, for example, Mexicans— Like you could see the difference if you look at the South Siders and the Crips and blacks, like a difference in the way they dress, the way they act—
Q: So even if you see a black fool dressed like a South Sider, you realize, "OK this fool's not no Crip or Blood"?
A: Yeah exactly! (SC 46 Street Tokers, twenties)

The practice of accepting African Americans goes back generations in some of the older *Sureño*-affiliated gangs in South Los Angeles, such as South Central's 38 Street Locos:

Q: Was there ever rules against black fools being from the neighborhood?
A: Nah, 'cause I got homeboys from my neighborhood since, like, the 1930s and they're black—like, black black! Prolly back in the '40s when there was the Zoot Suit Riots and stuff like that, prolly back

then it was like that. But I got homies that's like seventy, eighty
years old, and they been from my neighborhood for, like, years
and years and years. I dunno. It all depends on that black person.
Q: So if they grew up in the neighborhood?
A: Yeah. If they grew up in the neighborhood, then they put them
in. (SC 38 Street, twenties)

Even *Sureño*-affiliated gangs in South Los Angeles that have a reputation for
animosity against African Americans, such as Florencia, accept African
American members if they grew up with Mexican members and assume a
Chicano cultural identity:

Q: Does your neighborhood have any black members?
A: Yeah, I think they're just black, but they were raised around Mexicans. They're whole time, you know? They act like a Mexican. It's
funny, though. [*Laughs*] 'Cause, you know, you ever seen a black
trying to talk Mexican? It's funny, you know? [*Laughs*]
Q: But they're like that 'cause they grew up in the hood with all *raza*,
right?
A: Oh, yeah, because, you know, they're homies. It can't just be a
normal black person trying to get into the hood, you know? It
can only be someone that grew up and knows you real good, you
know? (SS Florencia 13, twenties)

However, in contrast, there are some older traditional *Sureño*-affiliated
gangs, particularly those from homogeneously Chicano communities on the
East Side, that do not accept African American members under any circumstances and whose members look disparagingly on African American members of *Sureño*-affiliated gangs, as well as *Sureño*-affiliated gangs who do
accept African American members. They thus refuse to acknowledge cultural identities and instead insist on primordial racial identity as absolute.
Such perspectives are typically remnants of previous generations who did
not grow up with the cultural diffusion that exists in the modern era. A
veterano from one of East Los Angeles's oldest Chicano gangs represented
this perspective without compunction:

Q: Has your neighborhood ever had anyone who was black in it?
A: Not to my knowledge, no.
Q: Is there a rule against that?
A: That's just the way it is. It's a unwritten rule.
Q: What do you think the homies would say if someone was like,
"Aye, I wanna get my homeboy in the neighborhood right here?"

A: Aye, he got to go, and you gotta go with him.

Q: What do you think about, like, in South Central it's pretty common for South Side neighborhoods to have black members in them?

A: Aye, that's on them. The East Side is different. You meet a person from the East Side, we have a whole different upbringing, morals, than other sections—South Central, the South Side, the West Side, Compton. All them other areas. It all began in the East Side, and them other cats just fucked it off.

Q: Do you think that's, like, a sign of weakness that these other neighborhoods put blacks down?

A: Yeah, because they, you know— When I meet a black homie from some other fuckin' place—like, "I'm fuckin' whatever from whatever"—I won't even shake his hand. To me he's still black, I don't acknowledge them. I never have. I never even tried to. For what? He's still a n—er!

Q: How does that work out when you're locked up? 'Cause there's fools who are South Siders but they're black.

A: I don't mess with them. Like I said, I won't shake their hand. I won't fuck with them. You can't be in my cell. You're black. That's it. Fuck you.

Q: How much do you think that's a common point of view? Like, do you know other South Siders who won't fuck with a homie if he's black?

A: Oh, yeah, I know for a fact. I know for a fact that a lot of homies feel like me. Yup. Stick with your own. (ES Clover Street 13, fifties)

While forty-one of the sixty-seven *Sureño*-affiliated respondents who were interviewed acknowledged that they do have African American members in their gangs, fewer *Sureño*-affiliated respondents reported formal or informal rules against accepting African American members than reported actually having African American members. Furthermore, there was a significant difference in *Sureño*-affiliated respondents from homogeneous East Los Angeles reporting formal or informal rules against accepting African American members when compared with *Sureño*-affiliated respondents from heterogeneous South Los Angeles. When compared with *Sureño*-affiliated respondents from East Los Angeles, *Sureño*-affiliated respondents from South Los Angeles were significantly less likely to report the existence of any formal or informal rules against African American members in their gangs. This lends support to the previous respondent's perspective that *Sureño*-affiliated gangs in East Los Angeles are less accepting of transracial membership than are *Sureño*-affiliated gangs in South Los Angeles. Clearly, the difference between the regions is their degree of demographic heterogeneity and corresponding cultural diffusion and familiarity.

Ironically, the refusal of leaders of one particular *Sureño*-affiliated gang in East Los Angeles, Barrio East Side State Street 13 (formerly known as Barrio State Park), to accept an African American member in the early 1990s was a significant historical crossroads that eventually led to the emergence of one of the largest gangs in East Los Angeles: Krazy Ass Mexicans (KAM) 13. That fateful decision to uphold rules against transracial membership ultimately resulted in the eventual loss of more than half of State Street's traditional territory to KAM, which was started as a graffiti crew in the 1980s by a group of mostly Chicano youth and one African American youth who grew up together in the Boyle Heights area just east of Soto Street, between the Interstate 10 freeway and Cesar Chavez Avenue (formerly Brooklyn Avenue). KAM was part of the widespread "tagbanger" subculture prevalent in Los Angeles that was brought to popular consciousness in a series of reports on the local Fox 11 News channel in the early 1990s.

Some of these groups, such as the one I was member of in the early 1990s, eventually cease to function as coherent entities and die out as members "age out" into more conformist lifestyles of union workers, small-business owners and operators, skilled laborers, and college professors. Other tagbangers eventually get absorbed into the larger hegemonic gangs in their area: a common career trajectory for gang members in Los Angeles is tagger to tagbanger to gangbanger. However, some tagbangers eventually morph into full-fledged gangs in their own right, surviving as a coherent group and taking on other established gangs in their area. Although this is rare; KAM is perhaps the most successful example of tagbangers that made a successful transition into a bona fide gang.

Unfortunately, and perhaps ironically, for State Street, the insistence on enforcing a ban on black membership ultimately led to the loss of much of their traditional territory, as KAM, led in large part by the African American boy to whom State Street *veteranos* had denied membership more than two decades earlier, grew into one of the largest and most violent gangs in all of East Los Angeles:

> Q: Can you be black and be from your neighborhood?
> A: Yeah, actually I had a really good friend, a really tight friend of mine growing up, that was kinda like my lil' soldier, like my lil' protégé growing up, and he was black. He lived actually on the other side of my neighborhood.
> Q: Was he from your neighborhood?
> A: He wasn't from my neighborhood, but he grew up with the other

side, with the other neighborhood [KAM]. He wasn't gangbang-ing when I was gangbanging, he was just kinda like fucking around trying to get down with us, for the simple fact he had a lot of heart. He was really down, and you know I schooled him, but just the fact that he was black— I would bring him around to my neighborhood, and my homeboys would be like, "Oh, why the fuck you bringing this fuckin' *mayate* to our neighborhood?" and just kinda dissing him in front of me. And I would feel bad because lil' homie wouldn't say anything because he had respect for all the older homies, but he was, like, all butt hurt over that shit, you know? The older homies were like, "You know there's no *mayates* in the neighborhood. That's never gonna happen." So he kinda just stopped kicking it with us and stood to the other side, and I would still be like, "What's up?" and still go over there and be like, "You're part of us. Why ain't you kicking it no more?" And he'd be like, "Oh, your homeboys are disrespecting me. They don't want no blacks in the neighborhood. So what's the point of me being over there? I'm just gonna stick to this side." And he ended up getting in the enemy neighborhood.

Q: He's from KAMsters?

A: Yeah, he's from KAMsters. He's a soldier to this day. You know what? He's really solid. I hear good things about him. He's actu-ally up there. He hit the system and he became a somebody be-cause he had to prove himself, you know? He was black and he was running with the homies, so he actually put in a lot of work where, like, to this day I hear he's really up there. He's a solid-ass dude. (ES State Street 13, forties)

In East Los Angeles, project gangs such as Primera Flats, Cuatro Flats, Big Hazard, and Varrio Nueva Estrada have commonly had a number of African American members who were or are accepted as full-fledged mem-bers of their neighborhoods because they grew up with Chicano members in housing projects in East Los Angeles, such as Aliso Village, Pico Gardens, Ramona Gardens, and Estrada Courts. In contrast, older gangs whose neighborhoods consisted mostly of single family homes and, later, private apartment complexes, such as East Side White Fence, State Street, and Clo-ver Street, tended to hold a strict line on not allowing African American members in their gangs.

Neighborhoods in Southeast Los Angeles such as South Gate, May-wood, Vernon, Cudahy, and Bell, which once had modest populations of Anglo-Americans and African Americans, have become almost entirely homogeneously Latino in recent decades, as they have been a common destination for first-generation immigrants and their families from Mexico and other parts of Latin America. However, in previous generations, when the presence of African American residents was not uncommon, their membership in local *Sureño*-affiliated gangs was not unheard-of. As the demographics of these areas have moved toward a more homogeneously Latino population, some of the older, more traditional local gangs in Southeast Los Angeles took on a more intolerant view of accepting black members. Earlier in our formal interview, a *veterano* from Kansas Street told me that the gang had had two African American members in the 1980s, whereas now such cross-racial membership would not only be unacceptable but, in fact, contemptible:

> Q: Was there an exception for those two black guys because they grew up in your neighborhood?
>
> A: I think because they grew up and they were, like, part of us, bro, you know? You grew up like us, you are like us, so to speak, right?
>
> Q: What if now somebody brought some black guy around—for example, from school?
>
> A: There'd be problems. Yeah, there'd be problems. They would probably fuck him up. I think the homies would have probably fucked him up and told 'em, "Nah, you can't be from my neighborhood." We would have probably just fucked 'em up just to fuck 'em up.
>
> Q: What do you think about other gangs that allow black guys to be from the neighborhood? Do you think it is a bad look? Do you think they do it because they are weak and recruit blacks? Why do you think people do that?
>
> A: Honestly, yeah, they don't care. Like 18 Street— Yeah, I think its weak, bro. I think it's because some people are hurt. I mean, yeah, they're hurting so bad for numbers that they'll lower their standards. (SS Kansas Street 13, thirties)

The perception that having cross-racial members is a sign of weakness in a gang was reported by twenty-one of the sixty-seven *Sureño*-affiliated respondents I interviewed, whereas only one Crip-affiliated respondent reported such a sentiment. However, he admitted that his gang had a number of transracial Latino members. As the respondent from Southeast Los Angeles reported, this sentiment was widespread among *Sureño*-affiliated respondents, particularly those who belonged to gangs that did not accept African American members. A significant difference was also found between the perceptions of *Sureño*-affiliated respondents from East Los Angeles and *Sureño*-affiliated respondents from South Los Angeles, with *Sureño*-

affiliated respondents from East Los Angeles more likely to hold contempt for *Sureño*-affiliated gangs that accept African American members than *Sureño*-affiliated respondents from South Los Angeles.

Predominantly African American Crip- and Blood-affiliated gangs are markedly more accepting of cross-racial Chicano members than *Sureño*-affiliated gangs are of accepting African American members, and transracial gang membership that crosses the black-brown binary is much more common in Crip- and Blood-affiliated gangs than in *Sureño*-affiliated gangs. However, as in *Sureño*-affiliated gangs that accept black members, Latino members of Crip- and Blood-affiliated gangs must demonstrate and display the appropriate repertoire of cultural literacy and praxis expected of a racialized Crip or Blood gang identity. In other words, cholos are not accepted as members in Crip- and Blood-affiliated gangs.

However, for Chicano, white, or Asian youths who grow up in predominantly African American neighborhoods and associate with primarily African American peers, joining a predominantly African American gang is a natural progression. Their African American peers will look on them as an "honorary black person," as one respondent put it—that is, thought of in terms of their culturally determined racialized gang identity rather than their primordial racial identity. When reflecting on their relationships with Chicano members of their gang in formal and informal interviews, Crip- and Blood-affiliated gang members universally pointed to cultural praxis as the tie that binds them to the gang:

Q: Does your neighborhood have any Latino members?
A: Yes. I'd say it's a small percentage, I could think of about four to five people right now, so I would prolly say 10 percent.
Q: And the reason they're from your hood and not from a Mexican gang is that they grew up with you guys?
A: Yeah, but, you know, the Mexicans we grew up with [are from] a Mexican gang in our neighborhood and we're not at war with them: the Harpys. So there is a Mexican gang there, but it's not a issue.
Q: What do you think caused those kids to choose to be from your hood and not from Harpys?
A: I think the friendships; who they chose as friends growing up.
Q: Do you think another part of that is that culturally they tend to act more black and carry themselves more like blacks do?
A: Right. I would say that, yes. But I think it's because of who they chose as their friends when they were in school, because two of them, they mothers are traditional Mexican women who speak

just a slight amount of English. It's primarily that they adopted the culture of the blacks. (WS Rolling 20s Neighborhood Bloods, fifties)

As another respondent described, the same goes in Watts, where African American project gangs traditionally have taken on more and more Latino members. As first-generation immigrant populations from Mexico and other Latin American countries have come to occupy many of the private housing and apartment stock adjacent to the public housing projects in Watts, Latino membership in the traditional Crip- and Blood-affiliated project gangs has become increasingly common. Those Latino youths who befriend African American peers in their formative years and adopt African American cultural identities will typically join the Crip- or Blood-affiliated gangs closest to their residence, if they decide to join a street gang, and they will be accepted by their African American peers as bona fide members:

Q: Your neighborhood has Mexicans in it, right?
A: Yes, it does.
Q: Are they accepted the same as black members?
A: Yes. Very much accepted.
Q: Everybody's the same?
A: Yes.
Q: And that's 'cause you grew up together, right? You've known them since you were little?
A: Yes.
Q: Do they have more of, like, a black style or they're not like cholos, right?
A: They're nothing like cholos, but they— They very much have a black style and a way of talking, but not— Not all of them, though some really, they're from the neighborhood and they let that be known and they still— You know how there are Mexican tradition about them, but they don't dress cholo or nothing.
Q: You think they adopt more black culture than Mexican culture?
A: Oh, yeah. Fo sho! (Watts Bounty Hunter Bloods, twenties)

Even Crip- and Blood-affiliated gangs that are particularly known for their animosity toward Latinos are known to accept Chicano members. The East Coast Crips, the archnemesis of Florencia 13, also accepts Latino members, just as Florencia accepts African American members, as long as they demonstrate the cultural repertoire commensurate to their adopted racialized gang identity:

Q: Does your neighborhood have any Mexican members?

A: Yeah, we do. About, like, seven.

Q: Out of how many?

A: Well, I know a couple from 89 [East Coast Crips]; I know one from 78 [East Coast Crips].[11] Yeah, I know some.

Q: So it's not totally out of the ordinary?

A: No, not at all.

Q: Are they accepted by everybody?

A: Yeah, they are.

Q: You think they act more like they black than they Mexican?

A: Yeah, most of 'em do. Most of 'em do.

Q: They're not all bald-headed, size-fifty pants pulled up to they chest and shit?

A: Oh, naw. Naw. Hell, naw! (East Coast Crips, thirties)

I have heard of only one instance of a member of an African American gang asserting that his gang does not accept Mexican members, and that was in a National Geographic documentary in which a Blood-affiliated gang member stated that Mexican members are prohibited in his gang.[12] I was unable to find any Crip- or Blood-affiliated gang members who would repeat that claim.

As discussed in Chapter 3, one of the most conspicuous and unambiguous indicators of the adoption of a transracial Crip or Blood identity is the common use of the word *nigga* as a term of endearment.[13] This must be differentiated from the racial epithet from which it was derived.[14] Casual use of this term of endearment in common vernacular is a conspicuous indicator of both the adoption of an African American cultural identity and a certain comfort level with African American culture and African American people. Even members of *Sureño*-affiliated gangs who grow up in demographically mixed communities with African American peers commonly use the term of endearment in their daily vernacular. This practice can get them into trouble in carceral environments with *Sureño*-affiliated gang members who are less accepting of indicators of affinity for an African American cultural identity and, in some cases, vigorously police those vernacular boundaries:

A: Mexicans— Most of the Mexicans that grew up in South Central, they act like blacks. That's what we say, you know? Everybody act

---

11. Pronounced "Eight-Nine" and "Seven-Eight," respectively.

12. *Inside Bloods and Crips* 2008.

13. Where *nigga* is used as a term of endearment rather than a racial epithet, I do not elide it.

14. See Smitherman 1977, 62; Smitherman 1994; Smitherman 2000, 210–212.

like— They say *nigga*, we don't look at 'em like, "Oh, he racist 'cause he say *nigga*." They say *nigga* to each other, you know? They could say it and don't nobody get offended. I could tell 'em— I always tell Mexicans, "Y'all can say it. It's white people that can't say it." [*Laughs*]

Q: If you grew up in the hood, you could say it, right?

A: Pretty much, yeah.

Q: So you think Mexicans that are from black gangs tend to act more black than Mexicans from Mexican gangs?

A: Yeah. People tell 'em that. Like the youngster I was telling you about from Playboys: when he got to prison 'cause he talk, now he talk black. Now, if he was a South Sider, you couldn't tell, and I would say that. That go back to the question you asked me earlier. Most of 'em— There's Mexicans in South Central that if they speak in the one room then the other one, you prolly couldn't tell if they was Mexican or black, right? And I remember he got into it with— He was trying to parole, and he got into it with some Mexicans. I think they was from over there in East LA. Something like that. And because one of these South Siders over there was like, "Why don't you go with the blacks 'cause, I mean, you act black anyway." . . . He had to step up to him [and fight] 'cause he was disrespectful.

Q: So he missed his parole day?

A: [*Laughs*] Yeah, you could say that. (ES Blood Stone Villains, forties)

While the individual from the Playboys this respondent referenced obviously was defending his honor by engaging in the fight after being accused of crossing the racial line that defines opposing racialized gang identities, it's important to recognize the policing of such boundaries by *Sureño*-affiliated gang members themselves, not because they mistake the term of endearment for a racial epithet, but because of their own antiblackness.

In Their Own Words

Of the three transracial black *Sureño*-affiliated gang members I interviewed, two had grown up in public housing projects in the Boyle Heights section of East Los Angeles. The fully African American respondent had lived in the projects his whole life, as had his parents. The respondent who was of mixed race—half–African American and half-Mexican—had likewise lived in the housing projects his gang claimed as their territory his whole life, with the exception of short periods in other areas after his family was evicted from the projects because of his gang membership. The Afro-Latino respondent had grown up in the Long Beach neighborhood that his gang claimed as its territory; his mother had likewise lived there since she had immigrated from the Caribbean as a child and was a member of the same gang. The mixed-race respondent was the product of a marital arrangement that must have been exceptional in East Los Angeles at the time:

> Q: Do you know how your parents met?
>
> A: At a bar. My mom worked at a bar that my dad used to go to. See, it's a trip to this day—well, if they were still alive—but my mom didn't know no English and my dad didn't know no Spanish. He never took the time to learn it. Before growing up, my mom would be like, "Aye, what is your dad saying?" and my dad would be like, "What is your mom saying?" you know? And I would be like, "Damn! When we're not around, how do you talk?" and she said they didn't. They used signs and stuff.
>
> Q: And they were married?
>
> A: Yeah.
>
> Q: Damn! So they met and fell in love and got married and all that but couldn't speak to each other?
>
> A: Yeah. [*Laughs*]

All three transracial *Sureño*-affiliated respondents felt that they had chosen to join *Sureño*-affiliated gangs and identify as cholos because they had been raised in a Chicano community; as a result of their upbringing in a Chicano social and cultural context, that identity came naturally to them. Each had strongly identified with a Chicano cultural identity, which explicitly aligned them with a *Sureño* racialized gang identity, irrespective of their own racial category in any primordial sense. From their perspective and that of their peers and community, cultural praxis trumps primordial racial identity. As one respondent put it, "I was born and raised in East LA, so everything I knew was Mexican."

The African American respondent self-identified as African American and did not explicitly deny or disidentify with blackness. The mixed-race respondent identified as "Hispanic" or "*raza*" but would identify as black in certain contexts, such as when he was with his African American family in a historically black community in South Los Angeles. This demonstrates the inherently arbitrary and therefore malleable nature of racial identity, as well as his ability to code switch between African American and Chicano communities on opposite sides of town:

Q: Under what circumstances would you identify as black to anyone?

A: Like, with my peoples, like, on my dad side. Naw, but they understand. They know I'm from a Mexican hood and everything.

Q: Oh, so it depends on what context you're in, huh? If you're around blacks, you'll tell 'em you're black, whereas if you're in the hood, you're *raza*?

A: Yeah. Yeah.

The Afro-Latino respondent emphatically disidentified with blackness, which he associated with African Americans, whereas Latinos of dark complexion like him were not genuinely "black" in his view:

A: My dad's dark. He's like a black guy.

Q: So you think your dad probably has some African heritage?

A: That's just— That's just how Panamanian, Belize, Honduras, Cuba— They're just, you got some dark, some white, you got caramel, you got toners like me.

Q: But it's not the same as black?

A: No, it's like a *moreno de Americo pero moreno de Latino*.[15] It's different.

However, because of his very black phenotypic appearance, he is often mistaken for African American, to which he immediately and emphatically objects. This is particularly significant in carceral settings, where sharp identity boundaries divide racialized inmate factions:

A: It's hard in prison sometimes, 'cause they'll just go by your color sometimes, you know?

Q: When you're locked up, people think you're black when they first see you?

A: Yeah, and then when they talk to me, they'll be like "Oh." Like, one time they trapped me in a black cell, and I walked to the door and I go, "What the fuck is this?" She [prison guard] was like, "Go inside." I'm like, "I'm not opening that door, man. You fuckin' crazy? I'm not one of them," you know? And, umm, she was like, "What are you?" I said, "I'm Caribbean." She was like, "Oh, you're an 'other' then." I'm like, "I'm not an 'other.' I'm a *Sureño*," you know? I'm going where I belong with the homies.

---

15. Translation: African American versus Afro-Latino.

The respondent was just as adamant about making clear to African Americans who tried to befriend him on the basis of shared racial identity that he wanted nothing to do with them:

> Q: When you first started getting locked up, how did people respond to you? Would anybody question you?
> A: Like, "Where you from?" I would tell them my neighborhood.
> Q: When they found out you're a South Sider there?
> A: They just walk away.
> Q: Have you ever ran into blacks in the system who are like, "Oh, you're black. You should . . . "
> A: Yeah.
> Q: What'd you tell 'em?
> A: I just tell 'em, "Fuck you."

His case is particularly interesting because, although he has a very dark phenotypic appearance that betrays modern Sub-Saharan African origin, he is a member of a *Sureño*-affiliated gang that has a history of intense racialized conflict with Crip-affiliated gangs.

As discussed in the previous section, transracial gang members are accepted as bona fide members of the community and are loved and defended as any member of the gang would be. While their primordial racial category may open them to slurs and attacks from rivals, the loyalty gang members have for one another is unmistakable for those who do have transracial homies. The oldest of the three respondents shared the following recollection from his formative years before going to prison:

> Well, I can say that I've been certain places where I've had— Me and some of my friends had altercations. And the only reason we had an altercation was that someone else, from somewhere else, called me the N-word, and my friends started fighting. And I found out afterward why they started fighting. So they were very protective of me and that term was never directed at me in the environment I grew up in. So they were less tolerant of anyone else using it toward me, and it was once told to me specifically like that: "We don't use that term, so we won't allow anyone else to use that term to you."

With regard to the kind of interracial bias and prejudice discussed in the previous chapter, the transracial respondents gave mixed responses. One of them was largely unbiased in socializing across racial lines as long as it occurred with black family in a black community where other *Sureño-*

affiliated gang members would not be around to judge. However, his position was context-dependent and would change when he was on the East Side:

Q: Would you ever consider living in a black neighborhood?

A: Well, I stayed in the Crenshaw district. See, it don't really bother me 'cause I guess I'm half-black, so, like, I don't even really trip. Like, I said I stayed in Leimert Park, and it's all blacks right there, but it doesn't bother me.

Q: Does anyone trip on you when you're over there?

A: Naw, 'cause all my nephews at my sister's house. It was like a kick-it house; all the blacks would come over. Smoke some blunts, drink some 40s [forty-ounce bottle of beer] with them, like that.

Q: So it doesn't bother you to kick it with them?

A: At first it didn't. I would keep on lying to myself—like, I would never smoke with a black fool. Got me fucked up. I would never put my mouth after a *tinto* [African American] just hit that blunt. But I was just lying to myself 'cause I was over there chilling for a few months.

Q: In the neighborhood, do the homies still trip on that? Like, if someone was to be kicking it with the black residents drinking and smoking after them?

A: Oh, yeah. I know I'll trip, to keep it real. I'll trip.

Q: But when you go over to your sister's pad over there in Leimert, you're over there, so it's not a issue?

A: Yeah, exactly.

In contrast, another transracial black respondent was adamant about maintaining boundaries between African Americans and Latinos. He had inherited this perspective from his mother, his homeboys, and his community at large, even though he had a phenotypic appearance that clearly indicated modern Sub-Saharan African origin—that is, he looked black but had a shaved head, cholo tattoos, and a formidable moustache:

Q: Do you date both Mexican and black girls? Does it matter to you?

A: No black girls.

Q: You don't date black girls?

A: I talk to— I, well— I— I.

Q: Would you have sex with one?

A: Not a full black girl.

Q: Only if she's—

A: Black, white. And Mexican.

Q: Mestizo or whatever?

A: Yeah. But she can't really be dark, dark as me.

Q: So all your girlfriends have been Latinas?

A: All Mexicanas and Latinas.

Q: So you wouldn't date or marry a girl that was black-black, like, [who] grew up with blacks?

A: No. Won't date a black girl.

Q: Why not?

A: My neighborhood is really racial. It's just, my neighborhood's just like the KKK, Nazi thing almost.

Q: Would you be opposed to your family members dating a black person—like, if your little sister wanted to date a black guy?

A: It'd be hard for me to get over it. Yeah.

Q: Would you say something to her about it?

A: Yeah.

Q: How about your mom? How does she feel about that type of thing?

A: Well, back in the day, before my mom changed [reformed] her life, she was like, uh, "I ever see you with a black girl in my house—aye, that's it."

Q: She told you straight up?

A: "Don't!" 'Cause she would be gone, and I would trip. She'd be like, "And you won't be my son."

The Mexican Crip I was fortunate to have interviewed was from a gang in South Los Angeles, where he had grown up in a predominantly African American community. He openly identified as both black and Mexican, and by that he didn't mean "Blaxican."[16] He said that he is a person of entirely Mexican origin who identifies as black, a perfect example of transracial gang membership—and an intriguing one, given the racial animosity between *Sureño*-affiliated and Crip- and Blood-affiliated gangs in Los Angeles. Further, this isn't just his perception. All of his African American peers consider him genuinely black. As he recounts, "Everybody that I hang around be like, 'He black. Yeah, you black.'" However, African Americans he doesn't know personally often question his blackness at first, reflecting the identity boundary policing that confers salience on racialized taxonomies. Only after getting to know him do they withdraw their objections:

Q: Have you ever felt any, like, exclusion from other black people?

A: Yes, I have actually, because they didn't know me.

Q: So if somebody doesn't know you, they might use that against you?

---

16. Romo 2011.

A: Yup.

Q: But the [black] people who you grew up with, they know you, so they don't say anything like that?

A: Yeah, yeah. But, like, if I was to go outside my circle and some-body don't know me, they might question me, like, "Who is you and why is he saying *nigga* and shit?" But, you know, once they get to know me, they understand.

The irony is that his phenotypic appearance is strongly suggestive of at least part modern Sub-Saharan African descent, though he is unaware of any direct ancestors from that region. His hair is "kinky" and he wears it in an Afro or woven into elaborate braids. His facial structure appears analogous to that found in the African Sahel rather than in *Indígenas* Mesoamerica, and I can think of numerous prominent African Americans whose skin tone is far lighter than his. If I did not know him and saw him walking down the street, I would assume he was African American or, at least, mixed-race based on his phenotypic appearance, not to mention his presentation of self.

Like all of the transracial gang members I interviewed, he felt that he had to go above and beyond to prove himself to his black peers, both those in his own gang and potential rivals:

Q: Do you think that you being Mexican from a black hood, like, you had to do more?

A: Yeah, I had to go hard. I had to prove myself to a whole lot of people—not only my gang, but a lot of other gangs, too.

Q: Do you think [black] people would try you more because you're Mexican?

A: Not just try me; like, ask to fight me then and there. But go on a basketball court, they prolly a lil' more aggressive toward me. If we sitting at the domino table, they might talk a lil' more shit to me, you know? Just like a lil' more aggressive with me. I had to stand up and poke my chest out, like, "I dunno what you think this is, but it ain't that!"

Perhaps not surprisingly, given his unique experience, he was adamant about protecting the victims of interracial bias, regardless of whether the victim or the aggressor was black or Latino:

Q: Is there anything about the way that black or Latino people act, or anything about them at all, that bothers you?

A: Only when somebody being racist. I don't care if it's a black person or a Hispanic person if he the one being racist. I won't like [a] black person being racist against a Mexican in front of me. I don't go for that. And I won't like a Hispanic Mexican acting racist to a black person. I don't go for that.

Q: Is that because of who you are, being Mexican from a black hood?

A: Yeah, you know, I'm Mexican, so I won't let a black person press up on a Mexican for no reason. But I mess with the black people, so I won't let a Mexican act racist toward them, either. It's like I'm stuck in the middle, you know? Just trying to hold each other back from that negativity.

His account of how he assumed a black transracial identity in the first place was intriguing in that it seemed rather arbitrary: it emerged out of his choice of sports in elementary school. As an avid basketball player in his youth, he gravitated toward the overwhelmingly African American peers with whom he played basketball in his community. He recounted:

Since I was about eight or ten years old, where we lived, it was predominantly blacks, you know? And I like to play basketball, so, you know, other people in the neighborhood, mostly blacks, liked to play basketball, as well. So, you know, I go on the court to play basketball, and I knew how to play, and they knew how to play, so I gravitated toward them because they was more around me. Since I was about ten years old, most of my friends were black, and my best friend was black, and I went to school mostly with blacks.

All of the respondent's uncles were actually *Sureño*-affiliated gang members from the San Fernando Valley, as were all of his cousins in the neighboring community of Watts. So had it not been for his love of basketball, he might well have joined a *Sureño*-affiliated gang:

When I was younger, I used to hang with my cousins. I got cousins from [the] Watts Varrio Grape Street [gang]. I used to hang with them. I'm talking about, I was, like, five years old, smoking weed with them at seven. The only reason I gravitated toward black people was 'cause of basketball. The basketball is what got me hanging with black people. You know, I be like, "What's up? Y'all playing ball today?" It's crazy, 'cause if I liked to play soccer when I was younger, I coulda gone the other way.

Not surprisingly, based on the data provided in Chapter 4, the respondent's mother, a native of Michoacán, initially opposed his friendships with black peers and relationships with black women:

Q: So in your family, was anyone in your family ever opposed to dating across racial lines?

A: My mother. She didn't like it at first. She was totally against it. You know, I remember this one time, this girl I had with me in my house was black, and [my mother] was, like— In Spanish, she told me, *"Por qué estás con esa mujer?"* [Why are you with this woman?] And I'm, like, "What do you mean?" She like, *"No deberías estar con esa mujer"* [You shouldn't be with that woman]. Like, "What you mean, ma?" She like, *"No está bien"* [It's not OK].

His mother eventually relented after he and his siblings started having children with black men and women. Antiblackness can only go so far:

Q: What happened? She just gave up at some point?

A: Yes, she did. She did. Her grandkids— Her daughters started being mixed with black people, so she had to. Yup.

Another issue that has received a great deal of lay commentary but no scholarly consideration to date is the supposedly standing green light *Sureño*-affiliated gang members have put on Mexican members of African American gangs. Folklore has it that, in carceral environments, transracial Crip- and Blood-affiliated gang members of Mexican origin are immediately attacked by rabidly racist *Sureño*-affiliated gang members. This respondent's experiences in Los Angeles County Jail and numerous prisons in California suggest that this is a gross exaggeration. If such a green light ever existed, it is clearly rarely enforced. During three prison terms and more county jail confinements than he could count, his affiliation as a Crip led to violence on only three occasions, all of which occurred in the Los Angeles County Jail. In the first incident, he recounted, he was the first to draw blood in anticipation of imminent conflict:

Back then, the jail system was real different. Back then the South Siders used to really trip on Mexicans being Crips. You know, like, if we come into a dorm or a row, they trip, like, "Yeah you. . . . OK, don't trip. When you rack it up [get settled] we gonna holler at [talk to] yo' peoples." So it was three different occasions. I was lucky I was in the dorms and the South Sider rep was really tripping on me, like, "He gotta roll it up!" [remove himself from the dorm by requesting a transfer]. And the black rep, he gave me an option. Like, this is, like, every time—well, two times—and the third time, I'm like, "I'm 'bout to get it poppin'. I ain't going nowhere. I'm 'bout to go over there and bomb on his ass. And once I go over there and sock him, they gonna come for your ass, too, so be ready." So the black rep came over and talked to me, and he told me, "Man, they trippin'. They said you gotta roll it up. They don't want no Mexican Crips up in here. But shit, you ain't gotta roll it up, but if you wanna stay in here, you gotta get it crackin'." And I'm like, "OK. All right." So they over there talking it out, talking it out. So now I'm over there waiting for the South Sider rep to go to the bathroom. So once he go to the bathroom, I go to the bathroom, too. He taking a piss, and I hit him from behind: Bing! Bang! Boom! I run back to the dorm, and we just, like, go up [start fighting]. It's, like, three blacks that got stabbed that day. I got stabbed. It went up! It was crazy!

The respondent ended up being moved out of the dorm, because, he suspected, the South Siders told the deputies that he had started the riot. As a result, he was sent to the hole, then transferred to another housing unit. The next time he made less of an attempt to avoid confrontation:

Well, the second one, a dude came and told me, like, whatever, but I didn't sneak up on a dude and hit him. So he like, "Man, they trippin' on you." And I'm like, "Man, I ain't goin' nowhere. We finna go up and just go up. Fuck it." He like, "Fuck it, then. We finna go up." So, like, he went and told the South Sider rep, "He ain't going nowhere. We finna go up." And they did that lil' call, and when they do that lil' call, boy, they be ready! All the South Siders, *paisas*, the ones that live in they neighborhood, they did they lil' call, and we just, shit, made a line. Boom! We clashed.

By the third time, there was no hesitation or discussion. Fed up with being confronted over his Crip affiliation, he responded with violence as soon as he was confronted about it. On two other occasions, *Sureño*-affiliated gang members pressed the issue, but no violence resulted because he refused to "roll it up." Those experiences notwithstanding, he was confronted only five times during over ten years of time in county jail and prison, only three of which actually resulted in violence.

If a standing rule to attack Mexican members of Crip- and Blood-affiliated gangs exists, as alleged, one would certainly expect it to be enforced in prison. But as the respondent recounted, he was never confronted over the issue in any of the prisons in which he was incarcerated between 2005 and 2020. When I asked him why he thought this was a non-issue in prison, he suggested that the structure provided by inmate organizations (so-called prison gangs) actually mitigates rather than encourages conflicts: "Never in prison. In prison, it's way more structured."[17]

When I asked who among the *Sureño*-affiliated inmates had made an issue about his being a Mexican Crip, the respondent suggested that only "racist" *Sureño*-affiliated inmates would press the issue—certain gang members whose zeal to enforce boundaries between racialized gang identities is so strong that it leads to violence. "I really can't remember where they were from," the respondent said, "but I do remember it's they neighborhoods are racist. . . . Oh, one was from Longo. What was the third one? I forgot. But they was all racist." This begs a question: racist to what end? Clearly, the *Sureño*-affiliated gang members who were making an issue out of his transracial gang identity were doing so as means of enforcing the boundary between racialized gang identities. Such boundary enforcement is necessary to maintain the salience of racialized identities; otherwise, the boundaries become blurred and permeable. Transracial identity is a threat to the race regime, whether gang members who enforce the invisible walls between them consciously realize that or not.

A Bridge Between

The pervasiveness of transracial gang membership in Los Angeles is undeniable. The prevalence of transracial gang membership can potentially serve as a bridge between African American and Chicano communities and play an important role in the dismantling of racialized gang identities. Of course, this is why some *Sureño*-affiliated gangs adamantly oppose accepting African American members and some *Sureño*-affiliated gang members make an issue out of the presence of Mexican Crips or Bloods in certain carceral environments. The existence of such transracial black members violates the boundaries and shatters the race-thinking logic of racial division many gang members zealously enforce. As gentrification and demographic transition push African American and Chicano populations into tightly circumscribed overlapping communities, one can only expect that the number of transracial gang members will increase, progressively undermining the racialized perceptions of what it means to be a *Sureño*-affiliated and Crip- and Blood-affiliated gang member. Gang members need only look among their own to realize that the invisible walls dividing them are a figment of their imagination.

---

17. I make this argument in Weide 2022.

7

The Peacemakers

Resistance and Resilience

When the prison doors fly open, the real dragon will emerge.

—Ho Chi Minh

While conflict between *Sureño*-affiliated and Crip- and Blood-affiliated gangs in Los Angeles has remained intractable for decades in some cases, the dynamics that drive these racialized conflicts are infinitely more complex than the simplistic race thinking that has framed them.[1] The essentialist discourses that inform these sectarian conflicts have been fueled for generations by professional ethnopolitical entrepreneurs, sensationalist media tropes, and overly zealous law enforcement who are either oblivious to the historical foundations that made the conflicts possible in the first place or are intentionally fanning the flames of sectarian conflict. If there is any hope for a cessation of hostilities between gang members in Los Angeles, perhaps the most promising source of relief is not intervention by state actors or well-meaning reformists but, rather, by gang members themselves. They alone have the inherent potential to reach the epiphany that, by opposing one another, they have become the instruments of their own oppression. The idea that criminalized communities themselves can intervene to mitigate intergang violence is far from a novel insight. The mitigating influence of so-called organized crime has been theorized since Marxist criminologists addressed the issue in the mid-1970s.[2] Likewise, the efforts of gang members and gang leaders in mitigating conflict and violence

---

1. The section of this chapter titled "United We Stand" is coauthored with Alex A. Alonso.
2. Quinney 1977; Spitzer 1975.

has been well documented since the late-1970s.[3] This chapter presents a series of narratives that reinforce these perspectives.

For decades, racialized conflict between *Sureño*-affiliated and Crip- and Blood-affiliated gangs was taken for granted by gang members and their communities, without any avenue to negotiate the cessation of hostilities between opposing racialized factions. This was due in part to the primary strategy used by the California Department of Corrections and Rehabilitation (CDCR) to control inmate populations: long-term isolation of anyone suspected of having a leadership role in gang politics.[4] For decades these men were held incommunicado, in extreme isolation, in the infamous Security Housing Units (SHUs) built specifically to house those accused of gang leadership at Corcoran State Prison and the paragon of prisoner isolation, Pelican Bay State Prison. Isolated from other prisoners and the outside world, they lacked the ability to communicate effectively with the general prison population or anyone else, which, of course, precluded any opportunity for negotiation.

Solidarity Forever

The situation started to change in 2011 when leaders of the four principal racialized inmate organizations in California—the Mexican Mafia, the Black Guerrilla Family (BGF), the Nuestra Familia, and the Aryan Brotherhood—had an epiphany. Entirely organically without external agitation, they arrived at the collective realization that the divisions and conflicts between them served only to advance the *divide and conquer* regime that had defined their lives up to that point. Ironically for the CDCR, their common condition in extreme isolation compelled them to this epiphany, growing to know and respect one another over decades of their shared isolation. For the first time in their lives, they realized the revolutionary potential of their solidarity and endeavored to put an end to generations of racialized conflict in California's prisons.

To advocate for their common interests, representatives of each of the four principal inmate organizations formed a collective, which they christened the Pelican Bay State Prison-SHU (PBSP-SHU) Short Corridor Collective. Their first act was to openly challenge the mundane circumstances of their extreme isolation. On July 1, 2011, approximately four hundred prisoners in the Pelican Bay State Prison-SHU program, representing each of the principal inmate organizations, declared a sustained hunger strike to

---

3. Afary 2009; Brotherton and Barrios 2004; Brotherton and Gude 2018; Curtis 1998; Hayden 2004; Jacobs 1977; Trammel 2012; Weide 2022.

4. Reiter 2012, 2016.

protest the conditions of their confinement.[5] Eventually, more than six thousand prisoners throughout the CDCR general population (GP) joined in the strike.[6] They demanded (1) an end to indefinite solitary confinement; (2) an end to the debriefing process, by which inmates were transferred out of GP in exchange for information on inmate organizations; (3) an end to collective punishment, by which all inmates in a given unit would be punished if an incident occurred there, whether or not they were personally involved; (4) the restoration of educational programs that had been abolished decades earlier; (5) an end to food restrictions for SHU inmates; and (6) CDCR compliance with recommendations proposed by the Vera Institute's Commission on Safety and Abuse in America's Prisons.[7]

Analogous to the Prisoners' Rights Movement of the 1960s, the impetus for the 2011 protest was a book provided by sociologist Denis O'Hearn detailing a hunger strike against harsh prison conditions carried out by members of the Irish Republican Army in the United Kingdom.[8] With knowledge of another recent successful hunger strike in Ohio, the Short Corridor Collective decided to execute the same tactic. The strike ended three weeks later, on July 20, 2011, after representatives of the collective met with Undersecretary of Corrections Scott Kernan. Rather than address the inmates' primary demands, Kernan instead offered to allow inmates to send a photograph of themselves to their families once per year and the ability to purchase beanies for the cold winter months, colored pencils, simple wall calendars to keep track of time, and pickles from the canteen.[9] However, in doing even this, Kernan broke a cardinal rule of prison administration in California: *never negotiate with gang members.*

Kernan abruptly retired mere weeks after meeting with the Short Corridor Collective.[10] Needless to say, the CDCR violated the agreement Kernan had made in good faith and followed through on none of the paltry concessions to which Kernan had agreed to end the hunger strike. After two months of waiting, the Short Corridor Collective concluded that the CDCR administration had no intention of addressing their concerns. On September 26, 2011, they declared a second hunger strike, this time with more than twelve thousand inmates participating. Again, they were told that their principal concerns would be addressed, but the CDCR granted only concessions

---

5. Reiter 2014, 2016.

6. Reiter 2014, 2016.

7. Jack Morris and Dolores Canales, prisoners' rights advocates, personal communication with the author, August 29, 2020.

8. Reiter 2014. Professor O'Hearn is now at Texas A&M University.

9. Reiter 2016, 196.

10. In December 2015, Kernan was appointed secretary of corrections of the CDCR by Governor Jerry Brown. He retired from the position in 2018.

that did not address the inmates' primary grievances—for instance, giving them access to handball courts and the opportunity to send a photograph of themselves to their families once a year. The strike was called off after three weeks, but the collective was under no illusion that the CDCR had any intention of addressing their principal demands. While SHU inmates were unable to secure any substantive concessions, they did garner the attention of the national media and public awareness of their plight. For men who had spent most of their lives in extreme isolation, public awareness of the conditions they endured was a victory in and of itself.

The following year, on August 12, 2012, the Short Corridor Collective released a document for public dissemination calling for an unconditional cessation of racialized hostilities among all GP inmates in CDCR and county jail facilities throughout the State of California. The "Agreement to End Hostilities," as the document was titled, stated:[11]

> To whom it may concern and all California Prisoners:
> Greetings from the entire PBSP-SHU Short Corridor Hunger Strike Representatives. We are hereby presenting this mutual agreement on behalf of all racial groups here in the PBSP-SHU Corridor. Wherein, we have arrived at a mutual agreement concerning the following points:
>
> 1. If we really want to bring about substantive meaningful changes to the CDCR system in a manner beneficial to all solid individuals, who have never been broken by CDCR's torture tactics intended to coerce one to become a state informant via debriefing, that now is the time to for us to collectively seize this moment in time, and put an end to more than 20–30 years of hostilities between our racial groups.
> 2. Therefore, beginning on October 10, 2012, all hostilities between our racial groups . . . in SHU, Ad-Seg, General Population, and County Jails, will officially cease. This means that from this date on, all racial group hostilities need to be at an end . . . and if personal issues arise between individuals, people need to do all they can to exhaust all diplomatic means to settle such disputes; do not allow personal, individual issues to escalate into racial group issues!!
> 3. We also want to warn those in the General Population that IGI will continue to plant undercover Sensitive Needs Yard (SNY) debriefer "inmates" amongst the solid GP prisoners

---

11. The original document is available at *Prisoner Hunger Strike Solidarity* (blog), https://prisonerhungerstrikesolidarity.wordpress.com/agreement-to-end-hostilities.

with orders from IGI to be informers, snitches, rats, and obstructionists, in order to attempt to disrupt and undermine our collective groups' mutual understanding on issues intended for our mutual causes [i.e., forcing CDCR to open up all GP main lines, and return to a rehabilitative-type system of meaningful programs/privileges, including lifer conjugal visits, etc. via peaceful protest activity/noncooperation e.g., hunger strike, no labor, etc. etc.]. People need to be aware and vigilant to such tactics, and refuse to allow such IGI inmate snitches to create chaos and reignite hostilities amongst our racial groups. We can no longer play into IGI, ISU, OCS, and SSU's old manipulative divide and conquer tactics!!!

In conclusion, we must all hold strong to our mutual agreement from this point on and focus our time, attention, and energy on mutual causes beneficial to all of us [i.e., prisoners], and our best interests. We can no longer allow CDCR to use us against each other for their benefit!! Because the reality is that collectively, we are an empowered, mighty force, that can positively change this entire corrupt system into a system that actually benefits prisoners, and thereby, the public as a whole . . . and we simply cannot allow CDCR/CCPOA—Prison Guard's Union, IGI, ISU, OCS, and SSU, to continue to get away with their constant form of progressive oppression and warehousing of tens of thousands of prisoners, including the 14,000 (+) plus prisoners held in solitary confinement torture chambers [i.e. SHU/Ad-Seg Units], for decades!!!

We send our love and respects to all those of like mind and heart . . . onward in struggle and solidarity . . .

PRESENTED BY THE PBSP-SHU SHORT CORRIDOR COLLECTIVE:
Todd Ashker, C58191, D4 121
Arturo Castellanos, C17275, D1-121
Sitawa Nantambu Jamaa (Dewberry), C35671, D1-117
Antonio Guillen, P81948, D2-106

AND THE REPRESENTATIVES BODY:
Danny Troxell, B76578, D1-120
George Franco, D46556, D4-217
Ronnie Yandell, V27927, D4-215
Paul Redd, B72683, D2-117
James Baridi Williamson, D-34288, D4-107
Alfred Sandoval, D61000, D4-214
Louis Powell, B59864, D2-117

Alex Yrigollen, H32421, D2-204
Gabriel Huerta, C80766, D3-222
Frank Clement, D07919, D3-116
Raymond Chavo Perez, K12922, D1-219
James Mario Perez, B48186, D3-124

This document is an unmistakably unequivocal statement of solidarity endorsed by all four of the principal inmate organizations within the CDCR GP facilities that explicitly recognizes and categorically rejects racial divisions between racialized inmate factions in carceral environments as a deliberate divide and conquer strategy perpetrated by the State of California.

The following year, on July 8, 2013, more than thirty thousand inmates throughout the CDCR system declared a prolonged hunger strike that lasted two months, resulting in the martyrdom of one of the strikers.[12] This third, but much larger act of collective resistance again garnered public sympathy and the attention of the national media and was eventually called off with the promise of legislative hearings on the conditions endured by SHU inmates serving indeterminate sentences in the SHU program.[13] On February 11, 2014, those hearings took place in the California State Legislature, where hundreds of prisoners' rights supporters packed the State Assembly to offer their support for the abolition of the SHU program in CDCR facilities. During the hearings, Assemblyman Tom Ammiano, numerous academics, and others lambasted CDCR officials for their intransigence.[14] Impatient with the lack of progress in legal efforts to ameliorate their conditions, representatives of the four principal inmate factions again took the initiative to increase pressure on CDCR to abolish the SHU program.

In 2000, SHU inmates Todd Ashker and Danny Troxell filed a lawsuit *pro se* challenging long-term isolation and solitary confinement. As a result of the public attention garnered by the first hunger strike in 2011, the Center for Constitutional Rights, a prestigious New York civil rights litigation firm, joined the case as counsel, along with the Bay Area nonprofit Legal Services for Prisoners with Children. The United Nations' Special Rapporteur on torture also weighed in, denouncing long-term solitary confinement as torture under the organization's definition. Criminologist Keramet Reiter, who testified in hearings held by Representative Ammiano and Senator Hancock in 2014, provides a deft description of the CDCR's attempt to neutralize the

---

12. For more on the strike, see *Prisoner Hunger Strike Solidarity* (blog), http://www.prisonerhungerstrikesolidarity.wordpress.com.

13. St. John 2013.

14. Reiter 2016. See also *Prisoner Hunger Strike Solidarity* (blog), https://prisonerhungerstrikesolidarity.wordpress.com/2014/02/11/solitary-confinement-cdcr-get-slammed-at-legislative-hearings.

lawsuit to abolish the SHU program through a series of legal maneuvers intended to undermine the standing of the plaintiffs in the case in *23/7* (2016), her invaluable book on solitary confinement.[15]

On August 16, 2012, Kernan's replacement as undersecretary of corrections, Terri McDonald, directed CDCR staff to modify the procedure for validating prison gang affiliation, the primary rationale for extended isolation and solitary confinement. Ostensibly, the new policy was a reform that would make the process for validation and indefinite isolation more objective. The CDCR immediately conducted a case-by-case review of inmates who had been in the SHU at Pelican Bay for ten years or more, who consequently made up a significant proportion of the plaintiffs in the lawsuit. By releasing these inmates from the Pelican Bay SHU and transferring them to other prisons, only to place them in isolation again, the CDCR attempted to remove their standing as plaintiffs in the lawsuit while maintaining the SHU program for the rest of the inmates held at Pelican Bay. The judge in the case didn't fall for the ruse and granted a motion by the plaintiffs to recognize the standing of the plaintiffs who had been surreptitiously relocated. Nonetheless, the CDCR continued to transfer inmates from the Pelican Bay SHU to SHU units at other prisons and, increasingly, to GP yards to separate and divide the strike organizers.

Facing certain defeat in federal court, the CDCR finally settled with the plaintiffs on September 1, 2015. The terms of the settlement effectively abolished the indefinite solitary confinement regime as it had existed for decades. SHU terms were capped at five years, even for the most serious offenses, and the release of all SHU prisoners who had been given those terms on the basis of gang validation—which was the vast majority of SHU inmates, including the representatives of the principal inmate factions—was mandated. For the first time in decades, members of the principal racialized inmate factions were released onto GP yards throughout the CDCR system. The bloodbath the CDCR had predicted would occur upon the release of these so-called "terrorists," as they had been described by a CDCR spokesperson, simply never happened.[16] Hundreds of bona fide members of the four principal inmate organizations have been released onto GP yards at prison facilities throughout the state over the past half-dozen or so years, almost entirely without incident. Only a handful of validated members and associates of inmate organizations have been victims of or accused of perpetrating homicides in CDCR facilities since being released from the SHU program onto GP yards.[17]

15. Reiter 2016, 194–203.
16. St. John 2015c.
17. Ormseth 2020; Reiter 2016, 201; St. John 2015a, 2015b.

As one gang member who was recently released from prison recounted, the agreement has been a tremendous success. It has led to better conditions of confinement for all prisoners, especially those who helped organize and negotiate the pact:

> Q: There's less tension than there used to be?
> A: Yeah. That's why they be doing the fifty-fifty yards now, because a lotta lifers that been in the SHU for years been isolated—people from the Mexican Mafia, Aryan Brotherhood, BGF, and they tired of being in the SHU or in the hole, so they the ones making calls, like, "Everybody just calm the fuck down and chill out. We trying to get out the hole." So, you know, they getting out the hole; they could make phone calls. 'Cause, you know, back in the day, lifers couldn't get conjugal visits, so now lifers can get conjugal visits because of stuff like that. So lifers get out; they tell their people, their homies, "Just chill out," you know? They trying to reform this shit from the inside so they could get their visits, get they phone calls, get they conjugals, and it really has helped out the prison system.
> Q: So you think it's coming from the top down?
> A: Oh, yeah. Definitely.
> Q: So if someone starts something for no reason, they end up getting dealt with?
> A: Yup. That's exactly how it going down right now.

As it turns out, the men whom law enforcement and prison authorities have told us for years were incorrigibly violent "terrorists" are, in fact, the peacemakers whose initiative is mitigating rather than exacerbating violence in carceral environments throughout California.

United We Stand

Coauthored with Alex A. Alonso

Following the third hunger strike in 2013, gentlemen from the Florence community in South Los Angeles were transferred out of the SHU program after decades of draconian isolation. As soon as they were transferred onto general population yards in 2016, they set about trying to contact a member of the East Coast Crips who could negotiate a cessation of hostilities between the rival gangs on the streets. Unfortunately, these efforts initially came to naught. Everywhere they turned, the gentlemen found themselves at a dead end, unable to establish contact with like-minded East Coast leaders.

Then, in 2019, by happenstance, an opportunity presented itself. The Youth Justice Coalition (YJC), a local nonprofit organization that provides meeting space for community groups and runs a continuation school for high school students, was evicted from its location in Inglewood as a result of plans to expand the Metro system into that city. As an alternative, Los Angeles County offered YJC the old Juvenile Justice building on Central Avenue and 76th Street, which had been vacant for years after being used as a juvenile court and jail for minors incarcerated in South Los Angeles. The Juvenile Justice building is located right on the border—the invisible wall— that divides Florencia from East Coast Crip territory. From the outset, there was concern from both the Florencia and East Coast communities that outsiders had been given use of a building in their community that they themselves had not been given an opportunity to use. When the YJC moved into the building, none of the primary staff members were native to the communities surrounding the new location. The closest indigenous connection YJC had to South Los Angeles at the time was through another nonprofit organization—2nd Call, a grassroots prisoner reentry and job placement service—to which YJC provides office space.

Within a week of the new location's opening, members of the Florence community paid a visit inquiring as to why they had not been offered space in the building to run their own community programs. In an attempt to find a compromise, Skipp Townsend, the executive director and cofounder of 2nd Call, reached out to a Florencia member who had recently been released from prison and was in 2nd Call's job placement program to earn a union job with the International Brotherhood of Electrical Workers (IBEW) Local 11. Over the years, 2nd Call has successfully placed hundreds of formerly incarcerated and gang-involved people in union jobs through IBEW and other local trade unions.

Through this contact, Skipp and his staff at 2nd Call were able to make contact with another member of the Florencia community who had recently been released from prison. He in turn connected staff from 2nd Call with the gentlemen in prison who graciously agreed to negotiate a resolution of the issue. However, the gentlemen asked for an important favor in return: "Find me someone from East Coast I can work with to end this war once and for all." Skipp and his staff happened to know the perfect person: Paul Gary "Lil Doc" Wallace, a widely respected member of the East Coast Crips who joined the gang in the late 1970s.[18] A committed family man and born-again Christian who had a sincere conversion after his most recent incarceration, Doc, as almost everyone calls him, was genuinely committed to doing right by his community. They asked Doc to facilitate the peace process

---

18. Weide received permission to use Paul Gary Wallace's name in this section.

and he agreed at least to hear out what the gentlemen had to say. They told Doc that he would be receiving a call from the gentlemen in the near-future and left it at that.

However, when the gentlemen called a couple weeks later, Doc didn't make the connection and thought someone had given his cell phone number to a rival. He was cordial in their first conversation but couldn't agree to negotiate a cease-fire because a beloved member of the East Coast Crips, thirty-year-old Raylorce Ysef "X-Ray" Gordon Jr., had been murdered on August 14, 2019, and it was automatically assumed that a Florencia gang member was responsible. In the ensuing days, three people were killed in two separate shootings in the Florencia community: Alfredo Carrera and Jose Antonio Flores Velasquez, both twenty-four, were killed on the 1100 block of East 68th Street, and Felix Valverde, thirty-two, was killed on the 9000 block of Compton Avenue. All three had been shot multiple times. None were affiliated with Florencia 13.

As it turned out, X-Ray's killers weren't affiliated with Florencia at all. He was killed in a personal dispute with members of another, unrelated *Sureño*-affiliated gang in South Los Angeles. Despite the wanton bloodshed for a murder in which Florencia was not in fact involved, the gentlemen maintained their position and, to demonstrate good faith, informed Doc that Florencia would stand down and not retaliate for the unprovoked murders that had just occurred in their community. This unambiguous demonstration of good faith broke the impasse and convinced Doc that Florencia was serious about negotiating an end to the decades-long war. Doc described the chronology of the events:

Q: Let's talk a lil' bit about how the beef got squashed. You know there's been this historic truce that y'all have agreed to. Can you break it down for me? Like, how did that start? How did the communication start? What was the backstory to it?

A: The thing was that right here at Chuco's, where I work—I got a office right here at Chuco's Youth Center—YJC—my coworkers from 2nd Call, they deals with a lot of the work here, gangs too. They was talking to the gentlemen from prison, and they wanted to talk to a East Coast Crip about a cease-fire and everything to stop the beef, and they told him about me. And they end up calling me from prison. And at the time, I forgot my coworkers even told me about him calling and getting at me. So I was mad thinking my homies gave them my number, you know?

Q: [*Laugh*] You like, "How they get my number?"

A: Yeah! They call me and talk to me and then we hung up. I start calling everybody from prison, like, "What y'all doing in there?"

What the fuck y'all telling these dudes to call me for?" You know, like you putting me on the spot, you know? Shit. Like, I'm trying to be low-key, and they like, "I didn't do it. I didn't do it. I don't know." Then, finally, you know, my coworker hollered at me, like, "Did they call you?" And I'm like, "Who?" And they like, "The gentlemen from prison. My friends from Florencia. They wanna have a truce. They said they talked with you." I was like, "Oh, yeah." And then it all connected for me. [*Laughs*] So when they called, I told him not right now because we had just lost our homeboy X-Ray from 1st Street.

Q: Was it Florence that hit him?

A: Yeah, but it wasn't even Florencios, from what we found out. It wasn't even Florencia. Basically, he had done something to some *eses*. . . . It wasn't no Florencios. It was a personal thing. They came back for him and called him to the car, so he go to the car when he shouldn't have, and by the time he saw they had a gun, he tried to get on, and they had opened fire on him. And being that it was Mexicans in the car, first thing we think is: "Oh, it was the Florencios!" So at that time, the gentlemen told me, "Hey, man, they told me you the man we need to talk to, 'cause we trying to squash this beef with us and raise some peace in the community. And we pretty much the ones that's pushing it. That's it. It's over. You got my word." And I was like, "Well, I'm all for peace, but not right now. I'm not trying to facilitate peace to my homies when y'all just killed one of the homies." That's where we left it at the time. They was like, "OK. I understand. Maybe somewhere down the line. But I'm'a tell my homies to stand down until we get this right." So I was like, "Yeah?" And he was like, "Yeah." I was like, "Yeah, right." You know?

Q: You were skeptical?

A: Yeah, and so they kept they word, like they had said. They homies was like standing down a little. I noticed it. I was like, "OK, this guy for real." You know? So I start presenting it to my homies that they really for real.

Doc took it upon himself to go throughout the East Coast Crip community, talking to the most respected and influential members of each set and, with faith and tenacity, convinced and cajoled each of them to back the peace process. This is a community that stretches for miles and contains thousands of active members from a dozen different sets.

That isn't to say that there wasn't some pushback. Many of the principals in the negotiations called these malcontents "protestors"—as in, they're protesting the peace process. However, it's understandable why some couldn't just let it go. Over the two decades the war had lasted, family and friends had been lost; innocent residents, including children, had been killed on both sides. Grief is an emotion that runs deep in the collective memory of a community whether it results from accident or intent. Others were personally responsible for the bloodshed and carnage and are serving life in prison as a result. Everyone on all sides had suffered tremendously because of the war; yet that is why it had to stop. Following the example set by the Short Corridor Collective, the epiphany spread, from prison yards to the streets, as gang members themselves realized that the divide and conquer regime had to come to an end and they were the only ones who could make that happen.

The two sides agreed to a face-to-face meeting at the YJC building on Central Avenue, which fortuitously had inadvertently presented the opportunity for negotiation between the two sides in the first place. On September 15, 2019, representatives of the Florencia and East Coast Crip communities met at YJC, with the Nation of Islam facilitating the meeting. The Honorable Minister Tony Muhammad of the Nation of Islam, a captivating man of incredible oratory, had been holding peace conferences at YJC between rival Crip- and Blood-affiliated gangs for six weeks before this meeting, so it was a natural progression to have a peace summit across racial lines.

Representatives on both sides exchanged pleasantries and sequestered themselves in a room to negotiate. The East Coast representatives expressed concern that their members were not able to travel freely and safely in certain areas of the community; they particularly wanted guaranteed safe passage through and use of the local Bethune Park, which they had not been able to enjoy for twenty years. Florencia representatives simply wanted an end to the bloodshed. Terms were agreed without dissent, and for the first time in twenty years they broke bread together and shared a meal. As Doc recounted:

> We met right here at Chuco's–YJC. I had the Nation of Islam here just for security purposes. Make your homies feel comfortable coming in, and make mine, too. Nobody gonna get searched, but just the fact that them standing there makes it look like— We can feel safe coming in here, not just coming as Florencia and East Coast Crips, and go up in here and pull heat on each other, you know? Have a massacre right here in the building. So, you know, it all turned out good. They all stood outside, you know, in the parking lot by the front door. Nation of Islam did their part making everyone feel comfortable. And then we all got together and had a dialogue about what we need to do and what not need to be done, far as coming in each other hoods, hanging out; stay away from us, we stay away from y'all. If it's peace, it's peace. We don't have to mingle. And then we had to

come back the second time because people was walking up in each other's hoods, mingling and doing everything like that. They brought that to our attention, so we was like, they all up at the gas station right now. So, yeah, I was in their hood walking around or whatever. So it was just got to the point where I was telling everybody, "If you gonna peace, you gotta peace all the way. You can't peace and then put a boundary on it. If we peacin', then you should be able to go up in each other's hoods, do whatever you wanna do, 'cause we at peace." So we left outta there that time like, "There it is, right there, man. We ain't even tripping, man. If we see you in the hood, we ain't tripping." So we shook hands and left outta that meeting.

They decided to meet again at the end of the month, this time with more attendees. "Let's bring the youngsters this time" was the call to give the younger active gang members a chance to express their perspectives and concerns. On September 29, another meeting occurred with as many as fifty members from each side in attendance. The Nation of Islam facilitated again, and while no one on either side had intended to back down an inch, no one had to. Members of both communities were there in good faith, with the best of intentions, and participants unanimously report that the atmosphere was jovial. Photographs and testimonials of the event we have been privy to demonstrate as much.

While no major incidents had occurred in the two-week intermittence, there were some issues over "wall banging" (graffiti being crossed out).[19] As Doc recounted:

Then we came back again about wall banging. So we came back to talk about everybody writing on the walls, dissing still. I ended up saying, "When we come back to it, we need to really sit down and let the lil' homies talk, 'cause they the gang members. We older. . . . Shit, we married with kids. We ain't got no time to be catching a murder at our age. So let these youngsters speak." So when we came back for that third meeting, we let the youngsters speak, and, you know, Florencia they had their youngsters, too. They spoke and then ours spoke. I stepped in to facilitate the rest, and the Florencios stepped in to facilitate their side.

As we've experienced in our gang intervention work, wall banging can be a constant impediment to the peace process between rival gangs trying to settle their differences. The "protestors" on each side can sabotage the peace

---

19. Phillips 1999.

process by writing on walls; rival gangs that have not come to the negotiating table can instigate by faking cross outs; and many gang members we've talked to since the peace process started are convinced that the police have even faked cross outs to deliberately undermine the peace process.

The most harrowing incident to threaten the peace process reportedly occurred on October 4, 2019, when a Florencia member who had recently been released from prison, and may not have known about the truce, encountered some East Coast Crips at Bethune Park, where, according to the terms of the truce, East Coast was supposed to be guaranteed safe usage. There has been some suggestion that the Florencia member may have had prior bad blood with one of the East Coast members; in any case, an altercation broke out, punches were thrown, and someone produced a gun and fired, hitting the Florencia member who instigated the confrontation in the arm. After the incident occurred, the lines of communication that had been established were employed and the protocol that had been agreed to at the peace summit was followed: both sides deliberated and mutually agreed that the Florencia member who had provoked the confrontation had violated the truce and thus was responsible for the incident. Therefore, no retaliation occurred. Doc recounted the incident and its aftermath:

> Q: I also heard there was a minor incident where some dude from Florence had got out recently and either didn't know the truce was on or whatever the situation was.
>
> A: Yeah. He was young. He came home, and him and my homie— they couldn't see eye to eye never anyways— So he went to jail, got out, and saw the homie. So he push up on the homie with two other lil' homies from Florencia. He kinda pressed up on 'em gangbanging, tripping, and, you know, they got in a altercation. And one of them got shot in the arm from Florencia, and that was it. So we ended up meeting on that, and that lil' youngster that did that, he came to the meeting here. And the homies, you know, the shooter was here. So everything was like, they were all here, so we squashed that, too, because we was like, "Y'all was wrong. He shouldn't have pressed up on him."

The truce has been very well received not only by the community, but also by those who opposed it early in the peace process. Even the "protestors" had been converted, as an East Coast member who was an early skeptic conceded:

> Q: So you think it's gone over well? Most people are grateful that it's over?

A: Hell, yeah. A lot! Alotta people grateful. I could say, even the motherfuckers who played like they didn't want the peace treaty—they still wanna be at war— Shit, they grateful, too. They get to walk up and down the street and go to the store and ain't gotta watch over they shoulder, trying to see inside every car, so see what I'm saying? It's a give and take. Feel what I'm saying?

Q: They been converted! [*Laugh*]

A: They been converted! [*Laughs*] Slowly but surely, everybody coming on board.

Since the first face-to-face meeting was held more than two years ago, as of this writing, no further shootings have occurred between East Coast Crips and Florencia. None. We implore the reader to appreciate that these are two of the biggest gangs in Los Angeles County, each with thousands of active members. Yet the discipline to maintain the truce has been so absolute that not a single shooting has occurred between these two gangs since the unfortunate incident at Bethune Park in October 2019. Doc enthusiastically recounted the success of the truce in an interview conducted in the spring of 2020:

Q: So y'all been bumping into each other since then and the truce has held?

A: Oh, yeah. It's held up good. Nobody shooting and killing. It's held up good. And it's mainly been because we let go of trying to do it over here. OK, we peacin', but what you doing over there? It's like, "We peacin', man. Just let it go."

Q: How about the wall banging?

A: That's coming down, too, and the Facebook stuff. All of it—kinda everything; it's really over now. We at a point now to where, like I said, the protestors—

Q: The peanut gallery has spoke? [*Laughs*]

A: Yeah, and ain't nobody listening. [*Laughs*] We ain't tripping, though. We ain't shooting them, and they ain't shooting us. That's all that matters. We really peacin' and, you know, the community really loves it.

This is especially noteworthy considering the circumstances created by the COVID-19 pandemic. Communities are stressed and struggling as they never have been before, and violent crime is on the rise both in Los Angeles and nationwide.

Not only has the truce held, but Florencia and East Coast Crips members who grew up together, and were estranged for twenty years, have suddenly found opportunities to reach out to old friends on the other side of the invisible wall and they're loving it, as one East Coast respondent noted:

> Q: Have y'all interacted with the Florences? See 'em at the store, at the park, that kinda thing?
>
> A: Yeah. I mean, we done grown up with each other, see what I'm saying? So with that, there ain't no war no more, so if I were to see a motherfucker that I grew up with, it's like, "What up, *nigga*?" Like, "What up? I ain't seen you in forever!" You know like, woopty-woop! Just kick back and go down memory lane with that motherfucker, know what I'm saying? Just be cool. So it's, like, kinda like a good thing.

Once a cessation of hostilities across racial lines is established, solidarity has the chance to face the light and grow organically on its own, no matter how long it lingered in the darkness. For the first time in a generation, childhood friends can reach out to one another across racial and gang lines, sharing their lives as they did before the war started. These relationships will no doubt be important in maintaining the truce in the coming years.

That would make a happy ending for the book. But unfortunately, the future is fraught with peril. On July 16, 2020, Paul Gary "Lil Doc" Wallace was indicted on federal RICO charges alleging that he was involved in two murders—one of which occurred more than seventeen years prior and for which state charges had been dropped—along with numerous other criminal acts. We've spoken with his attorneys and a colleague who specializes in defending RICO cases. We all agree that the indictment is incredibly peculiar.

The timing of the indictment is certainly suspect, ten months after the truce was established between Florencia and the East Coast Crips. Further, Doc was charged as the sole defendant in a RICO indictment, which is unheard-of in Los Angeles RICO cases involving gang allegations. If there were convincing evidence of his involvement in either of the murders alleged in the indictment, he would have been tried in California Superior Court years ago with gang enhancements and, perhaps, special circumstances, which carry the penalty of execution, at worst, and life in prison without parole, at best. This leaves the obvious impression that the U.S. Department of Justice brought the indictment against him surreptitiously to intentionally undermine the peace process between Florencia and East Coast Crips. That is certainly what the gang members and communities involved think and what many of the gang intervention professionals we work with think.

Having read the indictment and followed the case ourselves, we find that narrative disturbingly plausible.[20]

The indictment of Mr. Wallace has had a chilling effect on the peace process since he was taken into custody. Many of those involved in the cease-fire negotiations believe that the indictment was brought to remove him from the peace process and so, understandably, they are concerned about exposing themselves to being indicted, as well. Worse yet, Doc was a key peacemaker in the resolution of hostilities between the East Coast Crips and other African American gangs with which they had engaged in decades-long blood feuds. Leaders of gangs throughout South Los Angeles have the same impression, so the indictment has had a generally chilling effect on the potential for peace among rival gangs far beyond the Florencia and East Coast Crip communities.

The gentlemen in prison who facilitated the cease-fire agreement between Florencia and the East Coast Crips, along with the signatories to the "Agreement to End Hostilities," are serving life sentences in prison, having been denied parole consistently for decades simply because they refuse to renounce their associations. These men, on all sides of the color line, are deserving of a Nobel Peace Prize. Instead, their peacemaking efforts are rewarded with RICO indictments and perpetual parole denials.

---

20. Paul Gary "Lil Doc" Wallace was convicted of RICO conspiracy involving murder on April 18, 2022.

CONCLUSION

Reform or Revolution?

The end of an academic book is typically where scholars present their suggestions for policy reforms that are rarely implemented and easily reversed. This is not that kind of book. There are many things that government at all levels and ostensibly concerned parties could have been doing to avoid the racial division, animosity, and sectarian conflict described in this book, but actions speak louder than words. Sectarian conflict such as that described in this book is the intended outcome of a system of labor management and social control deliberately conceived to sabotage solidarity and provoke racialized divisions among labor populations to guarantee the financial interests and personal security of the American oligarchy in perpetuity.

The course of action the oligarchy and their proxies in government, the media, and academia can be expected to pursue to maintain the status quo is clear. The ruling classes of every society since the dawn of sedentary agriculture have had to contend with the threat of popular revolt. In the modern era, identity politics is their best vehicle for encouraging division and undermining solidarity among discarded labor populations who present the greatest existential threat and to whom the capitalist economy has the least to offer. Therefore, the American oligarchy can be expected to continue to generously sponsor professional ethnopolitical entrepreneurs in the academy, media, and nonprofit-industrial complex who propagate identity politics, racial division, and, ultimately, sectarian conflict. These ruling-class collaborators are the vanguard of capital, charged with deflecting opposition to runaway wealth stratification, burgeoning neofascist movements around the world, and impending worldwide ecological collapse, by focusing discourse exclusively on racial disparities absent class analysis—and they are very effective in that role. The identity politics they espouse has successfully cleaved opposition to state violence along racial lines in recent years and continues to fuel the war of all against all on the streets of our communities among our friends, family, and neighbors.

Likewise, law enforcement can be expected to continue to prosecute the kingpin strategy that is the mainstay of U.S. foreign and domestic criminal justice policy, doing everything in their power to dismantle the structure and solidarity within and among street and inmate organizations that could potentially present a direct threat to the personal security of the American oligarchy. Members and associates of the four principal racialized inmate organizations in California prisons weren't held incommunicado in extreme isolation by the California Department of Corrections and Rehabilitation (CDCR) for decades on end to prevent violence. That much should be obvious in recent years, with Segregated Housing Unit prisoners being released onto General Population (GP) yards throughout the CDCR system, almost without incident. Rather, the most acute source of violence in CDCR facilities today is the entirely manufactured provocation resulting from the forced integration of GP and Sensitive Needs Yards (SNY) in recent years. Members and associates of the principal inmate organizations have been subjected to such intense criminalization and draconian isolation since the collapse of the Civil Rights Movement because they are the *social dynamite* that represents the greatest existential threat to the American oligarchy.[1] These men aren't a criminal threat; they're a political threat. They have endured every possible deprivation, degradation, and torment the state is capable of manifesting while steadfastly retaining their dignity and integrity. These are men who cannot be broken, no matter what the state does to them. As such, they possess the potential to unite righteous black and brown gang members in solidarity and coordinated rebellion against the ruling classes. As George Jackson's biographer Jo Durden-Smith described the dynamics of the prison context so eloquently:

A prison population which is riven by race hatred is more controllable than one united in its hatred for its keepers. . . . Men like George Jackson threaten the power of the guards to manipulate men under their subjection. He had every reason to know at first hand the skill with which they contrived disunity. And as he matured and educated himself he came to see that, if the prisons were to be breeding grounds for the kind of revolution he wished to see outside, then the

---

1. Spitzer 1975.

kind of interracial fighting that could be prodded into life by any guard at any time he wished would have to stop. The common oppressor would have to be identified.[2]

From the Civil Rights Movement era to the present, those who have attempted to politicize and organize gang members in solidarity have always suffered the most intense and extreme state repression in our society. The worst possible scenario for the American ruling class is the one for which men such as Alprentice "Bunchy" Carter, Fred Hampton, George Jackson, and Rudolfo "Cheyenne" Cadena sacrificed their lives: pan-racial class solidarity that results in coordinated revolt among the most marginalized, most criminalized, most demonized members of our society—black and brown gang members.

The American oligarchy narrowly avoided such an unmitigated catastrophe when rebellions engulfed cities across the nation in the summer of 2020 after the murder of George Floyd in Minneapolis. Here in Los Angeles, Black Lives Matter–LA leaders steered the main contingent of protestors and rioters into marching around in circles east of La Cienega Boulevard, in the Fairfax District, where they chanted and scribbled harmless slogans on walls, broke bank windows, and looted pharmacies and small businesses. The fact that the vast majority of protestors allowed themselves to be led around in circles clearly demonstrates the absence of any class-consciousness that could have presented an existential threat to the Tinseltown oligarchy—the hallmark of identity politics. Imagine if, instead, the mob had charged west of La Cienega into Beverly Hills postal code 90210 to raid and pillage the estates of some of the wealthiest people in the world; then swept west along the Sunset Boulevard corridor, in an orgy of unbridled expropriation, through some of the wealthiest communities in the world, all the way to Malibu. That is the apocalyptic scenario the American oligarchy fears most: a direct threat to their own homes, property, and families. Black Lives Matter–LA leaders saved the Tinseltown bourgeoisie from the apocalypse of revolutionary expropriation here in Los Angeles in 2020, but the rage of the most marginalized, demonized, and criminalized members of our society continues to simmer below the neoliberal façade of reform and token representation. It is a rage that cannot be diverted forever.

The analysis presented in this book also has ramifications for the conceptualization of violent crime in our communities. If sectarian conflicts over groupist identities—whether they are racial identities, gang affiliations, or otherwise—exist essentially to divert the frustrations of subordinate labor populations against one another, then the ultimate responsibility for

---

2. Durden-Smith 1976.

violent crimes lies not with those who commit them, but with the ruling classes whom such sectarian conflict is intended to safeguard. If racialized identities and divisions were invented to prevent another sacking of Jamestown, then the culpability for the violence that results from racialized sectarian conflict such as that described in this book lies first with the purveyors of the divisive racialized identities that make such sectarian conflicts possible, not with the gang members who take ethnonationalist ideology to its logical conclusion—a war of all against all. The violence pervasive in marginalized black and brown communities throughout the United States that conservatives decry and liberals lament is a function of the capitalist system itself, which is why sectarian conflict, and gang violence particularly, is endemic not just in the United States but across the capitalist world.

As the narratives presented in this book demonstrate, law enforcement has consistently served to antagonize rather than mitigate sectarian conflict between gang members across racial lines. If the objective of law enforcement was in fact violence reduction, rather than conflict escalation, I would expect a markedly different approach to racialized gang conflicts. Law enforcement would support rather than suppress those who take an active role in facilitating cease-fire agreements between opposing gangs. Law enforcement would use the discretion inherent in their authority to *not* pursue conspiracy cases against gang members who facilitate peace rather than perpetuate conflict among gangs. The most significant obstacle to convincing gang members to come to the table to negotiate cease-fire agreements among themselves is the fear that they will be targeted by law enforcement for doing just that.

If law enforcement were serious about mitigating racialized gang conflicts and the violence that results, it would refrain from incendiary rhetoric and racially charged narratives that serve only to further inflame racialized conflict when it occurs rather than mitigate it. When conflicts do occur across racial lines, law enforcement would make every effort to deescalate rather than agitate racialized animosities. Law enforcement would beseech the media not to publish incendiary, racially charged narratives that further inflame racialized conflicts when they do occur. Such sensationalist moral-panic journalism only exacerbates sectarian conflicts. It never mitigates them. However, as I have demonstrated, law enforcement does the exact opposite of what would mitigate racialized gang conflicts, thereby exacerbating gang violence by constituting it as racial conflict and undermining attempts to intervene by punishing the peacemakers.

Hate crime laws that are always used disproportionately to target one side of a conflict, thereby inflaming resentments and hardening hostilities on the other, ought to be abolished outright. Charging both sides to a conflict equally, if such equality of criminalization could be achieved, is no solution. Equality of criminalization is not justice any more than is equality of victimization by state violence. The criminalization that hate crime laws represent inevitably serves the interests of the state, not of the victims of sectarian violence in our society. As prison abolitionist Jason Lydon writes:

> Hate crime law sets up the State as protector, intending to deflect our attention from the violence it perpetrates, deploys, and sanctions. The government, its agents, and their institutions perpetuate systemic violence and sets themselves up as the only avenue in which justice can be allocated; they will never be charged with hate crimes.[3]

We don't need ethnonationalist identities as vehicles for liberation any more than we need the punitive apparatus of the state to guarantee our collective security. We need to completely reimagine the terms of our entire society, from our educational institutions to our system of political organization, to our efforts to resist our collective subordination. Instead of teaching ethnonationalist ideology and racial pride, universities should be reinvented as sites of revolutionary catechism. We don't need ethnic studies to teach and learn about the horrifying history of colonialism, slavery, labor exploitation, and political repression or about the valiant resistance and rebellions of those who have sacrificed their lives and freedom in the struggle for liberation. And even if we do, must ethnic studies function as a site of ethnonationalist indoctrination? Instead of abandoning the field entirely, ethnic studies could be transformed into a site of contestation to critique and dismantle, rather than reify and perpetuate, the salience of ethnoracial taxonomies. At the least, ethnic studies requirements could mandate that students learn about cultures and histories other than those they identify with, yet that is too often the opposite of what happens in practice. Instead of encouraging cultural diffusion, class-consciousness, and pan-racial solidarity, ethnopolitical entrepreneurs in the academy denounce even the suggestion of anyone enjoying the full range of cultural praxis the human race has to offer with the identitarian slur "cultural appropriation."

Political blocs could be organized on the basis of commonality of class position and material circumstances rather than into competing racial-interest factions. Instead of racializing resistance to state violence with nationalist mantras such as #BlackLivesMatter, dividing those who actually suffer from state violence into opposing racialized camps, social movements could be predicated on class solidarity. We deserve a movement against state

---

3. Lydon 2014.

violence that includes every victim, every family, and every community that is victimized by state violence, irrespective of identity. Instead, privileged spokespersons platformed by corporate media and grant-funding institutions, who are neither indigenous to the communities for which they speak nor have ever suffered the kind of state violence of which they claim exclusive spokespersonship, shamelessly exploit the state-sanctioned murders of black men and women across the country for their own career advancement, fundraising, grant hustling, consulting enterprises, political influence, and personal notoriety. The hustle train of racial justice "coalitions" such as Black Lives Matter is anything but. Rather, they seed resentment in African American communities toward those who do not share a black identity, breed resentment among those who are genuinely committed in their abolitionist politics and opposition to state violence but disillusioned by the leadership of Black Lives Matter, and they breed resentment in the Chicano community, whose victimization by state violence is effectively erased from public discourse. As a recent column in the *Los Angeles Times* asked, "What will make people care about police shootings of Latinos?"[4] The familiar BLM mantra betrays the obvious impediment, "We're talking about Black Lives right now!"

That's exactly why a contingent of cholos in East Los Angeles took to Whittier Boulevard during the George Floyd rebellion to (from their perspective) defend their community. "From what?" is the question. They obviously saw no commonality in the brutal experiences members of the Chicano community have had with the police and the brutality suffered by African Americans at the hands of the police. They see African Americans only as adversaries, against whom their community must be defended. This perspective cannot be explained by simplistic accusations of antiblackness or racism alone. It is a reaction to the framing of state violence *as a racial issue* by ethnopolitical entrepreneurs, such as the leaders of Black Lives Matters, elevated on a pedestal by the media, academia, and the nonprofit-industrial complex. Perhaps nothing symbolizes the divisive role of ethno-nationalist identities in the capitalist economy as clearly as a contingent of cholos posted up on Whittier Boulevard posing for photos with the police, standing side by side in defense of Niketown, against people rioting over the police murder of an African American man. Reactionary politics begets reactionary praxis.

Imagine a world, if you will, where the movies, media, and TV content we consume emphasizes the primacy of our common material position relative to the ruling classes rather than our purported cultural and racial differences, encouraging resistance to the capitalist system rather than assim-

---

4. Arellano 2021.

ilation into it. Instead of ethnonationalist idols such as Marvel's Black Panther and DC Comics' Aztek, we could have heroes for our children that reflect a hybridization of identities and cultural practices. Instead of media content that indoctrinates our children with divisive ethnoracial identities, we could consume media content that deconstructs our divisions. But identity is a potent marketing vehicle and a cash cow always ready to be milked.[5] Whether "Buy Black" or "Latinos, Inc.," identity is big business in a society where identity is everything. We drape ourselves in garments saturated with identitarian iconography. We decorate our homes and adorn our bodies with cultural symbols of the ethnonationalist identities we claim. We consume identitarian scholarship and entertainment. Indeed, the cultural accoutrements and putative practices of racialized identities taken together constitute an entire identitarian economy of their own.

Why are we bombarded with all this ethnonationalist propaganda in every aspect of our lives? Because it all serves a very essential function for the racial capitalist society in which we live—*divide and conquer*. Race thinking may have a logic of its own, but it requires constant reinforcement and provocation to maintain its salience, or else the boundaries that make groupist identities relevant succumb to the organic progression of cultural diffusion and the natural human inclination toward solidarity rather than division. For oppositional identities to retain salience and reinforce conceptualizations of groupist identity between populations on opposing sides of sectarian conflicts, they require zealous identity-boundary maintenance, the perpetuation of biases and prejudice among opposing populations, provocation from law enforcement and other state actors, and a steady stream of divisive propaganda from the media and academia. As the late Norwegian anthropologist Frederick Barth observed, boundary enforcement is what makes ethnoracial identities meaningful.[6] Professional ethnopolitical entrepreneurs in the media and academia certainly enjoy the material privileges generated by the cult of identity—their careers and livelihoods depend on it—but gang members in Los Angeles and partisans to other sectarian conflicts around the world suffer the consequences.

Indeed, the ultimate evolution of racial oppression is when those who suffer from its pernicious effects themselves become the instruments of their own oppression, the enforcers of the racial regime that they themselves endure. This is the defining feature of the race concept in late modernity. There's nothing new about racist terrorism, state violence, and white supremacists marching through the streets with burning torches. What is new about the racial regime we endure today is that those who suffer most from

---

5. Davila 2001; Pitcher 2014; Widdowson and Howard 2008.
6. Barth 1969, 14–15.

racial oppression and economic privation have themselves seized the gauntlet of race thinking and embraced the racialized identities and divisions that make their economic, social, and political subordination possible. Rather than denouncing racialized division, they embrace it. Despite our best efforts to intervene in specific sectarian conflicts anywhere in the world, as long as the race concept, nationalist ideology, and the groupist identities they engender retain salience, they will always lie waiting to ignite division and sectarian conflict at the first spark of provocation. Ultimately, the capitalist economy has little of material substance to offer the discarded labor populations of the world other than the consolation prize of identity—at the expense of class-consciousness and solidarity.

Trapped in the iron cage of race-thinking hegemony, befuddled by the subtle incantations of *racecraft*, we ourselves act as the instruments of our own oppression. We could imagine so much more for ourselves and our children. Rather than bestowing on our children names that reflect their ethnoracial heritage, we could choose names on the basis of the lives lived by those who bore them, irrespective of origin. Instead of teaching our children languages that coincide with ethnoracial identities we acquired by accident of birth, we could raise a generation of polyglots, speaking languages that span the globe. Instead of encouraging our children to take pride in our ancestry, whether real or imagined, we could be encouraging our children to take pride in their own accomplishments. Instead of limiting our children to our cultural practices, we could expose them to the full range of cultural diversity the human race has to offer and let them weave the canvas of their lives as it suits them. Instead of thinking of ourselves in terms of exclusive, insular, oppositional racialized categories, throwing up invisible walls that divide us from those with whom we share our lives and communities, we could appreciate the commonality of our material circumstances vis-à-vis the ruling classes, as well as our shared cultural practices and experiences, different flavors forever in flux, mixing and mashing in a genuine and organic melting pot of cultural diffusion rather than an *exclusive society* predicated on division and mutual hostility.[7] Instead of reifying ethnonationalist identities, we could be dismantling them. Instead of policing color lines, we could be erasing them.

I harbor no illusions that parties to sectarian conflicts in Los Angeles, or anywhere in the world, will willingly discard their oppositional identities overnight. As Antonia Darder and Rodolfo Torres lament, "In a country like the United States, which is filled with historical examples of exploitation, violence, and murderous acts justified by both popular opinions and scientific ideas of 'race,' it is next to impossible to convince people that 'race' does

---

7. Young 1999.

not exist as a 'natural' category."[8] Therefore, as long as oppositional identities exist, I expect a permanent and lasting peace between gang members in Los Angeles—or partisans to sectarian conflict in any corner of the capitalist world, for that matter—will continue to be elusive. There can be no enduring peace in a society predicated on identity division and sectarian conflict.

In this book I have provided the historical analysis and theoretical tools necessary to dismantle these sectarian identities and the nationalist ideology that informs them. It is up to gang members and partisans to sectarian conflicts around the world to apply this analysis in their own lives. Only they possess the positionality to interrupt the cult of identity by joining in solidarity and coordinated resistance based on the common class position they share vis-à-vis the ruling classes. As the narratives recounted in the previous chapter demonstrate, gang members have taken the first step across racial lines toward that epiphany, despite every effort exercised by state actors to sabotage their solidarity.

Despite the unremitting threat of state repression, the Pelican Bay Short Corridor Collective has served as a model for efforts to settle long-standing rivalries and create solidarity among rival gang members across gang lines and across racial lines in communities throughout Los Angeles County. Following the example set by the Short Corridor Collective, dozens of rival gangs in Los Angeles have formed collective cease-fire agreements in recent years to bring sectarian conflicts to an end and build solidarity amongst former rivals. These encouraging developments are occurring on both sides of the color line. Many of my colleagues and I, both in prison and on the streets, have been deeply involved in these efforts. We find ourselves at another crossroads in history, where, for the first time since the collapse of the Civil Rights Movement, we have the opportunity to bring black and brown communities together in solidarity, across gang lines and across racial lines, igniting a social revolution from below against the status quo. At this critical juncture in human history, as we face runaway wealth stratification, burgeoning neofascist movements around the world, and imminent ecological collapse the likes of which human civilization has never known, we cannot afford to miss that opportunity.

The thrust of this book has not been to perpetuate the sycophancy of expecting that the government, police, media, academia, nonprofit-industrial complex, or any well-meaning outsiders can or will offer any miraculous panacea. Rather, if a solution to sectarian gang conflict is to be found, it must be realized by gang members themselves—in spite of all those forces aligned against their solidarity. Their liberation is ultimately contingent

---

8. Darder and Torres 2004, 137.

on their own discovery of the revolutionary potential they possess to dismantle the ideas, ideology, and identities that have kept them in a state of conflict for generations. The ideological iconographies and conceptual constructs that shape gang members' hostility toward one another—the boundaries drawn by centuries of historical division, ethnopolitical entrepreneurs, government agents, and incendiary media tropes that stoke resentment among communities of color—are ultimately social constructs and thus are entirely capable of being deconstructed, both conceptually and materially. The candid and reflective voices of the gang members presented in this book, coupled with a critical analysis of the historical foundations of contemporary racial divisions, demonstrate that the time is ripe for gang members in Los Angeles and partisans to sectarian conflicts throughout the capitalist world to discard divisive groupist identities and nationalist ideologies and instead join in solidarity, realizing the existential threat that their very existence represents to the continued wealth accumulation and personal security of the oligarchy of every country, the world over.

REFERENCES

Adler, Patricia A., and Peter Adler. 1987. *Membership Roles in Field Research*. Newbury Park, CA: Sage.

Adorno, Theodor, and Max Horkheimer. (1944) 1997. *Dialectics of Enlightenment*. New York: Verso.

Afary, Kamran. 2009. *Performance and Activism: Grassroots Discourse after the Los Angeles Rebellion of 1992*. Washington, DC: Lexington.

Ahrens, Gale. 2003. *Lucy Parsons: Freedom, Equality and Solidarity, Writings and Speeches, 1878–1937*. Chicago: Charles H. Kerr.

Alexander, Harriett. 2021. "BLM Founder Is Branded a 'FRAUD' after Buying a $1.4 Million Home in an Upscale Mostly White Enclave in LA." *Daily Mail*, April 10. https://www.dailymail.co.uk/news/article-9456145/Shell-pick-white-people-complain-BLM-founder-buys-1-4M-LA-home.html.

———. 2022. "Black Lives Matter 'Transferred Millions to Canadian Charity Run by the Wife of Co-founder Patrisse Cullors to Buy Toronto Mansion Formerly Owned by the Communist Party.'" *Daily Mail*, January 30. https://www.dailymail.co.uk/news/article-10457275/BLM-transferred-millions-Canadian-charity-run-wife-founder-Toronto-mansion.html.

Allen, Theodore W. (1994) 2012. *The Invention of the White Race, Volume 1: Racial Oppression and Social Control*. New York: Verso.

———. (1997) 2012. *The Invention of the White Race, Volume 2: The Origin of Racial Oppression in Anglo-America*. New York: Verso.

Alonso, Alex. 2004. "Racialized Identities and the Formation of Black Gangs in Los Angeles." *Urban Geography* 25, no. 7: 658–674.

———. 2010. "Out of the Void: Street Gangs in Black Los Angeles." In *Black Los Angeles: American Dreams and Racial Realities*, edited by Darnell Hunt and Ana-Christina Ramon, 140–167. New York: New York University Press.

Altman, Ida, Sarah Cline, and Juan Javier Pescador. 2002. *The Early History of Greater Mexico*. New York: Pearson.

Alvarez, Luis. 2008. *The Power of the Zoot: Youth Culture and Resistance during World War II*. Berkeley: University of California Press.

Anderson, Benedict. (1983) 2016. *Imagined Communities: Reflections on the Origin and Spread of Nationalism*. New York: Verso.

Appiah, Kwame Anthony. 2018. *The Lies That Bind: Rethinking Identity*. New York: Liveright.

Appleby, Joyce. 2010. *The Relentless Revolution: A History of Capitalism*. New York: W. W. Norton.

Arellano, Gustavo. 2021. "What Will Make People Care about Police Shootings of Latinos?" *Los Angeles Times*, April 20.

Ashbaugh, Carolyn. (1976) 2012. *Lucy Parsons: An American Revolutionary*. Chicago: Haymarket.

Austin, Curtis J. 2008. *Up against the Wall: Violence in the Making and Unmaking of the Black Panther Party*. Little Rock: University of Arkansas Press.

Bakunin, Mikhail. 1848. "Appeal to the Slavs." https://www.marxists.org/reference/archive/bakunin/works/1848/pan-slavism.htm.

———. (1873) 1990. *Statism and Anarchy*. Cambridge: Cambridge University Press.

Balibar, Étienne, and Emmanuel Wallerstein. 1991. *Race, Nation, Class: Ambiguous Identities*. New York: Verso.

Banton, Michael P. 1983. *Racial and Ethnic Competition*. Cambridge: Cambridge University Press.

Barbato, Lauren. 2015. "Is Being Transracial Actually a Thing?" *Bustle.com*, June 16. https://www.bustle.com/articles/90610-is-being-transracial-a-thing-rachel-dolezal-has-officially-brought-the-term-to-our-vocabulary.

Barraclough, Geoffrey. 1984. *The Origins of Modern Germany*. New York: W. W. Norton.

Barreto, Matt A., Benjamin F. Gonzalez, and Gabriel R. Sanchez. 2014. "Rainbow Coalition in the Golden State? Exposing Myths, Uncovering New Realities in Latino Attitudes toward Blacks." In *Black and Brown in Los Angeles: Beyond Conflict and Coalition*, edited by Josh Kun and Laura Pulido, 203–231. Berkeley: University of California Press.

Barth, Frederik. 1969. *Ethnic Groups and Boundaries*. Boston: Little, Brown and Company.

Bauer, Susan Wise. 2013. *The History of the Renaissance World: From the Rediscovery of Aristotle to the Conquest of Constantinople*. New York: W. W. Norton.

Bean, Frank D., James D. Bachmeier, Susan K. Brown, and Rosaura Tafoya-Estrada. 2011. "Immigration and Labor Market Dynamics." In *Just Neighbors? Research on African-American and Latino Relations in the United States*, edited by Edward Telles, Mark Q. Sawyer, and Gaspar Rivera-Salgado, 37–59. New York: Russell Sage Foundation.

Becerra, Hector, and Richard Winston. 2014. "Ramona Gardens Firebombing Has Some Black Residents Fleeing the Area." *Los Angeles Times*, May 17.

Berger, Dan. 2014. *Captive Nation: Black Prison Organizing in the Civil Rights Era*. Chapel Hill: University of North Carolina Press.

Bergesen, Albert, and Max Herman. 1998. "Immigration, Race, and Riot: The 1992 Los Angeles Uprising." *American Sociological Review* 63:39–54.

Black Lives Matter–Cincinnati. 2018. "Why Black Lives Matter: Cincinnati Is Changing Its Name." *LibCom.org*, April 30. https://libcom.org/library/why-black-lives-matter-cincinnati-changing-its-name.

Black Lives Matter–Inland Empire. 2021. "To Ally with the Democratic Party Is to Ally against Ourselves." *Left Voice*, February 4. https://www.leftvoice.org/blm-inland -empire-breaks-with-black-lives-matter-global-network?fbclid=IwAR2Q-NG p8QZFlpvXJfhaIRgP6jHhslt-PY2OMCwDFyQtcEsGX7uShzGHxz0.

Blay, Zeba. 2015. "Why Comparing Rachel Dolezal to Caitlyn Jenner Is Detrimental to Both Trans and Racial Justice." *HuffPost.com*, June 12. https://www.huffpost.com/entry /rachel-dolezal-caitlyn-jenner_n_7569160.

BLM10. 2020. "It is Time for Accountability." https://www.blmchapterstatement.com.

Bloch, Stefano, and Susan A. Phillips. 2022. "Mapping and Making *Gangland*: A Legacy of Redlining and Enjoining Gang Neighborhoods in Los Angeles." *Urban Studies* 59, no. 4: 750–770.

Bloom, Joshua, and Waldo E. Martin Jr. 2013. *Black against Empire: The History and Politics of the Black Panther Party*. Berkeley: University of California Press.

Blumer, Herbert. 1958. "Race Prejudice as a Sense of Group Position." *Pacific Sociological Review* 1:3–7.

Bobo, Laurence. 1983. "Whites' Opposition to Busing: Symbolic Racism or Realistic Group Conflict?" *Journal of Personality and Social Psychology* 45:1196–1210.

Bonacich, Edna. 1972. "A Theory of Ethnic Antagonism: The Split Labor Market." *American Sociological Review* 37:547–559.

Boyd-Bowman, Peter. 1969. "Negro Slaves in Early Colonial Mexico." *The Americas* 26:134–153.

Bracey, John H., August Meier, and Elliott Rudwick. 1970. *Black Nationalism in America*. Indianapolis: Bobbs-Merrill.

Breen, T. H., and Stephen Innes. (1980) 2004. *"Myne Owne Ground": Race and Freedom on Virginia's Eastern Shore 1640–1676*. Oxford: Oxford University Press.

Bright, Brenda Jo. 1995. "Re-mappings: Los Angeles Low Riders." In *Looking High and Low: Art and Cultural Identity*, edited by Brenda Jo Bright and Liza Blackwell, 89–123. Tucson: University of Arizona Press.

Brotherton, David C. 2015. *Youth Street Gangs: A Critical Appraisal*. London: Routledge.

Brotherton, David C., and Luis Barrios. 2004. *The Almighty Latin King and Queen Nation: Street Politics and the Transformation of a New York City Gang*. New York: Columbia University Press.

Brotherton, David C., and Rafael Gude. 2018. *Social Inclusion from Below: The Perspectives of Street Gangs and Their Possible Effects on Declining Homicide Rates in Ecuador*. Report prepared for Innovation in Citizen Services Division of the Banco Interamericano de Desarrollo, April. https://publications.iadb.org/en/social-inclusion-below -perspectives-street-gangs-and-their-possible-effects-declining-homicide.

Brown, Michael K., Martin Carnoy, Elliott Currie, Troy Duster, David B. Oppenheimer, Marjorie M. Schultz, and David Wellman. 2003. *White-washing Race: The Myth of a Color-blind Society*. Berkeley: University of California Press.

Brown, Scot. 2003. *Fighting for US: Maulana Karenga, the US Organization, and Black Cultural Nationalism*. New York: New York University Press.

Brubaker, Rogers. 2004. *Ethnicity without Groups*. Cambridge, MA: Harvard University Press.

———. 2016. *Trans: Gender and Race in an Age of Unsettled Identities*. Princeton, NJ: Princeton University Press.

Bruce, Matt. 2021. "'Stop Monopolizing and Capitalizing off Our Fight': Tamir Rice's Mother Issues Stern Warning to Tamika Mallory, Ben Crump and Other Social Justice Activists." *Atlanta Black Star*, March 18. https://atlantablackstar.com/2021/03/18

/stop-monopolizing-and-capitalizing-off-our-fight-tamir-rices-mother-issues-stern
-warning-to-tamika-mallory-ben-crump-and-other-social-justice-activists.

Calhoun, Craig. 1994. "Nationalism and Civil Society: Democracy, Diversity and Self-
Determination." In *Social Theory and the Politics of Identity*, edited by Craig Calhoun, 304–335. Oxford: Blackford.

———. 1997. *Nationalism*. Minneapolis: University of Minnesota Press.

Campbell, Sean. 2022a. "The BLM Mystery: Where Did All the Money Go?" *New York*,
January 31. https://nymag.com/intelligencer/2022/01/black-lives-matter-finances
.html.

———. 2022b. "Black Lives Matter Secretly Bought a $6 Million House." *New York*, April 4.
https://nymag.com/intelligencer/2022/04/black-lives-matter-6-million-dollar-house
.html.

Chambliss, William J. 1975. "Toward a Political Economy of Crime." *Theory and Society*
2:149–170.

Chang, Edward T. 1999. "New Urban Crisis: Korean-African American Relations." In
Koreans in the Hood: Conflict with African Americans, edited by Kwang Chung Kim,
39–59. Baltimore: John Hopkins University Press.

Chang, Edward T., and Jeannette Diaz-Veizades. 1999. *Ethnic Peace in the American City:
Building Community in Los Angeles and Beyond*. New York: New York University Press.

Chibnall, Marjorie. (2000) 2006. *The Normans*. Oxford: Blackwell.

Choi, InChul. 1999. "Contemplating Black-Korean Conflict in Chicago." In *Koreans in
the Hood: Conflict with African Americans*, edited by Kwang Chung Kim, 157–177.
Baltimore: John Hopkins University Press.

Churchill, Ward, and Jim Vander Wall. 1988. *Agents of Repression: The FBI's Secret Wars
against the Black Panther Party and the American Indian Movement*. Cambridge,
MA: South End.

Clarke, John. (1975) 2006a. "The Skinheads and the Magical Recovery of Community."
In *Resistance through Rituals: Youth Subcultures in Post-war Britain*, edited by Stuart
Hall and Tony Jefferson, 80–83. London: Routledge.

———. (1975) 2006b. "Style." In *Resistance through Rituals: Youth Subcultures in Post-
war Britain*, edited by Stuart Hall and Tony Jefferson, 147–161. London: Routledge.

Coldham, Peter Wilson. 1992. *Emigrants in Chains: A Social History of Forced Emigration
to the Americas of Felons, Destitute Children, Political and Religious Non-conformists,
Vagabonds, Beggars and Undesirables 1607–1776*. Baltimore: Genealogical Publishing.

Combahee River Collective. (1977) 2017. "Combahee River Collective Statement." In
How We Get Free, edited by Keeanga-Yamahtta Taylor, 15–27. Chicago: Haymarket.

Conquergood, Dwight. 1997. "Street Literacy." In *Handbook of Research on Teaching
Literacy through the Communicative and Visual Arts*, edited by James Flood, Shirley
Brice Heath, and Diane Lape, 354–374. New York: Simon and Schuster.

Cornell, Stephen, and Douglas Hartmann. 2007. *Ethnicity and Race: Making Identities
in a Changing World*. Thousand Oaks, CA: Pine Forge.

Cronon, E. David. 1969. *Black Moses: The Story of Marcus Garvey and the Universal Negro
Improvement Association*. Madison: University of Wisconsin Press.

Crouch, David. 2002. *The Normans: The History of a Dynasty*. London: Hambledon Con-
tinuum.

Cuevas, Ofelia Ortiz. 2014. "Race and the LA Human: Race Relations and Violence in
Globalized Los Angeles." In *Black and Brown in Los Angeles: Beyond Conflict and
Coalition*, edited by Josh Kun and Laura Pulido, 233–251. Berkeley: University of
California Press.

Cummins, Eric. 1994. *The Rise and Fall of California's Radical Prison Movement*. Stanford, CA: Stanford University Press.

Curtis, Richard. 1998. "The Improbable Transformation of Inner-City Neighborhoods: Crime, Violence, Drugs and Youth in the 1990s." *Journal of Criminal Law and Criminology* 88, no. 4: 1233–1276.

Darden, Joe T. 1995. "Black Residential Segregation since the 1948 *Shelley v. Kraemer* Decision." *Journal of Black Studies* 25, no. 6: 680–691.

Darder, Antonia, and Rodolfo D. Torres. 1999. "Shattering the Race Lens: Toward a Critical Theory of Racism." In *Critical Ethnicity: Countering the Waves of Identity Politics*, edited by Robert Tai and Mary Kenyatta, 173–192. Lanham, MD: Rowman and Littlefield.

———. 2004. *After Race: Racism after Multiculturalism*. New York: New York University Press.

Davila, Arlene. 2001. *Latinos Inc.: The Marketing and Making of a People*. Berkeley: University of California Press.

Davis, Mike. 1990. *City of Quartz*. London: Verso.

Day, Meagan. 2020. "Corporations like Amazon Hire Union-busting Labor Spies All the Time." *Jacobin Magazine*, September 2. https://www.jacobinmag.com/2020/09/amazon-jeff-bezos-union-busting-surveillance.

Drummond, Tammerlin. 2015. "Legendary Black Revolutionary Freed 46 Years after UCLA Murders." *East Bay Times*, February 3.

Du Bois, W. E. B. (1935) 1992. *Black Reconstruction in America 1860–1880*. New York: Free Press.

Durden-Smith, Jo. 1976. *Who Killed George Jackson? Fantasies, Paranoias and the Revolution*. New York: Knopf.

Eisenstein, Elizabeth L. (1983) 2016. *The Printing Revolution in Early Modern Europe*. Cambridge: Cambridge University Press.

Elliot, John H. 2002. *Imperial Spain: 1469–1716*, 2nd ed. New York: Penguin.

Febvre, Lucien, and Henri-Jean Martin. (1958) 2010. *The Coming of the Book: The Impact of Printing, 1450–1800*. New York: Verso.

Ferrell, Jeff. 1995. "Style Matters: Criminal Identity and Social Control." In *Cultural Criminology*, edited by Jeff Ferrell and Clint Sanders, 169–189. Boston: Northeastern University Press.

Fields, Karen E., and Barbara J. Fields. 2014. *Racecraft: The Soul of Inequality in American Life*. London: Verso.

Fleischer, Matthew. 2007. "Children of the Revolutionary." *LA Weekly*, August 22. https://www.laweekly.com/children-of-the-revolutionary.

Frasure-Yokley, Lorrie, and Stacey Greene. 2014. "Black Views toward Proposed Undocumented Immigration Policies: The Role of Racial Stereotypes and Economic Competition." In *Black and Brown in Los Angeles: Beyond Conflict and Coalition*, edited by Josh Kun and Laura Pulido, 90–111. Berkeley: University of California Press.

Fredrickson, George M. 2002. *Racism: A Short History*. Princeton, NJ: Princeton University Press.

Freer, Regina M., and Claudia Sandoval Lopez. 2011. "Black, Brown, Young and Together." In *Just Neighbors? Research on African-American and Latino Relations in the United States*, edited by Edward Telles, Mark Q. Sawyer, and Gaspar Rivera-Salgado, 267–298. New York: Russell Sage Foundation.

Galindo, D. Leticia, and María Dolores Gonzales. 1999. *Speaking Chicana: Voice, Power and Identity*. Tucson: University of Arizona Press.

Gangland. 2010. "Shoot to Kill." Documentary, Gangland Productions, History Channel. First aired August 20.

Gans, Herbert. 1973. "Symbolic Ethnicity: The Future of Ethnic Groups and Cultures in America." *Ethnic and Racial Studies* 2:1–19.

Gilroy, Paul. 2000. *Against Race: Imagining Political Culture beyond the Color Line*. Cambridge, MA: Harvard University Press.

Gitlin, Todd. 1995. *The Twilight of Common Dreams: Why America Is Wracked by Culture Wars*. New York: Owl.

Goldman, Emma. (1931) 2006. *Living My Life*. New York: Penguin Classics.

Gomez, Laura E. 2007. *Manifest Destinies: The Making of the Mexican American Race*. New York: New York University Press.

Grant, Colin. 2008. *Negro with a Hat: The Rise and Fall of Marcus Garvey*. Oxford: Oxford University Press.

Grebler, Leo, Joan W. Moore, and Ralph Guzman. 1970. *The Mexican American People: The Nation's Second Largest Minority*. New York: Free Press.

Green, Donald P., Dara Z. Strolovitch, and Janelle S. Wong. 1998. "Defended Neighborhoods, Integration and Racially Motivated Crime." *American Journal of Sociology* 104:372–403.

Green, Lisa J. 2002. *African American English: A Linguistic Introduction*. Cambridge: Cambridge University Press.

Gunn, Tamantha. 2021. "Michael Brown's Father, Ferguson Activists Request $20 Million from Black Lives Matter." *Revolt.TV*, March 4. https://www.revolt.tv/article /2021-03-04/58475/michael-browns-father-ferguson-activists-request-20-million -from-black-lives-matter.

Haas, Jeffrey. 2010. *The Assassination of Fred Hampton: How the FBI and the Chicago Police Murdered a Black Panther*. Chicago: Lawrence Hill.

Hagedorn, John. 1988. *People and Folks: Gangs, Crime and the Underclass in a Rustbelt City*. Chicago: Lake View.

———. 2008. *A World of Gangs: Armed Young Men and Gangsta Culture*. Minneapolis: University of Minnesota Press.

Haider, Asad. 2018. *Mistaken Identity: Race and Class in the Age of Trump*. New York: Verso.

Hall, Stuart. (1980) 2019. "Race, Articulation, and Societies Structured in Dominance." In *Essential Essays, Volume 1*, edited by David Morley, 172–221. Durham, NC: Duke University Press.

Hampton, Fred. 1969. "It's a Class Struggle Goddamnit!" Speech given at Northern Illinois University, November. https://www.hamptonthink.org/read/its-a-class-struggle -goddammit-fred-hampton.

Haney-Lopez, Ian F. 2003. *Racism on Trial: The Chicano Fight for Justice*. Cambridge, MA: Harvard University Press.

Hannaford, Ian. 1996. *Race: The History of an Idea in the West*. Baltimore: John Hopkins University Press.

Hayden, Tom. 2004. *Street Wars: Gangs and the Future of Violence*. New York: Free Press.

Hebdige, Dick. (1975) 2006. "The Meaning of Mod." In *Resistance through Rituals: Youth Subcultures in Post-war Britain*, edited by Stuart Hall and Tony Jefferson, 71–79. London: Routledge.

———. 1979. *Subculture: The Meaning of Style*. London: Routledge.

Heideman, Paul M. 2018. *Class Struggle and the Color Line: American Socialism and the Race Question 1900–1930*. Chicago: Haymarket.

Hemming, A. D. 2015. "Time to Honor Lucy Parsons for Black History Month." *Counter

Punch, February 13. https://www.counterpunch.org/2015/02/13/time-to-honor-lucy -parsons-for-black-history-month.

Hipp, John R., George E. Tita, and Lyndsay N. Boggess. 2007. "Measuring Intra- and Intergroup Violent Crime for African Americans and Latinos in South Bureau Los Angeles." Report to the Los Angeles Police Department, September. Obtained from the authors.

———. 2009. "Intergroup and Intragroup Violence: Is Violent Crime an Expression of Group Conflict or Social Disorganization?" *Criminology* 47, no. 2: 521–564.

Hobsbawm, Eric J. 1990. *Nations and Nationalism since 1780*. Cambridge: Cambridge University Press.

Hochschartner, Jon. 2012. "What's Missing from Black History Month." *Red Phoenix*, February 10. https://theredphoenixapl.org/2012/02/10/whats-missing-from-black -history-month.

Horne, Gerald. 2014. *The Counter-revolution of 1776: Slave Resistance and the Origins of the United States of America*. New York: New York University Press.

———. 2018. *The Apocalypse of Settler Colonialism: The Roots of Slavery, White Supremacy, and Capitalism in Seventeenth-Century North America and the Caribbean*. New York: Monthly Review.

Hutchison, Earl Ofari. 2007. *The Latino Challenge to Black America: Towards a Conversation between African Americans and Hispanics*. Los Angeles: Middle Passage.

Inside Bloods and Crips: L.A. Gangs. 2008. Documentary, Wall to Wall Media and Underworld Gangs II, National Geographic Channel. First aired June 8.

Isenberg, Nancy. 2016. *White Trash: The 400-Year Untold History of Class in America*. New York: Penguin.

Jacobs, James B. 1977. *Statesville: The Penitentiary in Mass Society*. Chicago: University of Chicago Press.

Johnson, Cedric. 2007. *Revolutionaries to Race Leaders: Black Power and the Making of African American Politics*. Minneapolis: University of Minnesota Press.

———. 2019. "Black Political Life and the Blue Lives Matter Presidency." *Jacobin*, February 17. https://jacobinmag.com/2019/02/black-lives-matter-power-politics-cedric -johnson.

———. 2020. "The Triumph of Black Lives Matter and Neoliberal Redemption." *Onsite .org*, June 22. https://nonsite.org/editorial/the-triumph-of-black-lives-matter-and -neoliberal-redemption.

Johnson, Gaye Theresa. 2014. "Spatial Entitlement: Race, Displacement and Sonic Reclamation in Postwar Los Angeles." In *Black and Brown in Los Angeles: Beyond Conflict and Coalition*, edited by Josh Kun and Laura Pulido, 301–314. Berkeley: University of California Press.

Jones, Jacqueline. 2017. *Goddess of Anarchy: The Life and Times of Lucy Parsons, American Radical*. New York: Basic.

Jones-Correa, Michael. 2011. "Commonalities, Competition, and Linked Fate." In *Just Neighbors? Research on African-American and Latino Relations in the United States*, edited by Edward Telles, Mark Q. Sawyer, and Gaspar Rivera-Salgado, 63–94. New York: Russell Sage Foundation.

Jordan, Don, and Michael Walsh. 2008. *White Cargo: The Forgotten History of Britain's White Slaves in America*. New York: New York University Press.

Katz, William Loren. 2012. *Black Indians: A Hidden Heritage*. New York: Atheneum.

Kemp, Michael. 2018. *Bombs, Bullets and Bread: The Politics of Anarchist Terrorism Worldwide, 1866–1926*. Jefferson, NC: McFarland.

Kerr, Andrew. 2022. "BLM's Millions Unaccounted For after Leaders Quietly Jump Ship."

Washington Examiner, January 27. https://www.washingtonexaminer.com/news/blms-millions-go-unaccounted-for-after-leaders-quietly-jump-ship.

Kim, Victoria. 2010. "Racial Hatred Blamed in Girl's Slaying in Harbor Gateway." *Los Angeles Times*, August 12.

King, Maya. 2020. "Black Lives Matter Power Grab Sets Off Internal Revolt." *Politico*, December 10. https://www.politico.com/news/2020/12/10/black-lives-matter-organization-biden-444097.

Kocka, Jürgen. 2016. *Capitalism: A Short History*. Princeton, NJ: Princeton University Press.

Krige, Eileen Jensen. (1936) 1974. *The Social System of the Zulus*. Pietermaritzburg, South Africa: Shuter and Shooter.

Krikorian, Michael. 1996. "Dorsey Student Wounded in Attack Near Campus Dies." *Los Angeles Times*, February 9.

Lee, Heon Cheol. 1999. "Conflict between Korean Merchants and Black Customers: A Structural Analysis." In *Koreans in the Hood: Conflict with African Americans*, edited by Kwang Chung Kim, 113–130. Baltimore: John Hopkins University Press.

Leiva, Priscilla. 2014. "'Just Win Baby': The Raider Nation and Second Chances for Black and Brown LA." In *Black and Brown in Los Angeles: Beyond Conflict and Coalition*, edited by Josh Kun and Laura Pulido, 346–371. Berkeley: University of California Press.

Leong, Nancy. 2021. *Identity Capitalists: The Powerful Insiders Who Exploit Diversity to Maintain Inequality*. Stanford, CA: Stanford University Press.

León-Portilla, Miguel. (1962) 1992. *The Broken Spears: The Aztec Account of the Conquest of Mexico*. Boston: Beacon.

Liebler, Carolyn A., and Timothy Ortyl. 2014. "More than a Million New American Indians in 2000: Who Are They?" *Demography* 51, no. 3: 1101–1130.

Liebler, Carolyn A., Sonya R. Porter, Leticia E. Fernandez, James M. Noon, and Sharon R. Ennis. 2017. "America's Churning Races: Race and Ethnicity Response Changes Between Census 2000 and the 2010 Census." *Demography* 54, no. 1: 259–284.

Lipsitz, George. 2006. *The Possessive Investment in Whiteness: How White People Profit from Identity Politics*. Philadelphia: Temple University Press.

Lozano, Carlos. 2018. "Death Row Inmate Fatally Stabbed at San Quentin Was Responsible for Sensational Hate Crime Killing in Los Angeles." *Los Angeles Times*, October 6.

Lydon, Jason. 2014. "A Compilation of Critiques on Hate Crimes Legislation." In *Against Equality: Queer Revolution Not Mere Inclusion*, edited by Ryan Conrad, 177–180. Chico, CA: AK.

Maghbouleh, Neda. 2017. *The Limits of Whiteness: Iranian Americans and the Everyday Politics of Race*. Stanford, CA: Stanford University Press.

Maghbouleh, Neda, Ariela Schachter, and René D. Flores. 2022. "Middle Eastern and North African Americans May Not Be Perceived, nor Perceive Themselves, to Be White." *Proceedings of the National Academy of Sciences of the United States of America* 119, no. 7. https://www.pnas.org/content/119/7/e2117940119.

Malatesta, Errico. 1914. "Anarchists Have Forgotten Their Principles." *Anarchy Archives*. http://dwardmac.pitzer.edu/Anarchist_Archives/malatesta/ForgottenPrinciples.html.

Marcuse, Herbert. (1964) 1991. *One-Dimensional Man*. Boston: Beacon.

Marks, Jonathan. (1995) 2008. *Human Biodiversity: Genes, Race and History*. New Brunswick, NJ: Transaction.

Marrow, Helen. 2009. "New Immigrant Destinations and the American Color Line." *Ethnic and Racial Studies* 32, no. 6: 1037–1057.

Martinez, Cid. 2016. *The Neighborhood Has Its Own Rules: Latinos and African Americans in South Los Angeles.* New York: New York University Press.

Martinez, Cid, and Victor Rios. 2011. "Conflict, Cooperation and Avoidance." In *Just Neighbors? Research on African-American and Latino Relations in the United States,* edited by Edward Telles, Mark Q. Sawyer, and Gaspar Rivera-Salgado, 343–361. New York: Russell Sage Foundation.

Marx, Karl. (1867) 1976. *Capital, Volume I.* New York: Penguin Classics.

Mathurin, Owen Charles. 1976. *Henry Sylvester Williams and the Origins of the Pan African Movement, 1869–1911.* Westport, CT: Praeger.

McClain, Paula D., Niambi M. Carter, Victoria M. DeFrancesco Soto, and Monique L. Lyle et al. 2006. "Racial Distancing in a Southern City: Latino Immigrants' Views of Black Americans." *Journal of Politics* 68, no. 3: 571–584.

McClain, Paula D., Gerald F. Lackey, Efren O. Perez, and Niambi M. Carter et al. 2011. "Intergroup Relations in Three Southern Cities." In *Just Neighbors? Research on African-American and Latino Relations in the United States,* edited by Edward Telles, Mark Q. Sawyer, and Gaspar Rivera-Salgado, 201–240. New York: Russell Sage Foundation.

McDermott, Monica. 2011. "Black Attitudes and Hispanic Immigrants in South Carolina." In *Just Neighbors? Research on African-American and Latino Relations in the United States,* edited by Edward Telles, Mark Q. Sawyer, and Gaspar Rivera-Salgado, 242–263. New York: Russell Sage Foundation.

McWhorter, John. 1998. *Word on the Street: Debunking the Myth of a "Pure" Standard English.* New York: Basic.

———. 2017. *Talking Back Talking Black: Truths about America's Lingua Franca.* New York: Bellevue Literary.

Meier, Matt S., and Margo Gutierrez. 2000. *Encyclopedia of the Mexican American Civil Rights Movement.* Westport, CT: Greenwood.

Menchaca, Martha. 2001. *Recovering History, Constructing Race: The Indian, Black and White Roots of Mexican Americans.* Austin: University of Texas Press.

Mendoza, Ruben G. 2000. "Cruising Art and Culture in *Aztlán*: Lowriding in the Mexican American Southwest." In *U.S. Latino Literatures and Cultures: Transnational Perspectives,* edited by Francisco Lomeli and Karin Ikas, 3–35. Heidelberg, Germany: Carl Winter-Verlag.

Mendoza-Denton, Nancy. 2008. *Homegirls: Language and Cultural Practice among Latina Youth Gangs.* Malden, MA: Blackwell.

Michaels, Walter Benn. 2006. *The Trouble with Diversity: How We Learned to Love Identity and Ignore Inequality.* New York: Picador.

Mills, C. Wright. (1959) 2000. *The Sociological Imagination.* Oxford: Oxford University Press.

Mindiola, Tatcho, Jr., Yolanda Flores Niemann, and Nestor Rodriguez. 2002. *Black-Brown Relations and Stereotypes.* Austin: University of Texas Press.

Moore, Joan W. 1978. *Homeboys: Gangs, Drugs, and Prison in the Barrios of Los Angeles.* Philadelphia: Temple University Press.

———. 1991. *Going Down to the Barrio: Homeboys and Homegirls in Change.* Philadelphia: Temple University Press.

Morgan, Edmund S. 1975. *American Slavery, American Freedom.* New York: W. W. Norton.

Morin, Jason L., Gabriel R. Sanchez, and Matt A. Barreto. 2011. "Perceptions of Competition." In *Just Neighbors? Research on African-American and Latino Relations in the*

United States, edited by Edward Telles, Mark Q. Sawyer, and Gaspar Rivera-Salgado, 96–123. New York: Russell Sage Foundation.

Morning, Ann. 2015. "It's Impossible to Lie About Your Race." *Huffington Post*, July 1. https://www.huffpost.com/entry/its-impossible-to-lie-about-your-race_b_7708598.

Morris, Richard B. 1946. *Government and Labor in Early America.* New York: Harper and Row.

Murch, Donna Jean. 2010. *Living for the City: Migration, Education, and the Rise of the Black Panther Party in Oakland, California.* Raleigh: University of North Carolina Press.

Newton, Huey P. (1972) 2002. "On Pan-Africanism or Communism." In *The Huey P. Newton Reader*, edited by David Hilliard and Donald Weise, 248–255. New York: Seven Stories.

Northrup, Solomon. (1853) 2014. *12 Years a Slave.* Los Angeles: Graymalkin Media.

Olzak, Susan. 1992. *The Dynamics of Ethnic Competition and Conflict.* Stanford, CA: Stanford University Press.

Olzak, Susan, and Suzanne Shanahan. 1996. "Deprivation and Race Riots: An Extension of Spilerman's Analysis." *Social Forces* 74:931–961.

Olzak, Susan, Suzanne Shanahan, and Elizabeth H. McEneaney. 1996. "Poverty, Segregation, and Race Riots: 1960–1993." *American Sociological Review* 61:590–613.

Ormseth, Matthew. 2020. "Danny Roman, Mexican Mafia Member and South LA Gang Chieftain, Is Stabbed to Death in Corcoran." *Los Angeles Times*, June 11.

Ortega, Adolfo. 1991. *Caló Orbis: Semiotic Aspects of a Chicano Language Variety.* New York: Peter Lang.

Pagán, Eduardo Obregón. 2003. *Murder at the Sleepy Lagoon: Zoot Suits, Race, and Riot in Wartime L.A.* Chapel Hill: University of North Carolina Press.

Palmer, Colin A. 1976. *Slaves of the White God: Blacks in Mexico, 1570–1650.* Cambridge, MA: Harvard University Press.

Park, Kyeyoung. 1999. "Use and Abuse of Race and Culture: Black-Korean Tension in America." In *Koreans in the Hood: Conflict with African Americans*, edited by Kwang Chung Kim, 60–74. Baltimore: Johns Hopkins University Press.

Parsons, Lucy. (1886) 2003. "The Negro: Let Him Leave Politics to the Politician and Prayers to the Preacher." In *Lucy Parsons: Freedom, Equality and Solidarity, Writings and Speeches, 1878–1937*, edited by Gale Ahearns, 54–55. Chicago: Charles H. Kerr.

Pastor, Manuel. 2014. "Keeping It Real: Demographic Change, Economic Conflict, and Interethnic Organizing for Social Justice in Los Angeles." In *Black and Brown in Los Angeles: Beyond Conflict and Coalition*, edited by Josh Kun and Laura Pulido, 33–65. Berkeley: University of California Press.

Patterson, Orlando. (1982) 2018. *Slavery and Social Death: A Comparative Study*, 2nd ed. Cambridge, MA: Harvard University Press.

Penland, Paige. 2003. *Lowrider: History, Pride, Culture.* St. Paul, MN: Motorbooks Journal.

Pensinger, Brenda J. 1974. *Diccionario Mixteco-Español, Español-Mixteco.* Mexico City: Instituto Lingüístico de Verano.

Peralta, Stacy, dir. 2008. *Crips and Bloods: Made in America.* Documentary, Docurama Films.

Perelman, Michael. 2000. *The Invention of Capitalism: Classical Political Economy and the Secret History of Primitive Accumulation.* Durham, NC: Duke University Press.

Phillips, Susan. 1999. *Wallbangin': Graffiti and Gangs in LA.* Chicago: University of Chicago Press.

Pinderhughes, Howard. 1997. *Race in the Hood: Conflict and Violence among Urban Youth.* Minneapolis: Minnesota University Press.

Pitcher, Ben. 2014. *Consuming Race*. London: Routledge.

Plascencia, Luis. 1983. "Lowriding in the Southwest: Cultural Symbols in the Mexican Community." In *History, Culture and Society: Chicano Studies in the 1980s*, edited by Mario Garcia, 141–175. Ypsilanti, MI: Bilingual Review Press.

Polkinhorn, Harry, Alfredo Velasco, and Malcolm Lambert. (1983) 2005. *El Libro de Caló: The Dictionary of Chicano Slang*, rev. ed. Moorpark, CA: Floricanto.

Pool, Bob. 2008. "Witness to 1969 UCLA Shootings Speaks at Rally." *Los Angeles Times*, January 18.

Proudhon, Pierre-Joseph. (1840) 1873. *Qu'est-ce que la propriété?* Paris: Lacroix.

Quillian, Lincoln. 1995. "Prejudice as a Response to Perceived Group Threat: Population Composition, Anti-Immigrant and Racial Prejudice in Europe." *American Sociological Review* 60:587–611.

———. 1996. "Group Threat and Regional Changes in Attitudes toward African Americans." *American Journal of Sociology* 102: 816–861.

Quinney, Richard. 1977. *Class, State and Crime: On the Theory and Practice of Criminal Justice*. New York: David McKay.

Quinones, Sam. 2007. "Girl's Accused Killer Straddles Racial Line." *Los Angeles Times*, March 10.

———. 2010. "Six Florencia 13 Gang Members Sentenced to Life in Prison." *Los Angeles Times*, February 8.

———. 2014. "Race, Real Estate and the Mexican Mafia: A Report from the Black and Latino Killing Fields." In *Black and Brown in Los Angeles: Beyond Conflict and Coalition*, edited by Josh Kun and Laura Pulido, 261–297. Berkeley: University of California Press.

Quinones, Sam, Richard Winton, and Joe Mozingo. 2013. "Attack on Family in Compton Latest Incident in Wave of Anti-Black Violence." *Los Angeles Times*, January 25.

Reed, Adolph, Jr. 2000. *Class Notes: Posing as Politics and Other Thoughts on the American Scene*. New York: New Press.

———. 2015. "From Jenner to Dolezal: One Trans Good, the Other Not So Much." *Common Dreams*, June 15. https://www.commondreams.org/views/2015/06/15/jenner-dolezal-one-trans-good-other-not-so-much.

———. 2016. "How Racial Disparity Does Not Help Make Sense of Patterns of Police Violence." *Onsite.org*, September 16. https://nonsite.org/editorial/how-racial-disparity-does-not-help-make-sense-of-patterns-of-police-violence.

———. 2019. "The Myth of Class Reductionism." *New Republic*, September 25. https://newrepublic.com/article/154996/myth-class-reductionism.

———. 2020. "Socialism and the Argument against Race Reductionism." *New Labor Forum* 29, no. 2: 36–43.

Reed, Touré F. 2020. *Toward Freedom: The Case against Race Reductionism*. New York: Verso.

Reiter, Keramet A. 2012. "Parole, Snitch or Die: California's Supermax Prisons and Prisoners, 1997–2007." *Punishment and Society* 14, no. 5: 530–563.

———. 2014. "The Pelican Bay Hunger Strike: Resistance within the Structural Constraints of a U.S. Supermax Prison." *South Atlantic Quarterly* 113, no. 3: 579–611.

———. 2016. *23/7: Pelican Bay Prison and the Rise of Long-term Solitary Confinement*. New Haven, CT: Yale University Press.

Robinson, Cedric. (1983) 2000. *Black Marxism: The Making of the Black Radical Tradition*. Chapel Hill: University of North Carolina Press.

Robinson, Paul. 2010. "Race, Space, and the Evolution of Black Los Angeles." In *Black Los Angeles*, edited by Darnell Hunt and Ana-Christina Ramón, 21–59. New York: New York University Press.

Rodriguez, Nestor, and Tatcho Mindiola Jr. 2011. "Intergroup Perceptions and Relations in Houston." In *Just Neighbors? Research on African-American and Latino Relations in the United States*, edited by Edward Telles, Mark Q. Sawyer, and Gaspar Rivera-Salgado, 155–175. New York: Russell Sage Foundation.

Roediger, David R. (1991) 2007. *The Wages of Whiteness: Race and the Making of the American Working Class*. New York: Verso.

Roediger, David R., and Elizabeth D. Esch. 2012. *The Production of Difference: Race and the Management of Labor in U.S. History*. New York: Oxford University Press.

Romo, Rebecca. 2011. "Between Black and Brown: Blaxican (Black-Mexican) Multiracial Identity in California." *Journal of Black Studies* 42, no. 3: 402–426.

Rosenthal, Keith. 2011. "More Dangerous than a Thousand Rioters." *Socialist Worker*, September 22. https://socialistworker.org/2011/09/22/lucy-parsons.

Sánchez-Jankowski, Martín. 1991. *Islands in the Street: Gangs and American Urban Society*. Berkeley: University of California Press.

———. 2016. *Burning Dislike: Ethnic Violence in High Schools*. Berkeley: University of California Press.

Sandoval, Denise Michelle. 2003. "Cruising through Lowrider Culture: Chicana/o Identity in the Marketing of Lowrider Magazine." In *Velvet Barrios: Popular Culture and Chicana/o Sexualities*, edited by Alicia Gaspar de Alba, 179–196. New York: Palgrave Macmillan.

———. 2014. "The Politics of Low and Slow/*Bajito y Suavecito*: Black and Chicano Lowriders in Los Angeles, from the 1960s through the 1970s." In *Black and Brown in Los Angeles: Beyond Conflict and Coalition*, edited by Josh Kun and Laura Pulido, 176–200. Berkeley: University of California Press.

Santa Cruz, Nicole. 2018. "Jury Acquits Palos Verdes Estates Man of Murder in Suspected Gang Killing in South LA." *Los Angeles Times*, July 23.

Sawyer, Mark Q. 2011. "Politics in Los Angeles." In *Just Neighbors? Research on African-American and Latino Relations in the United States*, edited by Edward Telles, Mark Q. Sawyer, and Gaspar Rivera-Salgado, 177–197. New York: Russell Sage Foundation.

Seale, Bobby. (1970) 1991. *Seize the Time: The Story of the Black Panther Party and Huey P. Newton*. Baltimore: Black Classic.

Shakur, Assata. 1987. *Assata: An Autobiography*. Chicago: Lawrence Hill.

Sherwood, Marika. 2011. *Origins of Pan-Africanism: Henry Sylvester Williams, Africa and the African Diaspora*. New York: Routledge.

Smedley, Audrey. 2007. *Race in North America: Origin and Evolution of a Worldview*, 3rd ed. Boulder, CO: Westview.

Smitherman, Geneva. 1977. *Talkin and Testifyin: The Language of Black America*. Detroit: Wayne State University Press.

———. 1994. *Black Talk: Words and Phrases from the Hood to the Amen Corner*. Boston: Houghton Mifflin.

———. 2000. *Talkin that Talk: Language, Culture and Education in African America*. New York: Routledge.

Soustelle, Jacques. (1962) 1970. *Daily Life of the Aztecs: On the Eve of the Spanish Conquest*. Stanford, CA: Stanford University Press.

Spitzer, Steven. 1975. "Toward a Marxian Theory of Deviance." *Social Problems* 22, no. 5: 638–651.

Stern, Fritz. 1979. *Gold and Iron: Bismarck, Bleichröder and the Building of the German Empire*. New York: Vintage.

Stewart, Ella. 1989. "Ethnic Cultural Diversity: Ethnographic Study of Cultural Differences and Communication Styles between Korean Merchants and African American Patrons in South Central Los Angeles." Master's thesis, California State University, Los Angeles.

Stiner, Watani. 2021. "Testimony of Lies, Conspiracy Theories and COINTELPRO." Video posted March 21. https://www.youtube.com/watch?v=Hd33sXS53NU&t=3297s.

St. John, Paige. 2013. "Inmates End California Prison Hunger Strike." *Los Angeles Times*, September 5.

———. 2015a. "Hugo Pinell, Infamous 'San Quentin Six' Member, Killed in Prison Riot." *Los Angeles Times*, August 13.

———. 2015b. "Slayed Inmate Hugo Pinell Was a Target of Prison Gangs, His Lawyer Says." *Los Angeles Times*, August 13.

———. 2015c. "California Agrees to Move Thousands of Prisoners out of Solitary Confinement." *Los Angeles Times*, September 1.

Stone, Michael. 1990. "Bajito y Suavecito: Lowriding and the 'Class' of Class." *Journal of Latin American Popular Culture* 9:87–88.

Sue, Christina A. 2013. *Land of the Cosmic Race: Race Mixture, Racism and Blackness in Mexico*. New York: Oxford University Press.

Swearingen, M. Wesley. 1995. *FBI Secrets: An Agent's Expose*. Boston: South End.

Tackwood, Louis. 1973. *The Glass House Tapes*. New York: Avon.

Telles, Edward E., and Vilma Ortiz. 2008. *Generations of Exclusion: Mexican Americans, Assimilation, and Race*. New York: Russell Sage Foundation.

Trammel, Rebecca. 2012. *Enforcing the Convict Code: Violence and Prison Culture*. Boulder, CO: Lynne Rienner.

Trotman, C. James. 2011. *Frederick Douglas: A Biography*. New York: Penguin.

Tucker, Robert C., ed. 1978. *The Marx-Engels Reader: 2nd Edition*. New York: W. W. Norton.

Umemoto, Karen. 2006. *The Truce: Lessons from an LA Gang War*. Ithaca, NY: Cornell University Press.

Vaca, Nicholas. 2004. *The Presumed Alliance: The Unspoken Conflict between Latinos and Blacks and What It Means for America*. New York: HarperCollins.

Van Young, Eric. 2002. *The Other Rebellion: Popular Violence, Ideology, and the Mexican Struggle for Independence, 1810–1821*. Palo Alto, CA: Stanford University Press.

Vaver, Anthony. 2011. *Bound with an Iron Chain: The Untold Story of How the British Transported 50,000 Convicts to Colonial America*. Westborough, MA: Pickpocket.

Vigil, James Diego. 1988. *Barrio Gangs: Street Life and Identity in Southern California*. Austin: University of Texas Press.

———. 2002a. "Community Dynamics and the Rise of Street Gangs." In *Latinos: Remaking America*, edited by Marcelo M. Suárez-Orozco and Mariela M. Páez, 97–109. Berkeley: University of California Press.

———. 2002b. *A Rainbow of Gangs: Street Cultures in the Mega-City*. Austin: University of Texas Press.

———. 2007. *The Projects: Gang and Non-gang Families in East Los Angeles*. Austin: University of Texas Press.

———. 2011. "Ethnic Succession and Ethnic Conflict." In *Just Neighbors? Research on African-American and Latino Relations in the United States*, edited by Edward Telles, Mark Q. Sawyer, and Gaspar Rivera-Salgado, 325–341. New York: Russell Sage Foundation.

Vinson, Ben. 2017. *Before Mestizaje: The Frontiers of Race and Caste in Colonial Mexico*. Cambridge: Cambridge University Press.

Ward, T. W. 2013. *Gangsters without Borders: An Ethnography of a Salvadoran Street Gang.* Oxford: Oxford University Press.

Washburn, Wilcomb E. 1957. *The Governor and the Rebel: A History of Bacon's Rebellion in Virginia.* New York: W. W. Norton.

Waters, Mary. 1990. *Ethnic Options: Choosing Identities in America.* Berkeley: University of California Press.

Webb, Gary. 1998. *Dark Alliance: The CIA, the Contras, and the Crack Cocaine Explosion.* New York: Seven Stories.

Webb, Stephen Saunders. 1984. *1676: The End of American Independence.* New York: Alfred A. Knopf.

Weide, Robert D. 2020. "The Invisible Hand of the State: A Critical Historical Analysis of Prison Gangs in California." *Prison Journal* 100, no. 3: 312–331.

———. 2022 (forthcoming). "Structural Disorganization: Can Prison Gangs Mitigate Serious Violence in California Prisons?" *Critical Criminology* 30, no. 1.

Widdowson, Frances, and Albert Howard. 2008. *Disrobing the Aboriginal Industry: The Deception behind Indigenous Cultural Preservation.* Montreal: McGill-Queen's University Press.

Wood, Ellen Meiksins. (1999) 2017. *The Origin of Capitalism: A Longer View.* London: Verso.

Wood, Peter H. 1996. *Strange New Land: Africans in Colonial America.* Oxford: Oxford University Press.

Wright, John. 2007. *The Trans-Saharan Slave Trade.* New York: Routledge.

Young, Jock. 1999. *The Exclusive Society: Social Exclusion, Crime and Difference in Late Modernity.* Los Angeles: Sage.

Zamora, Sylvia. 2011. "Framing Commonality in a Multiracial, Multiethnic Coalition." In *Just Neighbors? Research on African-American and Latino Relations in the United States,* edited by Edward Telles, Mark Q. Sawyer, and Gaspar Rivera-Salgado, 299–321. New York: Russell Sage Foundation.

Zaretsky, Eli. 1994. "Identity Theory, Identity Politics: Psychoanalysis, Marxism, Poststructuralism." In *Social Theory and the Politics of Identity,* edited by Craig Calhoun, 198–215. Cambridge, MA: Blackwell.

Index

ROBERT D. WEIDE is Associate Professor of Sociology at California State University, Los Angeles.